Powerful
Peacemaking
A Strategy for a
Living Revolution

DEDICATION

To my granddaughters Crystal, Raquel and Chanelle, I dedicate this contribution to an environment that nurtures their love and courage.

To Babette and Billy,
With appreciation for your good work and deep caring. You both model what a powerful peacemaker is like!

George Lakey

Powerful Peacemaking
A Strategy for a Living Revolution
George Lakey

New Society Publishers

Philadelphia, PA   Santa Cruz, CA

Inquiries regarding requests to reprint all or part of *Powerful Peacemaking* should be adressed to: **New Society Publishers, 4722 Baltimore Avenue, Philadelphia, PA 19143, USA**.

ISBN: 0-86571-096-1 Hardcover.
      0-86571-097-X Paperback.

Printed in the United States of America.
This book is printed on partially recycled paper.

Cover design by Brian Prendergast, Syracuse Cultural Workers.

New Society Publishers is a project of the New Society Educational Foundation and a collective of the Movement for a New Society. New Society Educational Foundation is a nonprofit, tax-exempt public foundation. Movement for a New Society is a network of small groups and individuals working for fundamental social change through nonviolent action. To learn more about MNS, write to: Movement for a New Society, PO Box 1922, Cambridge, MA 02238. Opinions expressed in this book do not necessarily represent positions of either New Society Educational Foundation or Movement for a New Society.

ACKNOWLEDGEMENTS

This book's transformation couldn't have happened without the pushing (gentle and otherwise) and support of many people. To those who urged from a distance as well as those who sat in my living room and discussed the early drafts, to those who generously agreed to be interviewed for the last chapter so the dialogue could begin even before the reader turned the last page, to my movement and academic mentors who modelled a commitment to excellence, to the collective at New Society Publishers and their combination of vision and guts, to my "political" and "non-political" friends and family who experience a living revolution as a loving revolution—I proudly acknowledge my thanks. My daughter Ingrid, whose bright awareness of herself and others and deep caring for the world inspire me continually, gets special mention for the ray of sunshine that she is.

FOREWORD

Joanna Macy

Imagine for a moment that there will be future generations and that they will possess the means of understanding our own. For that to occur, omnicide by nuclear holocaust or ecological disaster will have had to have been averted. And they, the future ones, will look back at the process by which our own generation managed to pull away from the abyss. They will see by the records how we dismantled our instruments of mass annihilation and converted our polluting technologies, how we chose life; they will see.

Looking back, they may well see that we in the late 1980s were farther along in that process than it can seem to us now. They may guess at the anguish and powerlessness widely felt in the face of preparations for World War III and the accelerating destruction of our biosphere. They may imagine how paltry and disconnected seemed our efforts to stem the tide, and how frequent our despair. But from their future vantage point, they—our descendants—will also be able to trace deeper and vaster forces at work in us now, forces that as they unfolded ensured for them a chance to be born and a world to inhabit.

What are these forces? How may we detect them, so that we can take heart and give them play?

Some substantial answers to those questions can be discerned in this book and in the thought and experience which it distills for us. Cataloguing abundant examples of nonviolent social change and drawing out the lessons they offer, George Lakey holds up a mirror in which we can see our own struggles and challenges in a wider context. His functional analyses help us comprehend the interlocking psycho-social forces that fuel the war system. He clarifies the stages through which a revolutionary struggle must move to enlist popular participation in the deconstruction of that system—stages we can recognize as already occurring in incipient form. He highlights the kinds of choices to be made along the way if real change is to occur. These tough choices are necessary if the revolution we would make is to be more than a "turning over of the dungheap" which substitutes one oligarchy for another. We recognize that the values necessary to those choices are rapidly emerging in our time.

Colleagues of mine, seeking to develop children's capacity to envision the future and making no reference to possible disaster, asked a fifth grade class to describe in writing what they imagine the world will be like when they grow up. Ninety percent of the children expected that a nuclear war would occur and that they would not survive it. The only hope some saw lay in an extraterrestrial rescue mission. Many adults in our society also cling to hope in a power external to themselves: in the "experts" or in a smiling President or divine intervention.

That is hardly the kind of assurance we find in this book. The hope it gives us is not that we will be rescued but that the job to be done, while vast and hard, is not beyond our own power as ordinary people. And we do not need to get elected or enlightened to find that power. Its ingredients are present in us already as ideas and values that are fundamental to the strategies Lakey presents.

Let me consider here just four of these ingredients: a willingness to face the crisis, a capacity to see and think systematically or holistically, a reconceptualization of the nature of power, and an awakening to the meaning and necessity of nonviolence.

We cannot correct what we do not allow ourselves to see. Of all the dangers confronting humankind—be they hunger, oppression, nuclear holocaust, or ecological destruction—none is so great as our denial of them. While this denial is still widespread—aided by rampant consumerism, drug abuse, fundamentalist cults and other forms of escape—it is harder to maintain with each passing day. Growing awareness of the environmental crisis and the chances of a nuclear winter propel more and more people to find the courage to acknowledge that we live in a world that can end. Describing his successful struggle with cancer, George Lakey tells of the power he found as he was able to "face the pathology." Confronting death, he learned to fear it less, while deepening his commitment to life. In the workshops I offer, where people tell the truth about what they experience happening to their world, the same kind of process occurs. As they stop repressing their pain for the world, energy is released, along with an invigorating readiness to survive and to act.

Meanwhile a quiet revolution is underway in our modes of perceiving our world and in the panoply of perils and problems assailing it. Instead of coincidental developments competing for our attention and conflicting in their demands, we are increasingly able to see them as essentially interrelated manifestations. This optic is a significant feature of powerful peacemaking. It is expressed in Lakey's portrayal of the mutual interplay between militarism and capitalism, violence and nationalism. Just as these abet and sustain each other so can, he argues, the alternative institutions of nonviolence, socialism, civilian defense, and transnationalism. Few readers will have difficulty in seeing these kinds of connections once they are pointed out because the world appears more and more as a network of interwoven events. If a paradigm shift is occurring in our modes of consciousness, it consists in just that: a growing capacity to apprehend the interdependence of all phenomena. We sense afresh the seamless, intricate web of life; we awaken to our deep ecology; we picture the holographic nature of the universe; we engage with the hypothesis that our planet itself is a living organism.

It is well to pause and appreciate that shift of mind, for it is intrinsic to the revolution. Without it we cannot build strategies or coalitions. Without it events appear chaotic, competing demands confuse and exhaust: Shall I work to save the whales or the rainforest? Shall I fight nuclear power plants or world hunger? Illiteracy or child abuse? Viewed systematically, however, these are not separate campaigns so much as different facets of the same struggle. We see their linkages, their intertwining roots, and we know that intervention at any point — including change in our own lifestyle—indirectly affects all others.

As a systems view of the world spreads, it brings a new understanding of the nature of power, one that is radically different than the linear, hierarchical notions to which we have been conditioned. This new understanding is, I consider, the major cognitive revolution of our time. The power that is ours for social change work is the power we see at work in evolution and ecosystems; it is not a property but a process; it operates not from the top down but from the bottom up; it is not so much power over as power with—or as systems theorists term it, synergy. It underlies the shift in relations between individuals and between groups that is both the means and the goal of a living revolution. Lakey's distrust of party politics and his cautions about co-optation are a reflection of this understanding of power. So are his long-term confidence about what happens to a government when sufficient numbers of people withdraw their consent and cooperation, and his belief in the people's capacity, when united, to outlast harassment and repression.
repression.
Along with this new concept of power comes a fresh and deeper appreciation of the necessity of nonviolence. Despite the militarization of our society (or perhaps because of it), a lively interest grows in finding peaceful means of settling differences; groups studying and training in mediation, conflict resolution, and nonviolent resistance spring up like green shoots in a wide range of localities and organizations. Lakey helps us see the long-term and revolutionary practicality of this approach. In case after case he shows the inherent strategic limitations of violence, the ways it backfires on its agents, even if it does not corrupt them: and he is all the more convincing by virtue of his belief in the essential, salutary role of conflict and confrontation in the redistribution of opportunities and resources. The strategies he presents do not require us to be saints, only to be smart enough and patient enough to see that violence is a dead-end street.
Despite the gathering darkness of our time, with militarism and exploitation bringing us ever closer to the brink, these shifts in values and perceptions are occurring. They don't make the front page or the evening newscast, but quietly they prepare us for the revolution that awaits us if our world is to survive. All we have to do is heed and

nourish these emerging values and trust them enough to act on them. The varied and progressive forms that such actions can take—from cultural work to protest demonstrations to tax resistance, from neighborhood cooperatives to radical caucuses to boycotts—are delineated in this book in ways that reveal their synergistic interrelationships and internal logic.

It is in confident action, no matter how small the step, that we break through feelings of futility and begin to experience our power. For that to happen, for us to be able to act with confidence and conviction, we need both long-term vision and practical guidelines. Because this book combines both, in ways that stimulate our own creativity, we can find in it an antidote to despair.

CONTENTS

INTRODUCTION

Since writing the first edition of this book, I have gotten in touch with my working-class background, taken a turn as primary nurturer of my children, and struggled successfully with cancer. I have published two more books and a number of articles, come out publicly as a gay man, and become a grandfather.

Along with changes have been continuities: I still organize campaigns for justice and peace, lead training workshops, and from time to time teach peace studies to college students. My concern for personal growth and cultural change has deepened through work with the Association for Humanistic Psychology and others.

My relationship with this book has, like the rest of my life, its changes and continuities. If I were now writing the book for the first time it would be different in some ways, yet its core would remain the same. I retain my faith in the abilities of large numbers of people to act effectively for peace and justice, when the time is right. I still look for innovation and freshness as a part of the spirit of revolution. I still root my analysis in the ecological perspective of the planet. I still find useful a historical and sociological framework for thinking about social change.

Our time is dangerous and millions of people are shaking off what Yale psychiatrist Robert Jay Lifton calls "psychic numbing"—the psychological denial of just how dangerous it is.[1] Being willing to see reality is an enormous aid to survival—and also very uncomfortable. Despair is tempting, cynicism is fashionable, and not everyone is able to stay with the discomfort of the truth long enough to do something substantial about it.

This book is for those ready to do something substantial. In this introduction I want to share something of my own experience of cancer because in that time of facing my personal death, I encountered some of the issues we face in the possibility, through nuclear or ecological destruction, of our collective death. The bottom line was knowing that, however slim the chance, I could still choose to struggle for life.

And so can we all.

I do not remember the surgeon telling me that the tumor he partially removed from my intestinal area was malignant. I do not remember telling the news to a friend immediately after, either; he said I looked pale and shaken. Mine is a long-lived family. I was 39; I wasn't prepared.

Yet, in another way, I was prepared. I had been living in a community of a hundred people, the Philadelphia Life Center, for six years. The community, most of which was involved with the Movement for a New Society, had responded to another crisis a few months earlier in the April 1977 occupation in Seabrook, New Hampshire of a nuclear power plant site. Movement for a New Society (MNS) people had developed the training model used by Clamshell Alliance and in response to the mushrooming activity, forty MNS members went to New England, did last-minute training, and then went to jail with the Clams and helped create a positive prison experience for the occupiers. There were jokes at the time about the National Guard armories being the "best social change schools in the country."

MNS responded with the same commitment and skill to my personal crisis as it had to the Clamshell Alliance's political need. Twenty-four hours a day for five days after surgery my community was close to me. Whenever I woke up, restless from the pain, one or several friends were there. While I slept they napped, or read, or prayed, or talked politics. The nursing staff was apprehensive: won't such a flood of visitors kill the patient? My friends were so sensitive, however, so careful to park their own anxieties outside while they came in to pay attention to me, that their influence was enormously healing.

The surgery was only the beginning. We followed up with chemotherapy, co-counseling, vitamins, meditation, exercise, spiritual healing, Jungian dream analysis, and oceans of love! I learned more about myself than I wanted to know. I also felt, more deeply than I thought possible, the reality of caring.

In May 1978, eleven months after surgery, my doctors felt confident that the cancer was gone; one referred to the victory as a "miracle." I had been put in touch with my deepest love for life and also my wish for death. I learned to trust my intuition again in a way I hadn't trusted it since I was nineteen, for as marvelous as my support community was, the decision to struggle for life was finally my own.

The facing of death was good for me; I learned to fear it less. At the same time, I've deepened my commitment to life. I cherish that experience for all humankind: a decreased fear of death and a deepened commitment to life. As each of us replaces despair with love, we move our dear planet a bit closer to a living revolution.

Some of the healing characteristics of my own struggle make strategic sense at this time of escalating arms races, spreading world starvation, and concentration of economic power. I find in this area as in so many that the feminist principle, "the personal is political," is sound. Six ways of overcoming my illness seem especially important to share as a metaphor for healing our planet: taking responsibility for illness, delighting in life, facing the pathology, envisioning health, accepting loving support, and thinking holistically.

TAKING RESPONSIBILITY

At first I resisted the concept of taking responsibility for my cancer. I was in pain from the surgery and scared by the diagnosis when someone suggested I look within for my part in causing the cancer to grow. It seemed like "blaming the victim"—here I was, flat on my back with tubes running in and out, and I should assume that I was responsible for the failure of my immune system?

In time I came to see the powerlessness of my victim stance. As long as I insisted on seeing the cancer as an alien force which invaded me and took me over, I was beaten before I started. I was no match for anything that overwhelming. When I began to understand that I shut down my immune system through unusual stress and growing despair, I realized that I had power in the healing process. I could examine whether I "needed" the cancer for some hidden purpose, or whether in my subconscious I wished to die. By looking at myself as an active participant in getting sick, I could become an active participant in getting well.

In the political sphere we also experience a frightening and painful reality. Humankind's experiment with civilization can be wiped out, and the everyday course of affairs results in the suffering of hundreds of millions from hunger, poverty, and environmental degradation. Women and minorities continue to be systematically hurt by sexism, bigotry, and discrimination. Since we are, objectively, victims in such a situation, it is natural to feel, subjectively, like victims. It is equally natural to feel powerless, since that is a characteristic of victimization. But it is as important for us politically as it was for me personally to stop defining ourselves as victims.

Giving up the victim's self-image is surprisingly hard. My experiences as a working-class boy and as a gay man have brought plenty of hurt to me and left me with a lot of righteous anger. When I am confronted with class snobbery or with heterosexism I feel victimized—and while I may feel powerless I nevertheless gain the satisfaction of feeling righteous.

The anger is natural enough; it needs expression. Bottling up anger, whether one is an activist or not, is unwise, for the reality is that we are being hurt every day in this system, whether by inadequate education for the young or neglect and poverty for the old. Letting out anger in constructive ways is one step to releasing ourselves from the experience of victimhood with its powerlessness and its righteousness. Another step is to take responsibility for our side of the structure of injustice. Just as I participated in the growing of my cancer, most oppressed people participate in the continuation of injustice. Gandhi said again and again that the people of India cooperated with the oppression of the British and that the Empire would stay in India as long as Indians "agreed" to it. He was not blaming his people. He was leading them. For as soon as they saw for themselves that they were willing their own weakness—through drugs, through individual self-seeking, through class exploitation, and so on—they found the means to develop their own power. And so Gandhi's work included not only massive direct action campaigns which confronted the British Lion with its inability to rule an aroused people, but also promoted education, women's equality, the end of untouchability, and so on. Gandhi did not succeed in building up the health of India, the immune system of its body politic, sufficiently so that class oppression and other evils could be thrown off. He did, however, stir millions from their unawareness sufficiently to see that their decisions and lack of them allowed the British to exploit them—and that the power to defeat the malignancy of empire was within themselves.

DELIGHTING IN LIFE

In the hospital room with the fear and pain I resolved to choose life and celebrate it. I asked a dear friend to make a large poster for the wall with times he remembered me embracing life. Members of the community brought guitars and sang the songs of joy and celebration I loved. I remembered asking for Pete Seeger's song over and over while I cried:

One blue sky above us
One ocean lapping at our shores
One earth so green and round
Who can ask for more?
And because I love you
I'll give it one more try,
To show my rainbow race,
It's too soon to die.[2]

Now I can see that I was mobilizing my spiritual resources, using song and symbol to reach to the deepest part. I learned a meditation for cancer patients in which the journey to my center was by way of my enjoyment of life's goodness. I went on retreat to a beautiful wood and meadowland, where I stood in the open field while the deer grazed, each accepting the others. When I was recovering, I went dancing again, and played the piano and cooked crêpes and made sly fun of my illness.

In social change this is not a new resource. The Scandinavian folk school movements nourishing the struggle in the early part of this century, the singing and dancing of revolutionists in Latin America, the celebration of culture in China—all have been reaching in one way or another for the delight of the present experience of life.

In August 1981, I joined political theater companies and other cultural workers in St. Peter, Minnesota for "the gathering." To open the festival, a pageant composed of local people and performers from distant places moved through the small town. Differences of lifestyle and vocation were accepted in the focus on the great themes of prairie, water, land. We converged on the town park, finally, and the singing began: "O beautiful, for spacious skies...." The tears got in the way of my singing, I was so moved by the spirit of authentic patriotism, a love of place which is not warped by scorn for other places.

FACING THE PATHOLOGY

The meditation I used encouraged me, after getting in touch with the joy and abundance of life, to face the pathology, to visualize the cancer. This is counter to a tendency in the New Age movement to discount the pathology by looking beyond it; in that tendency self-transcendence is an elaborate scheme of avoidance. I found in my healing that it was useful to look at my cancer and to realize that "the only way out is through." Because it came *after* I put myself in touch with life's joy and abundance, I did not look at the cancer through eyes of fear. But I did not belittle it and seek comfort in bravado. I took it seriously, as a worthy opponent there to challenge me. When an opponent comes forward in the martial art of *aikido*, one moves toward him or her to meet. After all, the opponent is a whetstone on which one can polish oneself!

In politics one can also find a wish to avoid, a hope for transcendence that relieves us of the need for struggle. I realize that looking at "it"—the military-industrial complex, racism, the rape of the earth, and more—is tough, and looking at it with eyes of fear may cause one to turn away. But developing the courage to look at it will mean having the courage to do something about it.

The decision to avoid and "transcend" cannot be a satisfactory solution because, in our heart of hearts, we know that we are flinching at reality. How can we experience peace of mind knowing that we lack courage, that our peace of mind is achieved through playing a game of self-deception, much as a rich business executive might avoid looking at the slums along the freeway? Such a peace of mind is simply pacification of awareness, "psychic numbing."

An alternative orientation to war and injustice is to become fascinated with it. Rather than avoiding looking at it, one can become mesmerized by it, researching the facts and figures compulsively, with horrified fascination—like someone who repeatedly goes to monster movies, touching again and again the dread, each time with the reassurance of survival. We all need reassurance. The problem with getting fascinated with the details of war and injustice is that one easily moves into the position of well-informed futility.

I have found it easier to face and examine the pathology with support than by myself. Analyzing the interlocking systems of war and injustice is a stressful activity, and there is growing evidence that we can handle stress in proportion to the size of our intimate support system. (One task of our intimate supporters is to keep in touch with the joy of living.) Others may not need community as I do. It is easy to notice whether we are avoiding the newspapers, not reflecting on the poverty and environmental decay we see around us, not reading the analyses which examine the larger outlines of the institutions which hinder a living revolution. We can also notice whether we are preoccupied with the details of analysis without taking action with others on strategies for change. We can search ourselves to see if we have taken the classic cop-out for intellectuals: to try to experience some control in an out-of-control situation through amassing more facts and clarifying more concepts.

What worked for me in facing my pathology was to learn—through co-counseling, journal-writing, discussions with medical people, Jungian dream analysis—what I needed to know for action, for healing. Looking steadily at the cancer *and* the dimensions of me that allowed it to grow gave me power.

ENVISIONING HEALTH

In my meditation, after experiencing the joy of life and facing the reality of the cancer, I pictured myself in good health. I visualized what my body and mind would be like, what my lifestyle and relationships and environment and work would be like. I had a small group of trusted friends meeting with me, helping me develop a way of being which would resist cancers more strongly. I looked to my roots as well as to my present, outside to the reflections of me as well as inside, to ask "who is this man whose potential I shall realize?" I also fell into ideological rigidity sometimes and asked "What would this man be like if he were politically correct?"

When I was flexible and creative, the process of envisioning was a source of strength for me, an inspiration and encouragement. When I wasn't blueprinting, but was seeking direction, I grew in confidence. Goal-setting is the activity of a powerful person, because setting goals implies the confidence of achievement.

In social change the need for vision is, if anything, greater than it was for me personally. Activist groups often feel less powerful to make changes than individuals in them feel about their own lives. Activist groups reduce their own vitality when they choose not to picture society without the Pentagon and yet work against weapons, choose not to picture society with meaningful work democratically organized and yet work against corporate irresponsibility. The bystander watching activists work for disarmament may well assume naïveté when the activists are not projecting a vision of how the world would resolve its conflicts without arms. The bystander watching work for economic justice is free to assume that socialists are looking to the Soviet model if the activists are not projecting a vision of a human, flexible, environmentally sound and democratically controlled economy. And we activists ourselves can get confused by the co-optations and counter-thrusts if we do not have a clear sense of structures and values we want to characterize neighborhood, society, and planet.

ACCEPTING SUPPORT AND LOVE

I am a giver. Temperamentally, I give love and service and often put others ahead of myself. I also have a hard time letting others take care of me, accepting one-way loving. The hospital bed was a trial for me in two ways, therefore: not only did I have to handle the pain, but (perhaps harder) I had to let people love me. Opening myself to that tender caring was scary; catching a glimpse of the reality that love is abundant in the universe was deeply moving. I cried more in the experience of that truth than in the pain of the surgery.

Emma Goldman did not want to be in a revolution she could not dance in. I do not want to be in a revolution I cannot dance and love in.

It is striking that Daniel Ellsberg, the Rand Corporation Vietnam war planner who helped write the Pentagon Papers, released the classified documents after attending the 1969 War Resisters

International conference and experiencing a gathering of joy, love, and courage in the face of one of its attenders being sentenced, that week, to three years for draft resistance. The clearest way to show those discontented with the status quo that there is the possibility of a living revolution is to show it in our conduct with one another.

THINKING HOLISTICALLY

When considering, with my support group, what means of treatment I would use, I had no wish to put all my eggs in one basket. Chemotherapy made sense to me because of the late diagnosis and quick growth of the cancer. Emotional work made sense because I am an emotional being. I was skeptical about spiritual healing because of my graduate school training but turned to it with hope when I found it good for me. Exercise, insight-work, vitamins—the cancer was a massive threat and I responded with a total mobilization. Perhaps the most important thing I did was to take myself that seriously, to get my intention to live that clear, to use a multidimensional strategy for healing.

Similarly, humankind is facing a massive, life-endangering threat. It is a good time for total mobilization. I can remember the homefront during World War II: recycling tin cans, planting victory gardens, missing my Dad, seeing the buzz of activity in which masses of people were focused on a collective goal. Careers were deferred, marriages and babies postponed, reduction of living standard accepted—the urgency of the times demanded such things.

Again, we are people needing to struggle, but the enemy is not another people. Their defeat would not mean our victory, not in a nuclear war. Their defeat is our defeat; our survival requires their survival. The enemy is the institution of war—always the enemy of human values, and now also the enemy of human survival. Governments which nurture that institution, such as those of the U.S. and U.S.S.R., are allied with each other against our values and against our survival.

Mobilization this time is in a different context and involves a different strategy, yet the urgency is at least as great. It may be time again to defer   careers,   reduce   living   standards,   avoid   preoccupying relationships, or whatever for each person gets in the way of streamlining and focusing, whatever gets in the way of clear intention.

Holistic health refuses to look at symptoms alone but looks at the body, mind, and spirit of the person, as well as their lifestyle, physical environment, and social context. We activist-healers need to go beyond the treatment of the symptoms that most alarm us (the nuclear arms race, violence against women, racist oppression) to deal with the whole situation of our society and planet. The holistic perspective is consistent with the ecological perspective with which I wrote the first edition of this book, and in preparing for the new edition, I am pleased to see how much the old one avoided preoccupation with symptomatic relief.

WRITING THIS NEW EDITION

Publishing a new edition of this book is a stimulating experience because of the stock-taking it requires. I ask myself where I am now compared with when I wrote the book (1968-72), and where the world is now compared with then.

We are now part of a long process of fundamental change which began before we were born and will continue after the giant corporations crumble. That process is like a river; sometimes it flows fast and sometimes slow. By revolution, I mean a fundamental transformation of society and values which happens at a point where the river of history is running swift. In my observation, the river since the 1950s has been moving faster: that is, a revolutionary situation has been developing. Since the early 1970s, the world situation has become more full of contradictions and more people see the danger than before. Fifty-three Nobel Prize winners said in 1981 that world starvation is growing at such a rate that the Holocaust will be small in comparison; they urged massive civil disobedience to force institutional changes which will let the hungry live.[3] The U.S. State Department and the Council on Environmental Quality issued a report to the President, *Global 2000*, in which they predicted a massive resource, population, and energy crunch if major changes are not made.[4] Third World countries are dumping-grounds for weapons, with the result that mini–arms-races are growing, the debts are being serviced on the people's backs, and governments face bankruptcy.

Most industrial economies, both capitalist and noncapitalist, are in trouble, and the discipline of economics is scattered and confused about what to do. In 1979, Dr. Juanita Kreps, outgoing Secretary of Commerce, told the *Washington Post* that economics was no longer working and she found it impossible to go back to her old job as professor of economics at Duke University because, "I would not know what to teach."[5] Former Treasury Secretary Michael Blumenthal, himself a Ph.D. in economics, said, "I really think the economics profession is close to bankruptcy in understanding the present situation—before or after the fact."[6]

In the meantime, unemployment continues at completely unacceptable levels. Even if economic policy-makers were to come up with measures which provided more jobs, there are very fundamental questions remaining about ecological and social justice. The International Labor Organization, for example, did a study for the July 1980 UN Conference on women, held in Copenhagen. The ILO reported that women provide two-thirds of the world's work hours, receive ten percent of all wages, and own one percent of all property![7]

The multinational corporations, which I described as a threat in 1973, have grown substantially; they use their political power to get tax advantages and to hinder environmental protection—and then use their profits to gobble up the smaller companies which are the actual producers of new jobs. According to Senator Edward Kennedy, the thousand largest U.S. companies used eighty percent of the total tax credit and fifty percent of industrial-process energy but created only 75,000 new jobs in seven years. In the same period, the country's six million small businesses, using far less process energy, created nine million new jobs![8]

The signals of crisis have grown so prominent and become so elaborate that a single chapter cannot do them justice. I have therefore focused my attention on a single institution—the war system—to enable a more thorough analysis and to illustrate my basic argument that radical transformation is, in these next decades, on the agenda of global history.

It may be that those with vested interests in the status quo will be able to see beyond their interests and participate in fundamental change which results in their own diminished wealth and power. But don't count on it. A few will transcend their class position and act in solidarity with the people's needs, but most of those who gain power and profit from the war system will resist transformation and will accept the rhetoric of peace but not the requirements of peace. Activists must, in that case, be prepared to use coercive force. We need to find means of power so great as to break the iron chains which now hold the institution of war in place.

Chapter Two will not offer the traditional answer to that problem of coercion, since this is a book about a *living* revolution. We will not get rid of the institution of war by making war on the war-makers. Chapter Two examines, with the help of case studies, the possibility of nonviolent coercion. In the historical cases I describe, including military dictatorships being toppled through nonviolent struggle, I also show that a spontaneous civilian insurrection is not holistic enough. We therefore need an organic stage-by-stage strategic framework. That framework forms the core of the book:

- Cultural preparation, or consciousness-raising
- Organization-building, or creating the embryonic structures of the new society
- Propaganda of the deed, or confrontation
- Mass economic and political noncooperation, or exerting coercive force
- Parallel institutions, or stabilizing the new structures for basic functions

This framework will not tell the reader exactly what to do next week for two reasons: the activist must always think specifically for her or his own situation; and this book is on the level of grand strategy—that is, it is most useful as a *framework* for developing a specific strategy. A specific strategy will be geared to a defined goal or set of goals, women's equality, for example, and take into account the particular resources of the campaigners and also the strategies of the guardians of the patriarchy.

This strategic framework aids us in working out a specific strategy by helping us to understand the *development* of the movement for change. The five stages are a developmental model of a revolutionary movement, from the earliest stage of consciousness-change to the most advanced stage of self-reliant governance. The model is of a movement growing organically over time, with reverses and interruptions of course, but experiencing increased capacity to realize its own values. In a way, it is like a developmental model of a person, or of a forest, with each stage building on the preceding.

The five stages are like other models in that they present a simplified picture of what in fact would be a complicated reality. No two infants are just alike, nor do adults go through their mid-life crises at the same time or in the same way. Knowing, however, that there is such a thing as a mid-life crisis, or that old age brings different opportunities from the teenage years, can make a difference in living one's life. A model is, therefore, simply a way of helping us know where we are and what kind of opportunities we can use next. While it is a simplification, the framework here is more complex than the way activists generally think about strategy; thoroughly understanding this grand strategy will enable the reader to go beyond your present thinking in working for a better world.

There are many reasons why the stages are in their present order. One of the commonest mistakes in activism is to skip stages or to get them reversed. The stages are not, however, watertight compartments any more than an adult is finished with the playfulness seen in the child. In one sense, the first stage, consciousness-raising or cultural preparation, should never stop, since a revolutionary movement will be stronger the greater the awareness of its members. The best use of the framework, therefore, is to describe the emphasis, the central activity of the movement, at a given time. If we imagine the movement to begin small as a self-conscious transformative group and then to grow, in a pluralistic society, into a mass movement, the stages will more accurately resemble a chambered nautilus.

Cultural preparation done with a small number of people leads to the possibility of strong organization-building, which enables propaganda of the deed (stage 3) to be done effectively. The effect of stage 3 awakens many more people to the crisis, which provides the opportunity for more consciousness-raising activities (stage 1) and organization of the new people (stage 2), who will after a time want to participate in nonviolent confrontation (stage 3), and so on. When the movement is ready and the historical situation is ripe, it becomes appropriate to move into mass noncooperation (stage 4), a stage often initiated not by organizational leaders but by an upsurge from the grassroots, as the Polish Solidarity movement of August 1980.

Stage 5, parallel institutions, can build on the stage 2 work of organization-building in this approach to revolution, thus creating democratic structures which embody the spirit of a living revolution.

For some readers a picture is useful; for others the strongest guidance comes from being asked questions, strategic questions, which are basic to fundamental social change. In the appendix are questions appropriate to each stage; the reader who works out answers to those questions will have a specific strategy to offer her or his movement.

CHAMBERED NAUTILUS

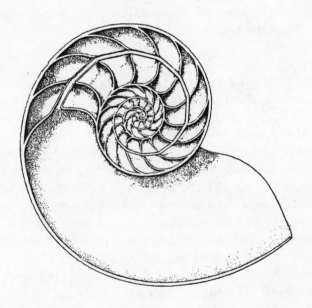

I

EMPOWERING OURSELVES
FOR PEACE

One of the most valuable lessons I've learned in twenty-five years of activism began in the mid-sixties. The war in Vietnam was already hot. Incumbent President Lyndon Johnson had run on a peace platform attacking presidential candidate Barry Goldwater's proposal to bomb North Vietnam, while, secretly, Johnson had already authorized such bombing to begin after the election was over. "Peace candidate" Johnson was elected and the war was escalated. The national radical pacifist Committee for Nonviolent Action decided to conduct civil disobedience at a Boeing plant in Morton, Pennsylvania, outside Philadelphia, where helicoptors were being built for use in Vietnam. I was a leader of that action.

Our message was simple and addressed mainly to the workers: Don't make those deadly helicoptors; lay down your tools and join us. We met considerable hostility. The long vigil line in front of the plant was pelted with eggs and tomatoes by townspeople who included relatives of the workers inside the plant. The tension grew after the arrests. Another leader and I were attacked as we headed for the train after ending the demonstration; fortunately we were only roughed up. We rode home feeling satisfied that we had made our moral point by challenging the workers and town in this way.

A year or so later a remarkable letter appeared in a Philadelphia newspaper's "letters" column. It was from the union at the Boeing plant and explained that the workers had no love for what they were making and had major reservations about the war itself. They were, many of them, however, family members who had dependents to feed and they were going to be responsible about that. They wanted anti-war activists to know about their dilemma.

About a year after that the head of the union local, John Taylor, conceived of a conversion plan. The workers did not want to be linked to military spending. Helicopter orders were slowing down and workers were being laid off; there was some urgency to Taylor's cause. With a Philadelphia architect, a plan was developed for modular housing to be made in the Boeing facility. A large tract nearby was being readied for residential development, so Boeing helicopters could even fly the houses to the site and lower them, unit by unit, to the foundations, ready for hook-up to utilities. It was a practical plan to meet a social and economic need.

The union took the plan to Boeing management, which turned it down. "Think," Boeing responded, "of how many houses we would have to build to get the profit we make on one helicopter." And the lay-offs continued until the workforce was only a fraction of its former self.

Where was I? I and other peace leaders had not responded to the letter in the newspaper by making contact with the workers. We did not know that they were now challenging Boeing management on what was to be produced at the plant, so we could not be an ally to them. We were elsewhere making a moral point about the war.

I now shake my head at how limited I was! Workers in military industry had a lot to teach me about the nature of the war system, about how industry which is organized from the top down and oriented to private profit is tied in with militarism.

FUNCTIONS OF THE WAR SYSTEM

The experience with the Boeing workers showed me one way I limit my power for peacemaking. I failed to look for *alliances* that would create a larger and more powerful force for change. I was partly blinded by self-righteousness: preoccupied by the moral rightness of my cause, I didn't notice what was before my eyes.

I was also lacking an analysis which would push me to look for alliances even when my righteousness was upon me. I was not observing the legitimate functions which the war system serves; in fact, the very idea of "legitimate functions" would have sounded dubious to me at the time. I was content to see war as either immoral or crazy—not as an institution which might have a certain rationality of its own.

In a way, I was like the U.S. progressives in the early part of this century who tackled big-city political machines. The reformers were appalled by the graft and corruption of the machines and, supported by muck-raking journalists, were able to force a number of them out of office. As sociologist Robert K. Merton has pointed out, the victories of the progressives were short-lived. New machines with new bosses came into power because the reformers had not looked at the system which produced the machines. The symptoms were obvious. Far from obvious were the *functions* which the machines were performing, some of which were legitimate functions. The machines provided upward mobility ladders for recent immigrants, softened the harshness of poverty for some, mediated between the confusing and impersonal bureaucracy and the neighbors on the block. Merton draws the conclusion that we will only be successful in abolishing an institution if we find out what its functions are and consider how they can be fulfilled in alternative ways.[1]

Three functions of the war system seem to me particularly clear: security, identity, and economy. These are basic human needs. We all need means of producing goods and services, we need measures to ward off attack and domination, and we need support for positive self-definition. These are individual needs which are also community needs, and insofar as a nation is a community (through shared tradition and values), a nation also has these needs.

As long as the military continues to fulfill these societal functions, it cannot be dislodged, no matter what the bad "side-effects" of militarism may be. A society will support disastrous policies as long as they meet these functional needs. Germans, for example, continued to support Hitler despite the terrible punishment they were taking in the Second

World War. They did so because his movement was meeting needs for identity, economy, and security better than any existing alternatives. Only with their leader dead and their cities in rubble did general compliance with Nazism dissolve. Other peoples, similarly, will go along with policies which take the heart out of the economy, increase the chance of nuclear holocaust, and sink us in despair—if there are no functional alternatives.

To understand the functions of the war system gives us power in several ways. We can increase the effectiveness of our educational outreach when we better understand where other people "are coming from." We no longer need to resort to concepts like "nuclear madness" which leave us frustrated and powerless. With a functional analysis we can build alliances with powerful groups in society by understanding how it is in their interest to support alternatives. We can also stay more steady in the midst of controversy because we can more easily sort out the legitimate concerns of our opponents from their negative desires for money or power.

Finally, we can dare to be abolitionists—to deepen the struggle against symptoms of the war system such as military intervention in Third World countries or the nuclear arms race—because a functional analysis points to the *fundamental* changes which can be made.

1) THE SECURITY FUNCTION OF THE WAR SYSTEM

Individuals as well as societies need defenses. Even on a psychological level, we need to be able to ward off attacks and efforts to subdue us. Therapist Jacqueline Larcombe Doyle has pointed out that healthy individuals have a variety of defenses which they use flexibly and appropriately. Neurotics are those who have one defense which they compulsively use—escape, for example—rigidly depending on it no matter what the situation.

Modern nation-states compulsively turn to a specialized response to difficult situations—war or the threat of it—and are as trapped as hapless neurotics who don't realize they have a choice. The legitimate function of security gets lost in the elaboration of the specialized and rigid response of a nuclear arms race.

There are plenty of experts who argue that participating in an arms race is extremely dangerous. For most people, however, a poor security system remains better than none.

A common argument made by peace advocates is that increased security will result from dropping out of the arms race while maintaining a military force. This view accepts the usefulness of the war system but argues against a particular strategy. Norway provides an example of a country which refused to participate in the European arms race of the late 1930s. It maintained a small army and neutrality. Its non-provocative stance was rewarded by a Nazi invasion and occupation.

Disarmament activists carry the idea of non-provocation farther and urge actual reduction of weapons. In the 1920s, disarmament movements became so strong that governments signed the Kellogg-Briand Pact which outlawed war and mandated the destruction of weapons. Governments began sinking their own battleships on the high seas. We know what followed—the largest and most destructive war in history.

Wars (and war preparations) will continue until there is an alternative security system.

WHAT IS TO BE DEFENDED?

When designing an alternative security system, it helps to ask exactly what we want to defend: the presence of multinational corporations in Third World countries? The freedom of the present dictatorships to rule in South Korea, Taiwan, El Salvador, Honduras, South Africa, etc.? The likelihood that Europeans will be the first to be destroyed in a nuclear war? The privileges and power of high military officers? The back-up of military force in case police power cannot restrain masses of Americans from struggling for a more just society (which is how the military was used in Poland against Solidarity)?

Clearly, there are many purposes of today's military which are questionable. We can perhaps agree, at a minimum, that we want to defend the human rights listed in the Constitution, to defend our freedom to steer our collective course from local to international levels through fair and clear rules that enable any minority to become a majority through persuasion. We might agree, in short, that we want to defend democracy.

Law professor Richard Falk points out the contradiction: when it comes to national security, *no* country is democratic! Major parties tacitly agree that the electorate must never face clear choices in national security, must never be given the chance to vote on whether to run an arms race, whether to support foreign dictatorships, whether to depend on dangerous Middle East oil or to pursue safe energy alternatives and conservation, for example. Electorates in Europe are similarly manipulated and lied to. No king or emperor, however tyrannical, ever had the power a British prime minister or French or U.S. president now has for destruction. The war system itself is a major subverter of democracy.

The means we invent to *defend* democracy need, therefore, to defend democracy rather than to subvert it. We need for our national security a democratic defense capability, one which does not separate out a specialized force as the agency for defense. We need what some Europeans are calling a "social defense," or what Harvard researcher Gene Sharp calls "Civilian-Based Defense."[2]

Civilian-Based Defense (CBD) is an approach to national security which meets threats through the flexible tactics of noncooperation applied by the people. The threats can either be external (an invasion from outside) or internal (an attempted coup d'état). CBD requires thorough training of the population in strategy and tactics of noncooperation and other methods of nonviolent struggle; in that sense every trained person is a member of the "reserves" and eligible for mobilization. Because training for CBD is related to training for nonviolent social change, CBD is a defense capability which encourages assertive and responsible citizenship, that is, democracy. (There are, however, some very significant strategic differences between CBD and nonviolent social change campaigns.)

As a defense technology, Civilian-Based Defense is at the crossbow-and-arrow stage. Although Swedish, Danish, and Dutch governments have funded studies, much more research and real-life testing needs to be done before societies will put their confidence in CBD. Already some features stand out, however:

- Civilian-Based Defense would be a stimulus for decentralization. The more dispersed power is, the more difficulty an authoritarian force would have in capturing it. CBD should be of great interest, therefore, to libertarians and the authentic conservatives who distrust a highly centralized nation-state.

- Civilian-Based Defense would cost very little compared with the present military budgets of most nations since the most important "weaponry" would be the solidarity and the new skills of the people.

- Civilian-Based Defense emphasizes struggle over institutions rather than geographical areas (in this way it is like guerrilla war strategy). The process of planning for defense in each workplace and institution would itself be a democratizing force within the institution.

- Civilian-Based Defense cannot defend exploitation of other countries. While there are some tactics of nonviolent intervention available, there is no capability for domination of other peoples to use their resources or gain their markets.

Could Civilian-Based Defense alone take care of national security needs? To attempt to use only CBD might fall into the trap of the neurotic individual who relies on only one defense. CBD makes sense in the context of other changes on both global and local levels. In Chapter Eight—"The World in Revolution"—I describe how CBD can be part of a whole program for transformation which draws on the best of the federalist, anarchist, and socialist perspectives.

2) THE IDENTITY FUNCTION OF THE WAR SYSTEM

Individuals and societies both need a sense of identity to hold themselves together and give purpose to their lives. Someone struggling with the question "What does my life mean?" is at risk; s/he may kill herself if s/he can't come up with an answer.

The war system helps provide an answer—which helps explain why war still commands the loyalties of so many. Peace activists are amazed that so many pro-lifers are also pro-war, but the apparent contradiction is eased when we notice that war helps to justify life by giving meaning to it. The institution of war influences identity through its reinforcement of national chauvinism and masculinity. National chauvinism offers people who feel bad about themselves (nearly everyone, on some level) the chance to feel better through identification with a state which can dominate others—if not alone, then in alliance with other states. Wars are so important in the recounting of a nation's history because wars reveal in heroic myth, if not always in successful outcome, that one's nation is superior after all.

Sociologist Elise Boulding has noted that polls consistently show women to be more dovish than men in attitudes toward foreign and military policy. Daniel Ellsberg has remarked on how frequently, during the Vietnam War, the wives of Pentagon and other government men disagreed with their husbands about the war and saw more clearly the folly of it all. This is an old connection: some of the organizers of the August 1914 peace parade down Fifth Avenue in New York City were outstanding leaders in the women's movement: Anna Howard Shaw, Jane Addams, Carrie Chapman Catt, Mary Beard, Charlotte Perkins Gilman.

When it comes to war, women have a decided advantage: they do not have to prove their masculinity. By "masculinity" I mean the character ideal which boys are taught to model themselves after. It includes such characteristics as competitiveness, being "cool" or unemotional (except for anger), doing abstract thinking, being responsible, taking the initiative. Masculinity exists only in contrast to femininity, for which girls are to strive. Feminine characteristics include cooperativeness, expressiveness, sensitivity, nurturance, and intuitive thinking.

Now we all know that, in fact, human characteristics are *not* distributed neatly between the sexes that way. A nursery school will often include girls who are aggressive and boys who cry easily. We also know that the culture does not leave them alone. The tomboy usually learns, over time, to become a lady, and the gentle boy develops armor to protect him from the jibes of his mates. They overhear the adults and learn that men who talk have "discussions" while women "gossip," that an assertive man is "independent" while an assertive woman is "pushy" or a "bitch." They to learn to value men and masculinity more than women and femininity.

Why is it so important to push boys into masculinity and girls into femininity at the cost of each person's individuality?

The masculinity/femininity dichotomy comes from a particular social structure called patriarchy—the domination of women by men. It is an ancient institution, predating capitalism and even urban civilization. Its nature is to maintain determining power in the hands of men—male boards of directors, male executives, male generals, male politicians, male religious leadership.

Patriarchy would never have lasted this long without a way of appearing to be "right and natural." Dividing human characteristics into two clusters and assigning them to the two sexes conditions us to think that it is natural for men to lead and women to follow.

Even though the spirits of men are hurt by pigeon-holing sex roles, the benefits largely go to men while women carry the main burden of the inequality. In the family, the man's name becomes the family's name; he gets paid for his job while the wife does not get paid for housework, even though the full-time housewife works for an average one hundred hours per week. When women go out to work, they receive 63 cents for each dollar a man receives and are more vulnerable to being laid off. Women form, in fact, a reserve labor pool for the capitalist economy, available for jobs when demand is high ("Rosie the Riveter" during World War II) and able to be pushed back when demand is low.

Few people realize how much our economy is subsidized by the unpaid work of women. Like slavery in an earlier day, it seems so natural. Economics writer Lisa Leghorn cites a conservative estimate of the annual value of women's unpaid work in the U.S.: in 1970 it was $650 billion! (On a global level, women work two-thirds of the total hours but receive only one-tenth of the income.) With economic exploitation on this scale, it is not surprising that there is widespread violence used by men against women. Individual instances of assault are colored by individual circumstances, but the overall picture shows a clear collective pattern: on the average, every 18 seconds a woman in the U.S. is beaten by a husband or male lover.[3]

Clearly, sex roles are far more than pink and blue baby blankets. They are one means of gaining acceptance of an institution of power, and even the way the characteristics have been distributed between the sexes reflects this power dynamic. The institution of power called patriarchy is a connecting link between militarism and masculinity.

Consider some of the characteristics assigned to the sexes:

MASCULINE	FEMININE
active	passive
competitive	cooperative
adventurous	nurturing
rigorous abstract reasoning	intuitive
task-centered	empathetic
unemotional	emotional
physically strong	physically weak
interested in sports	interested in art, music, and literature
self-assertive	self-sacrificing
rugged	graceful

Obviously the characteristics associated with power in our society are assigned to the masculine role. What corporation would hire a top executive whose personality profile was the list of feminine characteristics? When Edmund Muskie so much as cried in public during the 1972 Presidential race he was written off by many as a serious candidate, even though he obviously was competitive, self-assertive, and had many other masculine characteristics. If Muskie could cry in public, was he fitted to be the dominant figure in a dominant nation-state?

The nuclear arms race is, among other things, a contest for dominance. Former Defense Secretary Robert McNamara noted years ago that a few hundred submarine-borne missiles are adequate to deter Soviet attack, and his statement has so little impact on the men at the top because deterrence is not really their interest. Geopolitical dominance is their dream, and violence is their means. Daniel Ellsberg has described a number of times when the U.S. government threatened the use of nuclear weapons to get its way. Political scientist Richard Barnet describes what he calls the "hairy chest syndrome" among national security managers:

The man who is ready to recommend using violence against foreigners, even where he is overruled, does not damage his reputation for prudence, soundness, or imagination, but the man who recommends putting an issue to the UN, seeking negotiations, or—horror of horrors—"doing nothing" quickly becomes known as "soft." To be "soft"—that is, unbelligerent, compassionate, willing to settle for less—or simply to be repelled by homicide, is to be "irresponsible." It means walking out of the club.[4]

The "fit" between this theme of dominance in politics and in sexuality is striking. When renewed proposals for a bombing halt in Vietnam surfaced in his Administration, Lyndon Johnson reportedly reacted with anger and irritation. "Oh yes, a bombing halt," he would say. "I'll tell you what happens when there's a bombing halt: I halt and then Ho Chi Minh shoves his trucks right up my ass. That's your bombing halt."

Fear of homosexuality turns up repeatedly among supporters of violence. Psychologist Kenneth Smith did some pioneering research on homophobia (the fear of or contempt for homosexuals). In a study of college students he found that those who were most homophobic also were likely to agree with this statement: " 'My country right or wrong' is a very admirable attitude."[5]

During a speech on gay liberation, I was once heckled by a man who was as much puzzled as angry about what I was saying. Just as I was doubting that I would ever get through, his expression changed to amazement. "*Now* I see!" he exclaimed. "*You're* the most macho of all."

It was my turn to be puzzled. "You," he explained, "not only can get it over on a woman—you can get it over on a *man!*"

Sexuality, he had been taught by our patriarchal culture, is about domination. If I can not only dominate women through sex, but also men, I am the most manly of all.

This cultural linkage of sex with domination turns up in many places. "Fucking," for example, means sexual intercourse *and* exploitation: "She really got fucked" could mean either, depending on the context. This linkage enables us to understand a major source of homophobia among men. To be taken advantage of or dominated is to be like a woman. The connection is made not because gay men make love in the traditional heterosexual way, taking the role of women—they do not—but because that is what the uninformed straight world thinks. Because the traditional heterosexual model has domination and submission built in, the assumption is that everyone must do it that way. A gay man must be on the bottom, must have lost power, must...no longer be a man.

Once we perceive this deep cultural connection between domination and sex, we see violence in every direction. Rape is violence expressed sexually; it is often a means of enforcement and, like the lynching of blacks, is a way to keep the inferiors in their place. Rape regularly accompanies war. Violence is the only way a man can successfully defend himself against the accusation of homosexuality. Referring to the size of his bank account, the newness of his car, or his academic degrees won't do—only fighting will "clear" his name.

The patriarchal order appears to be both unnatural and unstable, judging from the amount of enforcement it requires. The daily pressure to conform to sex roles which begins in infancy and builds to intense peer pressure in adolescence, the beating of wives and mothers, raping to the point where one woman in four can expect to be raped in her lifetime, the beating of gay men—a tremendous amount of energy in this society goes into trying to hold the line.

Patriarchy is at this time a shaky institution, which is why the enforcement is so flagrant. It leans on a natural ally and another shaky institution—war—for support. The alliance is perhaps clearer in a country like Denmark, where the society is much more tolerant of lesbians and gay men than is the U.S. For many years, open gays have been employable by the government except in the two areas most involved with the institution of war: the military and the foreign service.

IS THERE A FUNCTIONAL ALTERNATIVE?

We all have a need to feel good about ourselves, to have a positive sense of who we are. We also, since we are not instinctual but historical persons who develop over time, need a positive sense of who we may *become*. Patriarchal culture has offered two character ideals, femininity and masculinity, so little girls and little boys may know what they are to grow into. The characteristics of those ideals are arranged in a way that supports the dominance of heterosexual men as a group. War and violence must be built into the "job description" of men because dominating institutions (racism, capitalism) use violence for enforcement as a last resort.

The obvious alternative to dominance is equality of sexes and sexual orientation. This can only happen by giving up polarized sex roles and offering a single character ideal which little girls and boys can look to for a positive sense of who they may become. This character ideal could be a combination of the best characteristics now located in femininity and masculinity, such as nurturance, cooperation, intuition, analytic reasoning, ability to feel feelings, physical strength, grace, initiative. I would like the new character ideal to include characteristics not now assigned to either sex: nonpossessiveness, non-attachment to material things. (In this society women and men are both expected to be jealous and to tie their identities to consumption.)

Because this new character ideal combines both feminine and masculine characteristics, it can conveniently be called "androgyny." Critics might say that there is nothing new about this character, that it has been celebrated in the past as most fully human, or most deeply Christian, or most psychologically integrated. This is a fair point. What is clearer now, thanks to the women's movement and to the lesbian and gay liberation movements, is how the polarization of human characteristics, felt so intimately in the experience of each of us, makes possible global destruction. "The boys with the toys" may actually blow us up.

What "the boys" need, as well as the rest of us, is a positive self-regard which includes deep acceptance of parts of ourselves which we may have been denying. We need to drop the inclination to project onto others the unacceptable parts of ourselves, labeling them "the enemy" and fighting them with all the energy of self-loathing. Freed of the task of appearing a "real man," men can relax and find out who they are as individual, unique beings. The human potential movement is providing resources and support for this process of individuation.

Getting to know and accept our individual selves is one major dimension of an alternative identity which does not need war and violence. A second dimension is positive group identity, pride in and acceptance of the specialness of "my people." A woman cannot accept herself fully without feeling sisterhood with other women, a worker cannot be proud of him or herself while being scornful of other workers as a class, an American cannot be fully self-accepting while muttering about "a nation of sheep." The past few decades have seen multiplication of resources for supporting positive group identity—in the growth of the Gray Panthers, women's groups, lesbian and gay groups, groups of the physically challenged, groups of people of color, men's antisexist groups, and so on.

A third dimension is species identity—experiencing solidarity with all of humankind. This may seem impossible, since we cannot at first hand experience humankind itself. What we can experience is human*ness*. And what gets in the way of recognizing the humanness in others is difference. Our ease or difficulty in handling difference is, I believe, rooted in the sexual difference; from the first movement the question is, "Is it a boy or a girl?" The cultural space for androgyny which has been growing since the 1960s encourages the conditions for species identity. Further, as Marshall McLuhan has pointed out, images transmitted by the mass media are shifting us toward the perception of a global village.

A fourth dimension might be called being identity—a solidarity with all living beings. There is, after all, a rape of the earth, a destruction of ecosystems, which is led by the same social forces which support the war system. Signs are growing of a cultural change in this area: Paul Winter's music in which human instruments mingle with the songs of whales and wolves; the increasing intervention by environmental activists such as Greenpeace on behalf of endangered species; the increase of vegetarianism.

A positive identity is growing: androgynous, accepting of self and others, and sensitive to our place in the universe. This is happening in the midst of television violence, horror movies, rising alcoholism and drug abuse, and other signs of disintegration of the old culture.

I do not know which will prevail. At times when I feel competitive, rigid, or violent, I especially notice the disintegration of the world "out there" and feel despairing. At times when I am in touch with my playfulness, my self-acceptance, my gentle strength, I notice the cultural movement for individuation and positive identification with group, species, and other beings. Then I feel hope. My decisions about how I experience my life affect how I see the world "out there." And

I become grateful to the millions before me who have taken the risk of being different, of reaching for more joy and communion than is in the patriarchal script.

3) THE ECONOMIC FUNCTION OF THE WAR SYSTEM

Individuals and societies both need a decent livelihood, ways of producing and exchanging that promote their well-being. A secure and adequate material basis for life usually translates into better health, less anxiety, and more optimism about the future.

The war system provides economic benefits to society. War offers to defend existing wealth, to provide continued access to resources available from outside the country, and to create jobs through soldiering and weapons manufacture. The tight connection between war and economy helps explain why war still commands the loyalties of so many people.

But how *well* does the institution of war perform its economic function, and for whom? The evidence is mounting that war performs poorly. Although many may benefit in the short run from an arms build-up, few gain in the middle run. If there is a nuclear war, no one gains in the long run.

In the short run, military spending can be used as a pump-primer for an economy in trouble. President Ronald Reagan, allegedly a fan of "supply-side theory," was in fact an oldfashioned Keynesian when he borrowed more money than any previous president. He injected the borrowed capital into the system through the nation's largest military build-up. While the economic recovery he created allowed poverty to grow, amidst double-digit figures of real unemployment, the spending spree on the military did benefit many people. Other military measures such as the Rapid Deployment Force created by President Carter were taken to ensure continued access to overseas resources at unfairly low prices, also benefitting (in the short run) a majority of U.S. citizens.

In the middle run, however, the impact of the war system on the economy is another story—a horror story. Deferred maintenance is the name of the game while the nation's infrastructure heads toward a nineteenth-century condition or worse. Manufacturing runs away to Third World countries where anti-union, low-wage, pollution-tolerant environments are created by military dictatorships supported by U.S. taxpayers. The touted "service economy" jobs which are supposed to replace manufacturing jobs often replace medium wages with low wages and are themselves moving to Third World countries via the technological marvels of satellite communications. The nation's productivity sags as internal "brain drain" depletes the civilian sector of innovative people who design wasteful weapons instead.

The government's Bureau of Labor Statistics tells us that, even in the short run, military spending costs us jobs. For each billion dollars of investment, 14,000 jobs are created in missile production, 16,000 jobs in fabricated metals, 28,000 jobs in apparel manufacture, 48,000 jobs in hospitals, 62,000 jobs in education, and 65,000 jobs in retail trade.

Because each billion dollars invested in the military is that much less capital available for the civilian sector—what economists call opportunity cost—a high military budget subtracts from the total jobs available. One study estimates that every time the military budget rises one billion dollars, 10,000 jobs disappear.[6]

Who benefits financially from the war system in the middle run? Workers in weapons plants benefit through the often-higher wages paid there, but the history of weapons manufacture is boom-and-bust, so job security is hard to come by. Many would prefer to make civilian products—products genuinely useful to society—but it is management's prerogative to decide what product will be made. When the Lucas Aerospace defense workers in England, for example, took the chance offered by unions to come up with ideas for what they would like to make with their skills and the Lucas facilities, they came up with hundreds of product ideas, almost none of which were military. (Lucas management turned down the workers' proposal to make these socially useful and marketable products.)[7]

The clearest benefits in the middle run go to the owners of the runaway shops and weapons companies. They make enormous profits and pay little in taxes. In fact the profits of the weapons manufacturers come from the taxpayers, so the war system functions as a mechanism for the redistribution of wealth—a kind of Robin-Hood-in-reverse.

The benefits of the cheap access to Third World resources are distributed likewise. Big-city children get to take a less expensive banana in their lunchpail to a school which is mired in hopelessness, with not enough books, overdue repairs to a decaying plant, underpaid teachers—because the nation can not at this point in history afford both good education and the war system.

The owners of runaway shops, on the other hand, can join the jet set and tuck their children into private schools.

What a society *needs* is a secure and adequate material basis for life, and I would add that all its members should participate in that. As the Scandinavians have demonstrated, there is really no reason for poverty, if sufficient wealth has been generated. In the U.S., sufficient wealth has been generated and there is no excuse for anything but a secure and adequate material basis for life for all.

The war system, despite its short-run functionality, is in the middle run clearly dysfunctional and needs to be replaced. Replacement means developing functional alternatives, and while there is not space here to describe every dimension, I can report good news in the area of *economic conversion.*

A functional alternative rapidly being developed both in Europe and the U.S. is generating socially useful products from facilities and skills that formerly served the war system. Economic conversion is not a new idea. Columbia professor Seymour Melman and others have been developing the concept for years, and there has been conversion legislation introduced into Congress since the early 1960s.[8] The International Association of Machinists—a union highly involved in military production—has been a major developer of the idea.

By 1984 enough work had been done to justify a major International Economic Conversion Conference, which was held at Boston College and which attracted 750 trade unionists, peace activists, and representatives from religious groups and groups fighting for economic justice. Participants came from 13 countries and 41 states of the U.S. The conference went beyond the specific application of conversion to military production to explore how conversion could aid every workplace which is threatened by cutbacks or closing. The key is advance planning by workers and community rather than letting the future of an enterprise depend on a whim of managers or "the play of market forces." When workers and community become bold enough to claim the right to plan for their future, they can just as well plan for the conversion of non-military runaway shops as for military installations.

One result of this new development is the introduction of conversion legislation in state legislatures and a push for county and municipal planning as well. Conversion has become one way in which activists can "think globally and act locally." And the more widespread conversion planning becomes, the less the military-industrial complex will be able to use the threat of joblessness to pressure for votes for the arms race. No longer will millions of workers, thousands of communities, and hundreds of members of Congress be held hostage to the war system. With plans already in place for alternative production, the threat will lose its sting. In fact, many localities will already be converting their facilities because conversion makes economic sense and is consistent with their values. Beating swords into ploughshares will at last be a practical goal.

FUNCTIONAL ANALYSIS: POWERFUL PEACEMAKING

Those turn-of-the-century reformers in the U.S. who attacked the big city political machines seemed very powerful at the time. They gained enormous attention in the press, they raised a large public outcry, and they often succeeded in turning out the corrupt bosses. Their power was more apparent than real, however, because the changes were largely cosmetic. The reformers lacked the understanding which a functional analysis would have provided them.

I realize that we sometimes fear knowledge—fear that seeing a problem in its full depth will result in feelings of helplessness and hopelessness. Information can, in fact, either empower or disempower us. Information which piles up fact after depressing fact about missile throw-weight or corporate exploitation or secret police tortures is unlikely to turn us on to our full power. On the other hand, information which explains how things work and demystifies the mechanisms of control does turn us on to our power, by giving meaning to our actions.

One powerful application of a functional analysis is that it spotlights alliances waiting to be built. Activists feel isolated when they don't see how the institution of war hurts a variety of people in a variety of ways; with a functional analysis they can see that it is to the benefit of many specific groups of people to support change. We can go beyond sloganizing (and wondering why all groups in society do not react the same to our slogan) to develop specific programs which respond to the needs of specific groups in society.

Another powerful application of a functional analysis is that it turns activism from a negative to a positive movement. The negativity of protest, with appeals to fear and guilt, has only a short-run value. Like the "no" of the two-year-old, it can help to assert the independence of mind which any activist needs. Powerful peacemaking, however, requires more than a stubborn "no"—it requires a creative "yes" to the institutions of peace and justice which are waiting to be built.

EXPECTING RESISTANCE TO POSITIVE CHANGE

Once I convince myself that a change will be for the better, I often expect that others will quickly agree. When they don't, I can choose to get discouraged...or I can ask myself what ties them to the status quo!

A functional analysis creates realistic expectations of resistance to change. If we think that the arms race is a product of "nuclear madness" and has no functionality, then we may be disheartened when we find a lot of resistance to the way of sanity. *Expecting* resistance gives us more power in dealing with it. Take, for example, the resistance to the functional alternative called economic conversion.

When he was Senator, Abraham Ribicoff sent a questionnaire to a sample of large corporations to find out whether they were developing conversion plans for the military part of their sales. The returns showed a nearly total lack of interest in conversion. In 1984 a broad coalition introduced conversion legislation to the Minnesota legislature, only to find it strongly opposed by the corporate lobby. We have already seen Boeing and Lucas Aerospace turning down their employees' plans for conversion. Why such resistance?

I see three main reasons why large corporations have so little interest in converting their facilities from military production to meeting vital human needs.

Militarism is more profitable. Corporations not previously involved in military contracting often try to get into the business because it is so lucrative. A headline story from the corporate world of 1982 was Bendix Corporation's bid to acquire Martin-Marietta in order to gain more military contracts. This is an old story; a Government Accounting Office study in 1971 showed that corporate profits average 56.1% return on equity investment for large military contracts.[9]

Military force can intervene abroad. U.S. corporations continue to invest heavily abroad, which puts strong pressure on U.S. foreign policy to support the governments which make good deals with corporations. These deals often mean a net outflow of wealth from poor countries to the U.S. and lessen the power of the country's citizenry to control their own economy. Understandably, resentment grows and citizens often mobilize to change the government even if it is a dictatorship, as it usually is. Since popular movements threaten the interests of U.S. corporations, these companies want their interests protected—and the Pentagon hopes to have the means to do it. From the point of view of the giant multinational corporations, therefore, it is more useful to have a far-flung military establishment than to have conversion.

This perceived need for military intervention becomes more pressing as non-renewable resources become more scarce. Jimmy Carter, appropriately enough, gave us both the picture of growing scarcity presented in *Global 2000: Report to the President* and the Rapid Deployment Force, a second Marine Corps for strengthening the government's ability to intervene in the interests of the corporations.[10]

Military projects don't compete. With existing economic institutions as they are, there is more productive capacity than can be used. The Government has for years stepped in to be the Big Consumer which buys up a lot of the production the rest of us cannot buy because we don't have the money. We might wish the Government would buy things that we can use instead of military hardware that just sits in silos or uses up oil in practice flights. But if the Government bought things the people can use—like fast, efficient, clean inexpensive public transport—it would be competing with private enterprise (the automakers). If the Government bought really good housing and made it available inexpensively, it would compete with the powerful slumlord interests. Since a rule of this Government (stated in the Employment Act of 1946) is not to do things which compete with private enterprise, it goes ahead buying nuclear missiles and submarines.

The economic result is that Government plays an important role in stabilizing the economy and providing a market which does not compete with existing civilian markets. The only people who suffer from this arrangement are...the people, because we don't get a lot of the things we need!

I could develop examples of resistance to other functional alternatives from those who benefit from the war system and/or have decided to protect it. We can expect that many of today's leaders will insist that weapons produce security, giant military corporations produce economic well-being, and stereotyped sex roles produce happy people. Their insistence is not always polite. It takes the form of slashing welfare rolls, attacking unions, red-baiting peace organizations, firing radical teachers, outlawing abortions, and reviving domestic spying.

Hope for change does not require naïveté. Instead, it requires realistic expectations and sound strategy. It is realistic to expect resistance to powerful peacemaking and to plan right now for that. Again, to use the psychological metaphor, a therapist knows that a client is ambivalent about getting well. On the one hand, a client longs to be free of painful compulsions. On the other hand, the client holds on and resists the intervention of the therapist. Internally, there is a conflict that may be intense, with dramatic signs of emotional crisis. For many clients, the only way out is *through*.

My theory of change assumes a crisis in society, assumes that the internal conflict will be heightened before it is resolved. The trick for the strategist—as for the therapist—is how not to lose the "client" in the process, how to keep the client from self-destruction.

In Chapter Two I present three case studies of societies in crisis, societies experiencing intense conflict over issues of democracy and justice. There is much to be learned that can be applied to our own situation.

II
POWER TO
FORCE CHANGE

A revolution means a drastic and relatively rapid change of power relations and values among a people. A revolution committed to life reflects that commitment even in its style. Like other revolutions, it breaks through the encrusted present, but it shoves aside the crust in its own way. The breakthrough of new life is powerful, but not in the way of the violent defenders of exploitation.

"We must destroy in order to build," some revolutionaries say. Metaphors are of course never precise, yet they affect us. An ecological imagination finds little appeal in images of destruction, since the margin of human life is already so narrow and violence is already so massive.

Marx's own organic metaphor—the birth of a baby—is better. A mother's womb is not destroyed in order to produce the new baby; a forceful wrenching occurs at birth but, if all goes well, not the mother's death.

A living revolution includes a forceful, wrenching, powerful process which allows the new life to breathe and grow. In this chapter, three large-scale examples of wrenching will show some limitations and possibilities: examples in France, El Salvador, and Guatemala.

A FRENCH SPRING, 1968[1]

In retrospect it is clear that there was increasing activity among French students in the spring of 1968, but at the time it made little splash. Nanterre, where much that was wrong in French university life appeared with particular clarity, erupted in the first days of May. Members of a group called the March 22 Movement began a three-day Campaign against Imperialism. The school, in a suburb of Paris, was closed by its administration, and the agitation boiled over into the Sorbonne, the center of the ancient University of Paris.

There, on May 3, a rally was held in a courtyard in support of Nanterre students who were to be brought before a disciplinary commission. The rector of the Sorbonne took the unprecedented act of calling the police to clear the courtyard, despite the peacefulness of the crowd and the Sorbonne's tradition of freedom from police activity.

The police "cleared" the courtyard by making arrests, to which the students responded at first peacefully but with growing indignation. Protests grew, and soon took the form of pelting police with stones, tiles, anything which lay near at hand. By the time it was over more than 1,000 students were involved, with 250 arrested and many students and some police injured.

In most French eyes the police had overreacted outrageously, and the national union of university professors joined the students' union in calling a strike in protest. The movement quickly spread to provincial universities, stimulating demonstrations and strikes at Aix-en-Provence, Bordeaux, Caen, Clermont-Ferrand, Dijon, Grenoble, Montpellier, Nantes, Rouen, Toulouse.

On May 6 in Paris about 4,500 students marched in protest. As they headed peacefully to the Sorbonne for a rally, they were met by a police charge which left the wounded scattered over the streets. Students fought back; the battle raged the whole night.

The next day about 30,000 students paraded up the Champs Élysées to the Arc de Triomphe to protest the police action. No violence occurred during the march, but when students returned to the Sorbonne they clashed with police again. The students were demanding three things: reopen the university, remove police from university property, and release arrested students. On May 9 an opinion poll published by *France-Soir* showed that four out of five Parisians supported the students' demands.

As demonstrations continued daily in the Latin Quarter, the movement gained momentum among students and teachers throughout France. A major impetus to the movement occurred the night of May 10, when thousands of students returned to the Latin Quarter from a march and attempted to encircle the police who were surrounding the Sorbonne. A few of the students began to build barricades. The action spread quickly. Paving stones were torn up, cars were overturned, and any materials lying around were pressed into service in the dozens of barricades erected that night. The students repeated their demand that the police leave the Sorbonne. Instead, the police began to clear the streets, taking barricade after barricade with the help of concussion grenades, heavy use of tear gas, and truncheons. Indignant residents threw flowerpots at the police and gave water for relief from the tear gas to the students.

The clashes continued most of the night. Radio reporters on the scene recounted them, blow by blow, to the French populace.

The drama was repeated the next night, this time with participation by some young workers. Daniel Cohn-Bendit, a young sociology student, declaimed in a speech at the barricades, "I call upon the working class to join our struggle." Reports of police brutality at the station house as well as at the barricades began to spread. Stories about the special riot police, some of whom got their training in the French war against the Algerians, were especially horrifying to the French public. The moment had arrived for participation by the factory workers. Union leaders called for a general strike on May 13.

The strike was illegal. In French law a general strike must be called with a five-day warning. But the then Prime Minister Georges Pompidou realized this was no time to be legalistic, and he sought to head off the growing student-worker alliance by releasing the imprisoned students, removing the police from the Sorbonne, and reopening the university. Pompidou publicly disavowed any responsibility for the violence of the police. This statement lowered the morale of the police still further; for days they had been subject to scorn from their children and neighbors when they went home from long shifts to catch some sleep.

Pompidou's concessions came too late. The twenty-four-hour general strike was judged even by conservative elements as 50 percent successful. In Paris a march headed by student leaders was joined by 800,000 to 1,000,000 factory workers and students. Politicians and union leaders were kept in the background by the student leaders, even though the strike was called by all of the French workers' unions. The students did not want the now-revolutionary content of their message to be blurred by the reformist leadership of the labor unions.

May 13 marked the beginning of the second stage of the insurrection. The dissidents took the offensive against all authority which presided over the status quo. Student leaders called on workers and students to cooperate in forming revolutionary action groups that would continue with tactics of direct action. Students began to occupy university buildings, turning them into forums where discussions could be held between students and workers on the kind of society which ought to be realized.

The strike of the workers, which was intended for only twenty-four hours, was resumed on May 14 in a number of factories throughout France. A new feature was added: on May 14 a group of young workers spontaneously occupied the Sud-Aviation plant at Nantes. Not since 1936 had France experienced the wave-upon-wave of sit-ins which followed. France's largest labor organization, the General Confederation of Workers (CGT), decided to run to the head of the parade to regain its leadership and put its organization and influence into the strikes and occupations.

On May 14, 40,000 workers and students demonstrated together in Toulouse, 12,000 in Strasbourg, 50,000 in Marseilles. Workers were joining students at the barricades, at rallies, at the Sorbonne, and on street corners to discuss the meaning of the events. Some students joined workers in the occupied factories, but the union officials tried to discourage this. A policy soon became evident which had enormous significance for the weeks following: the two main unions, the Communist-backed CGT and the Christian Federation of Democratic Workers (CFDT), felt the student revolutionaries were going too far and should be separated from the workers, and that the energies of the workers should be directed toward non-political, material goals.

On May 16 students occupied the Odéon, a state-subsidized theater not far from the Sorbonne. Their purpose was to invite the general public to join the students and workers in discussions. But on the same day a large student march to the Renault factory, which had just struck, was turned back by the unions, and students were denied entrance to the factory to talk with the workers.

Within the schools, education reform became the leading issue. Inspired by the occupation of the universities, high school students began to occupy their schools, often supported by the teachers. Discussions flourished between teachers and students on the shape the new education should take. This teacher-student alliance was reflected in the announcement on May 16 that deans of university faculties threatened to resign en masse if reforms were not carried out.

On May 17 railways and shipyards were occupied, and air traffic out of and into Paris was nearly brought to a halt. The farmers' union announced plans for demonstrations. Radio and television technicians prepared to occupy the studios.

In the next several days in Paris, garbage collectors, subway and bus operators, and bank employees went on strike. Technicians occupied theaters, and the Cannes Film Festival closed in sympathy with the growing movements.

By May 20 at least 2 million workers were on strike, and 250 factories occupied. Hardest hit were metal and chemical industries, coal mines, and public services. The army was being used to provide necessary public services, but there were rumors that the army could not be relied upon to restore order.

The socialists and communists, who had been in coalition before the outbreak, sensed a chance to succeed the Gaullist government, and on May 22 a parliamentary motion of censure failed by just eleven votes. The Communist Party, to the dismay of the revolutionary students, showed every intention of carefully moving the conflict back to the parliamentary arena.

By this time the state bureaucracy was becoming severely strained. The Minister of the Interior, responsible for the maintenance of public order, was put out of communication with the provinces because of strikes in his own transmission services. The Paris police union warned on May 23 that the police might be forced to question their orders if they were used continually against the strikers. In their statement the police hinted regret that they could not legally go on strike themselves to voice their grievances.

The government's situation was complicated further by the uncertain reliability of the troops. Most of the soldiers were young conscripts who could sense the mood of their fellow workers. Some soldiers customarily returned home at night to sleep and could feel the excitement firsthand. The army officers included many who were still unhappy about the French departure from Algeria and had little love for De Gaulle as a result.

With the government on the defensive, De Gaulle tried his customary weapon to restore order; on May 24 he proposed a referendum. The proposal was met with jeers. Students and workers marched again in Paris. The strike was joined by retail employees, restaurant workers, architects, and farmers. Amateur soccer players occupied their association's headquarters, professional dancers took over the Folies Bergères, and gravediggers occupied the Paris cemeteries.

Over the weekend of May 25–27 Pompidou held talks with unions and employers. The unions as well as the government wished to gain control of the rebellion, for the initiative still lay with the younger workers and students rather than with the union officials. The government made tremendous economic concessions to the labor movement in an effort to separate it from the students and cause the radical workers to forget their demands for political change and "worker power" within the work place. The government also issued a ban on demonstrations.

But the rank and file rejected the agreements on May 27, and workers joined students in defying the government ban on demonstrations by gathering in a Paris rally of 35,000. Two days later 500,000 workers demonstrated throughout France. No violent incidents were reported.

Word spread that President De Gaulle had consulted with the headquarters of his army of occupation in Germany in order to ensure the loyalty of at least that part of the army. Support was evidently promised; several political prisoners held for their anti-government activity during the Algerian War were finally released. Apparently De Gaulle was mending fences on his right.

On May 30, then, he was ready with both the carrot and the stick. In a forceful speech to the nation De Gaulle announced that the National Assembly was dissolved and the referendum abandoned, and that there would be general elections within forty days. The way to reform was open by the electoral process, the General was saying, and he was fully prepared to restore order with the army if necessary. He cleverly linked the Communist Party with the uprising, then warned that the Party was about to take over the country to destroy liberty forever.

The conservatives, reassured that their leader had things in hand, staged a huge pro-Gaullist parade in Paris. Politicians began to prepare for the election campaign and police began to clear strikers from communication centers through much of France. Gasoline, which had been in short supply, suddenly became available again, in time for the Whitsun holiday. The state-controlled radio and television continued to emphasize the destruction of automobiles and property by the students, and injuries suffered by policemen during the barricade fights. The Communist Party denounced De Gaulle's speech, but also tried to bring the strikes and occupations to an end.

With surprising suddenness a cooling wind blew over France, changing the climate for student revolutionaries and young workers alike. Some activists still tried to continue the movement. Railwaymen, for example, reoccupied the Strasbourg railway station after being expelled by the police, and engine drivers lay down on the track to stop a train. In some cases the workers, helped by students, fought the riot police which were sent to expel them from the factories. The brutality of the police started new waves of protest, expressed in massive demonstrations in Paris on June 10–12, and a one-hour work stoppage on June 13.

But De Gaulle's speech had begun the third stage of the struggle, which was defensive and essentially in reaction to the government's initiative. The public mood had changed in favor of the government, and the vast majority of the population seemed to favor a return to "law and order."

At its peak, the civilian insurrection involved ten million strikers (two-thirds of France's work force), hundreds of occupations, hundreds of thousands in the streets. The government was shaken, but did not fall.

The lack of revolutionary organization was a decisive handicap to the struggle. The forces in motion were not related to each other in an organic way, and were dependent for their unity on blunders by the government and a corresponding context of public sympathy. The most serious problem was the split, among students as well as workers, between the reformers and the revolutionaries. The supposedly revolutionary Communist Party refused to play a revolutionary rôle, which added further to the lack of cohesion.

The spontaneity of the struggle, however, was one of its most exciting aspects. It unleashed a power of innovation and a burst of communication which was previously hidden by bureaucracy and tradition. Associated in its origins with the young people, the spontaneity should remind cynical and tired radicals that all the calculations are not finished so long as the spontaneity of youth remains.

There was astonishingly little violence by the students and workers, and also less violence by the agents of repression than one might expect in a situation so threatening to the state. Estimations place the number of dead at five to ten, in a month-long struggle by millions! The three weapons most used in the struggle were strike, occupation and demonstration—all nonviolent methods. The barricades were considered by Trotskyist leader Alain Krivine and others as defensive, rather than as a means of forcing social change. Most of the workers and students realized that attempts to create an army of liberation would only ensure the intervention of the national army and might in effect be suicidal.

The generally nonviolent character of the insurrection seemed to have an inhibiting effect on the state, which left most policemen's guns unloaded and was extremely hesitant to use most of the army.

On the other hand, even the rebels' comparatively little violence was a disadvantage to them; it was used for propaganda successfully by the government, for it maximized the fears of important segments of public opinion and even antagonized some workers.

The revolt plainly succeeded in gaining some immediate changes. The unions were strengthened in a country in which unions have long been weak, and some material gains were made for workers, at least for the moment. Student power was increased in the schools and educational reforms were initiated. But these gains fell far short of the goal of the revolutionaries to bring down the regime, and indeed there was a turn to the right by the national government after the insurrection.

Have there been cases in which a civilian insurrection succeeded in bringing down a government? In the history of Chile, Haiti, Panama and Vietnam, governments have fallen largely because of such a rising. The following two cases of governmental collapse reveal more of the dynamics of civilian insurrection.

SALVADORANS THROWN OUT A DICTATOR[2]

On Palm Sunday, April 2, 1944, with the top officials of the administration away from the capital for the Holy Week holiday, the strategic First Infantry and Second Artillery regiments of San Salvador and Santa Ana garrison took up arms against the government. Rebel officers took control of the Air Force, the state radio station, the telegraph offices of San Salvador and Santa Ana, and the Santa Ana police headquarters.

So began the armed revolt against the hated rule of Hernandez Martínez. Airplanes bombed San Salvador; two square blocks of the city were destroyed. In Santa Ana civilians held a huge demonstration, threw out the old city council, and elected a new one.

The dictator, however, was able to rally parts of the armed forces which remained loyal to him and began a crackdown which defeated the rebels. Executions began immediately as martial law was declared and enforced by the police curfew.

One of the heroes of this revolt was tortured the whole night—from six in the evening until ten the following morning, when he was shot.

When he was brought out to be shot, both his arms had been broken, one knee smashed to splinters, his right hand was a bloody pulp. His finger-nails and toe-nails had been pulled out—wood splinters had been driven into the tips of his fingers, and they had filed his teeth. They had fractured his collar-bone; there was only a bloody, gaping hole where an eye had once been.

The priest who was attending him during his last moments noticed his trembling and asked, "My son, are you afraid to die?" This boy who the day before was filled with life, whose body had been smashed and twisted beyond repair, answered, "No, father. It is only my body which trembles. Not my spirit."

What was the setting for this tragic effort to overthrow the government?

The social picture of El Salvador was not pretty. The major export, coffee, was largely in the hands of a few families. The oligarchy had largely been content with the rule of General Maximiliano Hernandez Martínez, who came to power in 1931 through a military coup. One of Martínez' first acts was to suppress ruthlessly a revolt by poverty-stricken peasants. Crying "Communist," the General presided over a bloodbath in which eight to ten thousand were killed. So by the time of the April 1944 rebellion, Martínez had had a good deal of practice in putting down popular discontent.

To avoid open conflict he combined road-building and high pay for the army and public servants with repressive censorship and banning of political opposition. Even the traditional elections of county councils were abolished in favor of government appointments. But in twelve years a dictator accumulates a lot of enemies, and it was probably no help that he claimed miraculous powers, sometimes haranguing his officers on spiritualist themes.

World War II was in some ways a destabilizing influence. There were economic strains, and ideological control was harder to maintain. Because El Salvador's main ally, the United States, was engaged in anti-fascist struggles overseas, opponents to Martínez were able to hold anti-fascist rallies and often get away with it despite the subversive overtones.

Opposition crystallized when it became clear that Martínez planned to violate the constitution by continuing in office beyond his end of term in 1945. A conspiracy was organized to overthrow the dictator, led by professionals with key allies in the army and among business leaders.

Even though his regime had been showing some cracks, Martínez was still shrewd enough to deal with the military revolt of early April. He followed his victory with weeks of terror, hunting down those who had been involved. Some observers believed that the violence aroused lower class Salvadorenos, the group least committed to the opposition before the revolt. At the end of April, according to one account, "market people, shopkeepers and civilians on the street are openly decrying the executions and tortures." Members of the clergy joined the effort to save fugitives, as people ranging from market vendors to the archbishop pleaded for an end to the executions.

On April 24 the students took the initiative by going on strike against the repression. The following week they produced this leaflet:

Decree for a general strike including hospitals, courts, and public works....The basis of the strike shall be general passive resistance, noncooperation with the government, the wearing of mourning, the unity of all classes, the prohibition of fiestas.

By showing the tyrant the abyss between him and the people, by isolating him completely, we shall cause his downfall. Boycott the movies, the national lottery. Pay no taxes. Abandon government jobs, leave them unfilled. Pray daily for the souls of the massacred. The Archbishop has been humiliated.[3]

The leaflets were mostly produced on typewriters, with the request that each person receiving one make ten copies to distribute. The walkout by high school and university students was followed by bus drivers and taxi drivers. National and municipal government employees stayed home. Railway workers followed. Stores closed, garbage piled up in the streets, the courts were empty.

On May 2 a group of physicians sent a memorandum to the government demanding amnesty for the civilian prisoners. Martínez burned the memo in front of two of their leaders. Physicians joined the strike, and were joined by dentists, pharmacists, lawyers, banking employees, engineers. Teachers had already acted with their students and the schools were closed.

The strike committee of the students had a fairly clear strategy even though it was hastily put together. They reasoned that the transportation sector was the "Achilles' heel of the Salvadoran economy"; if it could be paralyzed, other sectors of the economy would follow. They also counted heavily on the physicians (some of whom had already been politically active), calculating that the loss of medical services and closing of drugstores would push the general public to take a stand, either declaring for Martínez or demanding his resignation.

The strike committee made a clear and conscious choice against violence. The failure of the military revolt taught them that Martínez could not be defeated in that arena; they also believed that refraining from violence would attract more supporters. When one committee member suggested sniping at the police, the others squelched the idea. They also decided against street demonstrations, thinking that too much bloodshed would be provoked, and so the phrase "*huelga do brazos caidos*" emerged: a strike with our hands at our sides. They knew, however, that this strategy was anything but passive, and they expected that Martínez would be toppled through the unarmed insurrection.

As it turned out, demonstrations did spontaneously occur. On May 5 a large crowd waited at the Church of the Rosary for the priest to come and say mass; the nervous authorities apparently prevented the priest from coming. The crowd then dispersed through the city to persuade stores to close which were still open.

Two days later a tragedy brought the insurrection to a head. A nervous or trigger-happy police officer fired without warning at a group of boys on the street, killing a seventeen-year-old instantly. Outraged, citizens poured into the streets. Thousands of people arrived at the boy's home that evening and at the funeral the next morning. The strike committee set up a peacekeeping force of some fifty students to reduce the chance of the crowd killing police; the students were kept busy, at one point preventing the lynching of the army chief of staff who drove to the crowd and urged them to abandon the strike.

From the funeral the crowd proceeded to a plaza across from the National Palace. Inside the palace five government employees presented their resignations and appealed to others to join them; by the time the crowd invaded the building later that morning calling for Martínez' resignation, they found the offices empty.

Martínez was finding his capability for ruling rapidly dissolving. He could not stem the tide, neither by martial law nor by his radio addresses attacking the rich and praising the poor, charging the strike was financed by the "Nazi arsenal." Police went to homes to find strikers and force them to return to work. Threats resulted in some merchants re-opening their shops, and some physicians were dismissed. The army leadership reportedly would have welcomed the opportunity to launch an all out attack on the strikers, but they lacked the excuse which would have been given by violence by the crowds, and they could not fully count on their troops to kill unarmed protestors wholesale. Martínez faced his cabinet, which recommended that he resign.

The Assembly accepted the resignation on May 9, but still the strike continued. The people would return to work only when Martínez left the country.

On May 11 sirens screamed and fireworks exploded; the hated dictator had fled to Guatemala. The new acting President ordered amnesty for all political prisoners, declared freedom of the press, and began planning for general elections. The general strike was over.

STRIKE ONE, STRIKE TWO . . . IN GUATEMALA[4]

Martínez might well have expected things to be calm in Guatemala. Surely the iron rule of President Jorge Ubico would make it a comfortable place for a dictator-in-residence.

Ubico had been elected in 1931. His first important act was to grant the United Fruit Company a major concession that the previous government had refused. As he consolidated his power, cancelling all legal limits on his tenure, the believers in democracy became restive. Ubico arrested hundreds of students, workers and prominent citizens, torturing and killing many of them.

The spy network was elaborate. Ubico dealt with some lawbreakers by transferring them from the jurisdiction of one court to another. During the transfer, which was done on foot over lonely roads, the political dissenters "tried to escape" and were killed in the attempt.

The army grew, and efforts were made to militarize the schools and universities. No form of citizen organization was permitted and even charity and cultural associations were suspect. Unrest surfaced again in 1940, but a firing squad put an end to the plans of politicians and army officers to stage a coup d'état. In 1941 the Congress again extended Ubico's term, this time to 1949.

Along with the coercive tactics, Ubico maneuvered to keep support from key sectors of society. His enforced scale of low wages and his taxation policies were bound to please the coffee-growers. United Fruit and the United States Embassy were friendly. Ubico made a show of great sympathy for the plight of the Indians, who formed about two-thirds of the population.

But World War II brought troubles for Ubico. Increasing United States activity included the construction of roads, bases and even a hospital. Thousands of U.S. troops, well-paid and housed, aroused the envy of the Guatemalan soldiers. Despite Ubico's fiscal policy, prices began to rise, while workers still earned between 12¢ and 50¢ a day.

Meanwhile, the air of Guatemala was full of wartime propaganda about the Atlantic Charter and the "Four Freedoms." As sociologist Richard N. Adams remarked: "In the Guatemala of Ubico, one did not generally advertise any freedoms, much less four of them, without evoking invidious comparisons."[5]

The downfall of Martínez in El Salvador may well have given the opponents of Ubico new hope, as well as a model for action. They began to surface before the month of May 1944 was out. Forty-five lawyers petitioned the President for the removal of a flagrantly arbitrary judge. Two hundred schoolteachers asked for higher pay. When their leaders were immediately charged with sedition before a military court, the teachers responded by refusing to participate in the rehearsals for the annual parade in honor of Ubico and were fired in large numbers. Meanwhile, a group of professional men quietly began organizing an opposition party.

When students at the San Carlos University in Guatemala City petitioned early in June for changes in their faculties, Ubico agreed to their still-moderate demands. The students, heartened by Ubico's concessions, escalated their demands. Every opportunity was used. Even the failure of the law school dean, an Ubico appointee, to award a gold medal to the chosen student because of the student's political convictions resulted in student agitation. The crisis came on June 22 when the students presented a sweeping program of university reform, threatening to strike if the government did not respond positively within twenty-four hours.

Whether goaded by the students or by rumors that a general strike was being planned for June 30 by an unidentified opposition group, Ubico acted the same day. The articles of the Constitution guaranteeing individual rights, including public assembly, were suspended—which made legal everything Ubico was already doing. The most active student leaders took refuge in the Mexican Embassy, but others began planning student action. University students and the schoolteachers went on strike on June 23.

On June 24 Ubico was presented with a petition for a return to constitutional liberty signed by 311 leading citizens of the capital. At noon the students led the first peaceful demonstration of protest. The procession marched past the U.S. embassy and, on the main street, became a mass gathering, with students reading the Atlantic Charter aloud.

That evening a second student demonstration occurred; there was more reading of the Atlantic Charter and for the first time the demand was made that Ubico resign. Students began distributing illegal mimeographed leaflets explaining their position to the general public.

That same evening the first police violence occurred. Provocateurs were encouraged by police to break up a festival of workers, after which the police came in shooting.

By the time morning arrived on Sunday, June 25, soldiers, cavalry and machine guns were menacingly evident in Guatemala City. Representatives of the dissident groups were summoned to meet with government officials. Demonstrations continued. Women dressed in mourning were fired upon as they marched from a downtown church to the National Palace. Many of the women were injured. María Chinchilla, a young schoolteacher, became the movement's first martyr.

On Monday all Guatemala City joined the movement of *brazos caídos* (hands at your sides). Stores, theaters, banks, schools, clinics, and offices were closed.

Ubico organized further reprisals. Highly respectable oppositionists had their automobiles taken into custody and were themselves followed by police agents. Since the majority of the large commercial firms belonged to foreigners, Ubico decreed the deportation of any foreigner who closed his business. The police went from door to door intimidating the merchants into staying open. When the railway workers joined the strike, Ubico issued a decree placing all personnel of transportation and communications companies under military law.

The students distributed more leaflets urging the public to continue its "dignified and peaceful attitude and to avoid any uncivil or hostile act that might prejudice the happy accomplishments of our objects and those of the people."

The army and the U.S. Ambassador remained loyal to Ubico, but it seemed almost everyone else had deserted him. His troops were powerless either to restore normal life to the city or to stop the continuing flow of petitions for his resignation. On July 1 Ubico turned the government over to a military triumvirate headed by his friend, Frederico Ponce.

The junta announced that constitutional rights would be restored and a new President elected as soon as possible. Meanwhile, however, Ponce planted soldiers outside the Congress to encourage the legislators to name him provisional President, and he began to meet secretly with Ubico. Five young lawyers who objected were jailed. Exiles began to stream back to Guatemala and new political parties were formed. Workers struck for higher wages during the summer. Ponce announced he would run for President on the ticket of the old Liberal Party.

By October it was evident that Ponce would not allow a free election. On October 16 students and teachers distributed mimeographed leaflets declaring a political strike. At the same time, a group of young army officers planned a military revolt. Aided by students and workers, they seized control of Guatemala City on October 18.

Ponce took refuge in the Mexican Embassy, and the diplomatic corps intervened to help a new provisional government take shape. The aims of the June insurrection seemed at last to be fulfilled early in 1945 when a new constitution was adopted and elections were finally held. Dr. Juan José Arevalo, a liberal democrat, was elected President and began a series of popular reforms.

LIMITS OF CIVILIAN INSURRECTION

France, El Salvador and Guatemala are among the many societies which have been convulsed by mass action, wrenched by the power of general strikes, boycotts, occupations, demonstrations. Clearly there is considerable coercive power available in these methods—in these cases two ruthless dictators were forced very much against their will to step down. Yet the source of the coercion seems puzzling to those who are used to equating coercion with violence.

With violent means such as conventional or guerrilla war, people gain their ends by destroying and destroying until the opponent gives up. Of course other factors, such as propaganda, are also important in military victory, but in most wars the intention is to destroy the army of the opponent. In this century the violence has often widened to destroy a good part of the society as well. The basic dynamic of coercion by violence, then, is destruction.

By contrast, the people of El Salvador and Guatemala were not depending on destruction; they scarcely destroyed anything. In striking and demonstrating they were relying on quite a different basis of coercion—*noncooperation*. They were unconsciously depending on the axiom in political theory that the oppressor depends for continuing rule on the cooperation of the oppressed.

Machiavelli long ago pointed out that the prince "who has the public as a whole for his enemy can never make himself secure; and the greater his cruelty, the weaker does his regime become."[6] Martínez and Ubico were not short of cruelty, or of weapons, but they could not overcome the determined refusal of their peoples to be ruled.

France, El Salvador, and Guatemala also show the limitations of civilian insurrection. In France the government was shaken but did not fall. In El Salvador the government fell but the resulting power vacuum was quickly filled by a rearrangement of the articulate forces (the ogliarchy, the army) over the heads of the people who had worked and sacrificed for change. In Guatemala much the same thing happened, except for the decidedly more progressive new government; but the basic social structure remains unaltered.

The chief limitation is that there is a strong tendency for the society, although shaken, to fall back into place roughly as before. The worst excesses of dictatorship may be eliminated, some reforms may be gained, but there is no revolution. The convulsion by the masses creates a power vacuum but cannot by itself fill that vacuum—only an organized movement can do that. Only a strong and united peoples' organization with a revolutionary program can provide the new life which becomes that new society.

The very swiftness of the insurrection is a limitation. For a heady moment people defy the regime, but more than a moment is required to change the habits of submission which are the foundation of oppression. There must be a succession of battles, a long march, a continuing revelation of the nature of power and authority. Else we will never learn to stand erect during the intervals between euphoria and rage.

The rapid pace of insurrectionary action leaves little time for the development of a revolutionary program. Daniel Cohn-Bendit kept insisting, during the French insurrection, that the program should arise out of the process of revolt itself, from the impassioned discussions at factory and barricade. But it is clearly impossible for new ideas and new feelings to be aired, digested and decided upon by millions of people in a matter of weeks! In 1968 the hope was that the French Revolutionary Action Committees would be able to gain full authority. If the Committees had done so, they would probably have found themselves doing a great many unrevolutionary things due to the lack of consensus on new departures—that is, for the lack of a program.

Of course some in the Bolshevik tradition believe that a small vanguard organization, taking advantage of the turmoil created by an insurrection, should take power and impose its program in the name of the masses. In doing so the vanguard could depend on the people's habits of submission to help to sustain it, once the insurrectionary mood had passed. It is doubtful, however, that even Lenin would have seized power in 1917 if he had not expected that this would touch off a genuine mass revolution in Germany, for the classical Marxist view is clearly weighted on the side of the full participation of the masses in their liberation.

If the new regime actually maintains the old habits of submissiveness in the people, and enforces top-down change by means of bureaucracy without participation of the people, can we say that it is fully revolutionary? The inevitable aftermath of political prisoners and suppression of free speech only raises more doubts.

Still another problem with civilian insurrection is that it focuses too much attention on the state. Despite the developments in France of a considerable number of parallel institutions—in some places the rebels were carrying out the normal government activities, and there were experiments with new forms of exchange—overwhelming attention was paid to the national state authority. Of course control of the state apparatus is important. But a form of revolution which develops other means of ordering the social life is considerably more revolutionary than that which concentrates on the state.

Perhaps the greatest limitation of all is the essentially local character of a civilian insurrection. In Guatemala the progressive developments that were triggered by the insurrection of 1944 continued for a decade, until the government of President Jacobo Arbenz decided to nationalize the idle lands owned by the United Fruit Company. Then, as Dwight Eisenhower publicly admitted, the U.S. Central Intelligence Agency organized a coup d'état. In 1953 the general strike and demonstrations in East Germany might have toppled Ulbricht's government if the Soviet Army had not intervened. If, in 1968, the French rising had resulted in a socialist revolution, NATO might have intervened.

The conditions for the beginning of an insurrection are national, but the conditions for success are often transnational. A genuine revolution will need to be transnational in character even when the major front is in one particular country.

What does all this mean for a strategy? To dismiss the importance of mass noncooperation is foolish; it is no small thing to topple a ruthless dictator or shake a modern industrial state. A means of coercing oppressors without large-scale destruction is exciting and hopeful, and a living revolution needs that power.

The power of noncooperation in the form of civilian insurrection is, however, clearly not enough.

Insurrection lacks the organic growth behind it of a cohesive mass movement with a revolutionary program. It lacks the time required to shake off the habits of submission on which all oppressive systems depend. It lacks the development of skills and knowledge in enough people to be able to inaugurate a genuine new order. It lacks the organizational forms which provide alternatives to state domination.

Finally, a spontaneous national convulsion lacks the transnational dimension which is required in this shrinking world. The Soviet and American empires, plus the ecological perspective, stand against all efforts to imagine ourselves on an island. Strategy for a revolution for life must be transnational as it develops a program and organizes for mass struggle.

III
CULTURAL
PREPARATION

People get ready for revolution by changing the way they look at themselves. Private problems become political issues as the people develop a collective will and an understanding of struggle. Latin Americans call this process *conscientización*. Solidarity and revolutionary program are rooted in the symbols of this first stage of our strategy—cultural preparation.

"It often happens," Mao Tse-tung has observed, "that objectively the masses need a certain change, but subjectively they are not yet conscious of the need, nor yet willing or determined to make the change. In such cases, we should wait patiently. We should not make the change until, through our work, most of the masses have become conscious of the need and are willing and determined to carry it out."[1]

Mass movements have historically been built on the material interests of people. Ideas changed too, but changed most easily among those whose interests were being frustrated by the system. Although Gandhi often talked like the remotest idealist, his campaigns were always fueled by the material interests of people: factory workers in Ahmedabad, peasants in Champaran, Indian traders in South Africa. The cadres of the Indian National Congress included many unemployed, educated youths.

People are sometimes have-nots in other than economic terms. In the United States, the service professions such as social work and teaching are increasingly recognizing their low status in the social control system of which they are a part, and their own powerlessness over it. Young people, especially students, know that society expects large things of them, including the risk of dying in war. Yet these demands are not matched by chances for youth to influence the institutions benefiting from their sacrifice.

When such tensions are heightened, as during the Vietnam War, workers for change can educate widely. The atmosphere for communication is important for persuasion. A confusing situation, where old images no longer work, opens people to new, more adequate images of the world. Cultural preparation is a stage when agitators use these images to explain, to discuss, and to ask questions.

People begin in this stage to achieve a common identity strong enough to support them in the struggle. Individuals see that frustration and misery are not simply their own lot, but that they are oppressed as a group. The youth locked into an anti-human school begins to see that his frustration is not simply his or her personal adjustment problem, but is a situation shared by a generation.

New group identities have provided the background of many movements. For the workers, class-consciousness had to exist before mass movements could be built. Sex-consciousness, or feminism, was an indispensable part of the movement for woman suffrage, and race-consciousness was essential for the growth of mass movements of blacks and chicanos in the United States. Most people must develop, it seems, a sense of their personal destiny as interwoven with that of a collectivity before they will act together.

People change not only their image of themselves, but also their image of the system. The increase in ecological disasters will produce a flurry of explanations and remedies. Some politicians will blame the individual motorist instead of Detroit and the highway lobby, in an effort to maintain the average American's faith in the rightness of capitalism. In the stage of cultural preparation agitators show with films and comic books, pamphlets and study groups, that those with most power in our society are most responsible for the mess we are in.

The most important education occurs when decision-makers are caught in the act of exercising that brutality which for the most part is well hidden.

Counting the innocent dead after a civil rights campaign or riot has taught many a black American the dismal truth about white power in the United States. But one cannot depend only on education-by-events. The African National Congress tried that in South Africa in the 1950s, engaging actively in cultural preparation only just preceding a campaign of protest. The ANC did not have a strong, continuous program for politicizing the people, and it suffered for it in the usually weak response to its calls for mass protest action.

The content of this kind of work, the tactics, and the agitators will all be discussed in this chapter. The spirit throughout this stage of cultural preparation is one of profound respect for the people themselves; no living revolution can be waged behind the people's backs, manipulating them into situations of struggle without their awareness of what the stakes are. Real education is an exercise in honesty.

THE NEW IMAGE

Education for oppression encourages blacks (or women, or workers) to think they are inferior. Education for freedom is development of self-respect. The system may give an illusory self-respect to those who achieve status and wealth for their private selves; I mean here the self-respect which is linked to a community.

What community? I have been referring to communities based on class, color, generation, sex. Another community has been dreamed of, thought about, even to a small degree worked for: the community of all humankind. Martin Luther King, Jr., pointed toward it:

We begin to glimpse tremendous vistas of what it might mean for the world if new programs of resistance succeed in forging an even wider alliance of today's awakened youth. Already our best younger workers in the United States are talking about the need to form conscious connections with their opposite numbers in other countries. There is not even an outline in existence of what structure this growing world-consciousness might find for itself. But a dozen years ago there was not even an outline for the Negro civil rights movement in its first phase. The spirit is awake now; structures will follow, if we keep our ears open to the spirit.[2]

It is not a new vision, of course. Around the turn of the century there seemed to be an internationalist socialism, but conditions were not yet ripe for such a development. World War I broke up the appearance of unity, and the domination of much of the Left by the interests of one state, the Soviet Union, further demonstrated the difficulty of escaping from the old national categories. Now, in the rapidly shrinking world, the nationalistic Left remains less able to use its international opportunities than is capitalism.

The collective identity appropriate to a revolutionary movement for world community is difficult to label. King used the term "world-consciousness"; others have used "humanism" to suggest that we are all part of the same overarching collective which transcends sectional loyalties such as class and nationality. Just as someone in the women's liberation movement considers her membership in the female sex to be crucial to her identity, this kind of revolutionist will have her sense of self wrapped up in her belongingness to all humanity.

Emerging world-consciousness is different from the old appeal to the common good which has been the ideological stock-in-trade of capitalists who want to deny the reality of class conflict. Workers, black people, and women have group interests which clash with those of owners, white people, and men in the present order. The conflicts based on those interests must continue until resolved, and the group indentities that give unity and self-respect must be strong. An oppressed black person does advance toward liberation when he or she becomes proud of membership in the black race.

But in the process of liberation from constricted, negative selfhood to a community of race, a person can gain a glimpse of what it means to say "brother," "sister" to a still-wider circle.

Western civilization made a mistake when it viewed human beings as totally different from nature, when it escalated the obvious differences into a fundamental break. Now we humans are learning through ecological crisis that we are also a part of nature. We cannot do violence to nature without doing violence to ourselves.

Similarly, the exaggeration of group differences to the exclusion of our common humanity would make likely our common destruction. We are, even when fighting with each other, sisters and brothers. Our fighting should reflect that.

While the *idea* of a brotherhood of man is old, we can now observe a *feeling* on the part of increasing numbers of people as enormous social and economic forces create similar life situations for people across various national frontiers. This is most clearly seen among young people in the West, who increasingly recognize themselves in others, despite differences of language and nationality.

Proletarian class-consciousness could not exist before the creation of the factory system. World-consciousness on a mass basis cannot exist before basic economic and social conditions support such a development. But, increasingly, interdependence in the world is a fact. More societies are becoming industrialized, with all the implications of that way of life. The development of mass media bringing even the faces of suffering Vietnamese into the television sets of Americans half a world away is another influence.

OPPOSING AND DISCREDITING THE OLD ORDER

In addition to a collective consciousness, revolutionary agitators need to stress the importance of struggle, of large-scale open conflict. Gandhi's own development showed quite a change in this respect: in the early period in South Africa he organized an Indian Ambulance Corps to help the British in the Boer War, thinking that "a sincere desire to be of help is bound to impress the other party, and is doubly appreciated when it is quite unexpected."[3] He was soon disillusioned about the possibility of gaining social change through reliance on generous acts, and by the 1930 civil disobedience campaign in India he was putting the issue harshly:

> It is not a matter of carrying conviction by argument. The matter resolves itself into one of matching forces. Conviction or no conviction, Great Britain would defend her Indian commerce and interests by all the forces at her command. India must consequently evolve force enough to free herself from that embrace of death.[4]

This conflict orientation is likely to contradict the ideologies even of the oppressed group. Some liberals whose children are risking cancer because of pollution may still believe in social change through committee attendance and reject the idea of open confrontation. Black Americans had a form of Christianity which was anti-conflict. In fact, their churches talked about "the sweet by and by" rather than social struggle in the bitter here and now.[5] One of Martin Luther King's major tasks was challenging this ideology, reinterpreting Christianity so that it was a faith to fight by, a support for action in the streets of Birmingham and Selma.

The people's attitude toward the regime is important. When the legitimacy of the government declines, the people are far more ready to act. As even Adolf Hitler acknowledged in *Mein Kampf*, "... in the long run, government systems are not held together by the pressure of force, but rather by the belief in the quality and the truthfulness with which they represent and promote the interests of the people."[6]

The legitimacy of the U.S. government is already in decline because its domination by the military is an open secret and the military's own competence is questioned by the Vietnam War.

In the summer of 1971, the Washington-based Potomac Associates brought out the study *Hopes and Fears of the American People*. According to William P. Bundy,

> Its key conclusion, based on impressive polling techniques, is that the American people, in the past the world's most perennial optimists,

truly believe that their country is in deep trouble, far worse off than it was five years ago, and unlikely to do more than recover lost ground in the next five years. A plurality thinks national unrest is at the point where it is likely to lead to a real breakdown, and loss of confidence in leaders of government and business is voted a major reason.[7]

Movement people may have difficulty seeing this process of eroding legitimacy because of their awe of the power which remains in the government's hands. It is discouraging to see the impressive apparatus of repression belonging to the state, but the fact remains that the state cannot continue without the cooperation of the people. In the metaphor of a house, the foundation is the people's consent, and no matter how impressive the roof of army, police, or secret files, if the foundation gives way, the house will fall.

Our task as agitators is not to create disaffection by fear, but rather by indignation that such foolishness and exploitation are still allowed to exist. Humor can help, for our rulers' behavior is often amusing. The pompous House Un-American Activities Committee a few years ago sputtered when the ladies of Women Strike for Peace distributed flowers in the supposedly intimidating committee room. The witch-hunters were not being taken with sufficient seriousness.

Events may occur which change the image of the ruling group. During World War II in Ghana, for example, the building of airfields showed to Ghanaians white men working with their hands and in other ways contradicting the picture of Europeans as a class ordained only to supervise and rule. The achievement of self-government in India and Burma in 1947 and 1948 had a strong effect also on the people of Ghana, and we have already seen the importance for Guatemalans of seeing El Salvador's dictator toppled by civilian insurrection in 1944. While organizers cannot create such events, they can make the most of them by interpretation.

In the American movement people sometimes emphasize to an almost paranoid extent the power and competence of our repressive institutions, while continually finding fault with the movement and its weaknesses. A more truthful and hopeful attitude is that the government is powerful but has increasing problems. The people's resistance will become more powerful than governmental repression, although it is not yet.

BOTH GOALS AND STRATEGY

In the cultural preparation stage the organizers need to develop a program. It may, like the *Communist Manifesto*, include both a theory of social change and a rough indication of the goals of the revolutionists. The dangers of formulating a program before the masses of the people are involved are obvious, but are offset to a degree when part of the program itself is the participation of the people in the shaping of the revolutionary goals and means.

An old problem in the creation of a program is how to relate long-term goals to short-term ones, and how to relate abstract political goals to immediate bread-and-butter goals. The African National Congress had great difficulty reaching the masses when it focussed on issues far from the masses' pressing daily questions of existence. The ANC called for a South African national political convention on political rights, for example, when most people were concentrating on immediate questions of economic livelihood. Both limited and basic goals should be outlined in the program and their relationship shown through an analysis of the political economic system. (In Chapter VI I discuss this problem more fully.)

The American peace movement has for years been dominated by idealists who were reluctant to make connections between war and American domestic issues. The government therefore had little difficulty in, for example, pinning the blame for inflation on the labor movement and welfare spending instead of on the war in Vietnam. The outstanding nonviolent leaders of poor people's groups, like Cesar Chavez and Martin Luther King, Jr., have found nonviolence in the context of their struggle rather than first accepting an ideology called pacifism and then trying to apply it to the situation of the poor. Pacifism as such is often a bourgeois comfort for those trying to escape conflict and unreason. Marxists are right to criticize a pacifism which sees the world as an unstructured mass of individuals and political power as residing in the breast of the single man.

Bourgeois pacifism is clearly an inadequate ideology for a revolutionary program. But nonviolent struggle as a strategic commitment is something else again. (One can see the difference when one realizes that most pacifists do not practice nonviolent resistance, and most people who do practice nonviolent resistance are not pacifists.) There are several very concrete advantages to a revolutionary movement's declaring a commitment to nonviolent action as strategy and discipline. Such a declaration might use other words (Kwame Nkrumah called it "positive action" in Ghana, and Gandhi called it *satyagraha*, or "truth force.") It needs to make sense in terms of the culture. But whatever the words, an explicit adherence to nonviolent struggle has three major advantages.

First, a stated commitment may serve as protection against the *agents provocateurs* planted in our midst. Governments and industrial firms have often used their spies to encourage the movement to use violence in order to discredit the movement and justify harsh repression.

During a Lawrence, Massachusetts, textile strike in 1919 the police placed machine guns at major intersections in the town. One worker argued strongly in the strike committee meeting that the workers should march on the machine guns and turn them around. The police are few and we are thousands, he urged, and we have learned in the war how to use them. We cannot let this provocation go unanswered.

Another worker on the committee disagreed strongly, arguing that mill owners could try to weave cloth with machine guns if they pleased, but the workers' power lay in their noncooperation. The committee voted with him. A. J. Muste, the leader of the strike, had clear evidence days later that the first worker was a Pinkerton detective who had been employed by management to gain influence among the workers for a moment such as this.

Similar stories can be told about the Indian independence struggle, the black people's struggle in the U.S., the South African Defiance Campaign of 1952, the Buddhist struggle in Vietnam. *Again and again the authorities show they would rather have a violent revolt on their hands than the nonviolent force they are confronting*. To turn the movement to violence these authorities employ spies to mix with movement people and urge violent tactics.

There is no real protection against the *agent provocateur* except a clear-cut adherence to nonviolent action. It is easy to destroy a movement through the planting of bombs if the movement is ambivalent about violence, or if it acts nonviolently but refuses to make an explicit statement about it. If, on the other hand, the movement has credibility as a nonviolent force, as with the movements identified with Gandhi, King, Cesar Chavez, it becomes much more difficult to make the charge of violence stick.

The second advantage seems, ironically, to be the opposite of the first. While the day-to-day decision-makers who wield the instruments of repression often prefer to deal with a violent movement, middle class elements who support the government generally are more relaxed about a nonviolent movement. Violence is the greater fear for retail store owners, professional groups, etc. (Some black leaders in the United States have taken advantage of this fear by warning these elements that, if concessions are not made to nonviolent movements, violence will follow.) The advantage, then, for the movement is that a declaration of adherence to nonviolent strategy lessens the fear of an important part of the community and makes it more difficult for the regime to justify repression of the movement.

The third advantage of making a clear-cut commitment relates to the psychological dilemmas of movement leaders. The inclination to violence may stem as much from the inner conflicts of the leaders as from any predisposition of the masses. Rebellion usually causes strong psychological stress within the rebel, especially if he is middle class and not really brought up to be a revolutionary.

One way to deal with an internal conflict is to act strongly in one direction, to try to burn one's bridges. The young man making his first bomb may be declaring as loudly as he can, to himself as well as to others, that he really *is* a revolutionary. When he plants the bomb, and kills, there is no turning back; the conflict may be resolved at last. (Frantz Fanon shows in his book *The Wretched of the Earth*, however, that internal conflict may even be heightened by the practice of violence. The decisive act may not be all that decisive.[8])

If the leadership ranks of the revolutionary movement are full of the sons and daughters of the middle class, conflicted about their rebellion, a strongly nonviolent line will help them maintain their own equilibrium.

CULTURAL RESISTANCE

It is one thing to look rationally at some practical advantages to a clear-cut commitment to nonviolent strategy, and another to see how it can be accepted by the people. In our culture, nonviolent action is usually thought of as passivity, as though a tension existed between *nonviolence* and *action*. Nonviolence is seen as *control*— do not hit back, control your anger, and so on. As a matter of history, nonviolent action becomes politically feasible as a technique of struggle only when it provides release, as it has in the cases described in this book.

This may account for the hostility to nonviolent struggle felt by many pacifists. It is not only that pacifists are often captive to their class interests and fearful, therefore, of mass action. It is also that their pacifism is an ideology of control as the answer to problems; they sense the exhilarated release of mass nonviolent action and regret that people have become so emotional!

There is a lot of confusion about this question of inclination toward nonviolent struggle. I have been told that it is a middle class approach to problems, characteristic of intellectuals rather than the common people. Historical fact shows otherwise. It has not been university professors who have led the way in direct action for higher pay, better conditions, academic freedom, and so on. In fact, I am sometimes depressed by the reluctance of college faculties to use the power they have to press for change; they have over the years preferred to talk about the basic goodwill of the administration and their own impotence. On the contrary, it has been manual workers who have waged most direct action in the United States, men and women without much formal education but with a willingness to struggle, nonviolently where that seemed effective, for their rights.

A recent example of this is the Mexican-American grape workers

strike in California. Before 1966 most people would have said that
the migrant farm workers could not adopt nonviolence as a strategic commitment, for their culture has stressed aggressive masculinity as a high value. But Cesar Chavez, the leader of the strike,
identified nonviolent struggle with manliness, and the workers saw
that it was so. "I am convinced," Chavez said, "that the truest act
of courage, the strongest act of manliness, is to sacrifice ourselves
for others in a totally nonviolent struggle for justice. To be a man
is to suffer for others. God help us to be men."[9]

In the preceding chapter we saw Latin Americans, who sometimes even think of themselves as violent people, practicing nonviolent resistance heroically.

The most striking case of nonviolent action being adopted in an
unlikely culture is that of the Pathans of the Northwest Frontier of
colonial India (now Pakistan). The Pathans were a Moslem people
who stressed the effective use of violence from childhood on. Violence was thoroughly integrated into the tradition and behavior of
the people. A brilliant young chieftain's son, Khan Abdul Ghaffir
Khan, participated in the Indian campaign of 1919–21, and was converted to Gandhi's social views. He started schools and made
speeches back home, and prevailed upon Gandhi to tour the area
to speak about the "soldiers of violence and the soldiers of nonviolence." Khan organized an association of men called Khudai Khid-
matgar (Servants of God). At first the men did social work, then they
developed a revolutionary posture. They wore red shirts for a uni-
form, drilled regularly, and took long marches in military style,
although carrying no weapons. The movement grew from hundreds to thousands, and participated in the 1930–31 campaign with
such heroism that Gandhi described them as his best "nonviolent
soldiers."[10]

The Pathans show that nonviolent action is a social invention that
can be picked up in a culture which is hostile to some of its implications. When people see an invention that is helpful, they may use
it despite its partial clash with traditional values. I say "partial"
because many cultures contain values which are consistent with
nonviolent strategy: bravery, truthfulness, determination, solidarity, compassion.

On the other hand, the openness may lie at the level of rough life experience, as reflected by this black youth who became active in the Southern civil rights struggle:

> When kids on the street want to beat you, start a fight and pick on you, the natural thing to do is to hit back. But if there are too many of them and you're surrounded, you'd better just stand there and take it. I've seen many times when someone has sworn to beat up and stomp another guy, but if the other guy doesn't hit back, the beating doesn't go too far. They may call you a lot of names, but it's pretty hard for them to keep beating you up when you aren't hitting back.[11]

Or the openness to a commitment to nonviolent struggle may be at the point of strategy. Persons who see the great strategic advantage of guerrilla warfare which refuses to meet the enemy at his point of greatest strength may be open to considering the advantages of nonviolent strategy which even more radically refuses to play the opponent's game. The strategic argument carries special weight when violence has already been tried and found wanting, as in El Salvador in 1944.

Difficult though this question of clear commitment to nonviolent struggle is, there is no escape through a pseudo-populist reference to "the people's" inclination to violence. The people have been striking and demonstrating and boycotting and nonviolently occupying for years and such incidents are noticeably on the increase. Black people in the United States now, for example, are far more involved in nonviolent tactics of protest than they were in the 1950s. The rhetoric of some articulate blacks has shifted in the last few years toward violence, and this indeed echoes the anger felt by the people. But actual participation of the masses in struggle can most easily be obtained through a nonviolent strategy.

OUR TACTICS AND OURSELVES

Movements develop a variety of methods for politicizing the people because they must relate closely to their cultures to be effective. Among the Pathans, the tactics were speeches and schools, uniforms and other symbols of solidarity. In Czarist Russia, under a different set of conditions, study circles and union organizations were key methods. In Ghana, daily newspapers became the major method of cultural preparation in the struggle for national independence.

The Cherokee Indian resistance to removal from Georgia, 1817–38, is a little known but interesting case of thorough educational work. When the Cherokees realized, in the first decade of the nineteenth century, that they would be pressured to give up their valuable lands to white men, they began to prepare for struggle. They invented an alphabet for the Cherokee language. Within three years the majority of people were reading and writing Cherokee. They translated books and published a newspaper. Dale Van Every in his book on Indian treatment wrote:

> Their national confidence was reinvigorated. They felt that they had justified their demand to be recognized as a distinct and free people. They had been reminded as no success in war had reminded them that they need feel no compulsion to recognize any inherent inferiority to whites.[12]

Because politicizing the people is so sensitively linked to the cultural pattern, revolutionary agitation is extremely difficult. The agitators tend to be not only alienated from the power institutions, but alienated from the people as well. For the Northern white radicals of the early sixties it required a lot of adjustment to work among fundamentalist Christian blacks of the Deep South. For today's young radicals the gap remains painfully wide between their life style and that of Middle America.

A method of cultural preparation which responds to this problem is street-speaking. Standing on a soapbox on a busy street corner is an exercise that develops the speaker as much as the movement. It has a long history in American radicalism: the Industrial Workers of the World used it successfully in the early years of this century, and Malcolm X spent much of his time street-speaking in Harlem. Street-speaking is much more personal than the mass media yet reaches more people than house-to-house canvassing. It is inexpensive. It responds to where the people really are, as contrasted to where we organizers think they are as we write our leaflets and slogans. It communicates our position in more depth than an ordinary demonstration can, and with less manpower. It reaches people who would never think of entering a meeting hall to hear a speech on the same topic.

I remember one afternoon in Philadelphia starting a vigorous street meeting which soon had five sub-meetings going around the edges. In one of them, discussing the race situation, were: a young black militant, a white railroad worker, a white suburban matron, a middle-aged black professional man, and a young white businessman, along with several onlookers. In what room in the country would these sorts of people meet to discuss a burning political issue?

When a hundred people gather for a typical demonstration in a U.S. city, there is almost no impact. If the one hundred formed ten street meetings instead, passers-by would learn that those "unpleasant" protesters are actually human beings with some facts on their side.

But just as important is the effect on the speakers themselves. By speaking several times the agitator gains in fluency, in ability to think fast on the spot, in motivation to learn more about the issue, in ability to deal with crowds and hecklers, and in understanding what is on the people's minds. This last is most important. When radicals do street-speaking we cannot be sectarian, cannot develop elaborate jargons which distance us from the people.

A speaker also learns to overcome fear, for nearly everyone is fearful before standing on a chair on the street. Fear is probably the reason why it is not done more. But fear is the central weapon of repression, and we in the movement will get nowhere if we are unable to overcome our fear. Street-speaking gives everyone easily available practice in overcoming fear.

I have stressed this method because it responds to a central problem of our movement: the tendency for activists to isolate themselves and lose touch with the mainstream of society. The occasional crusading political campaign, like that of Eugene McCarthy in 1968, does at least get many activists outside their own circles, but the campaign is not very useful to the revolutionist because it presses toward the lowest common denominator in content and fails to build revolutionary organization. A personal discipline which helps is for each activist to make a point of returning home from time to time to try to interpret what he is doing to his relatives and former neighbors. But this has the weakness of all personal disciplines: it is not underpinned by community effort. Systematic street-speaking can be a community activity, on the other hand, and can make a sizable contribution to democratizing our movement.[13]

Before all great historical movements there is a period of fermenting, a time when objective forces and the work of visionaries change the consciousness of masses of people. This stage of the revolution for life finds agitators busy making connections— between the symptoms of unease and the causes, between the unhappy individuals and the community they need, between the partial identitites and the full identity of humanity. A revolutionary program emerges, not as a blueprint but as a beginning to be modified by discussion with the people and by experience.

Agitators stress in this stage the importance of conflict, but insist that the nonviolent way encourages life even while it sloughs off the old skin which now oppresses everyone. Agitators are most helpful when they breathe the same air (even though polluted) as others in society, when they understand the language and even the most irritating of the arguments. They choose methods of agitation which counter their own elitist tendencies by putting them in genuine conversation with the people. Their styles, even though diverse because of the heterogeneity of the people, have in common the buoyancy of hope, and openness to new insights, and a commitment to life.

In the United States some aspects of cultural preparation have been going on for decades. Other aspects have been neglected, such as ecology, strategy, nonviolent power, planetary identification, and decentralist programs for the political economy of the new society. Most lacking has been a theory which integrates all these aspects and shows why they interrelate.

The heterogeneity of the United States means that cultural preparation does not have a clear beginning and ending. Some parts of the population will have highly developed revolutionary consciousness when other parts are just beginning to identify the sources of their discontent. The agitator who decides to keep educating until the entire task is completed is in danger of avoiding his or her own opportunities to move on to organizing and action, and the revolutionary strategy may sound hollow from such a person. Perhaps the slogan for the agitator should be: Share the skills of education and move on!

IV
BUILDING
ORGANIZATIONAL
STRENGTH

As the consciousness of oppression spreads, more people are ready to organize themselves for revolutionary change. Organization is essential for a struggle movement, for only through organization is it possible to generate enough force to slough off the old order and create new institutions. Isolated, spontaneous incidents of resistance can no more accomplish substantial change than can occasional rioting—each is a witness which can be appreciated in symbolic terms but does not change structures.

Revolutionaries are experimenting with various organizational approaches in America today. Some are in tight-knit conspiratorial groups while others are active in progressive community associations. Some are gaining experience in national protest organizations. Some are active in campus student organizations while others are in labor unions. The political party method attracts some; others organize residential communes.

THE U.S.A.: A RADICAL ORGANIZER'S PUZZLE

Organizing a broad movement for fundamental change has always been difficult in the United States, because the class structure has never become really transparent. The hodgepodge of races and ethnic groups in the U.S. has obscured the reality of class domination of our society. In Scandinavia or England, by contrast, the cultural sameness of the population made it easier for workers to see that they had the same lot in life; union-organizing was easier and it was even possible to organize labor parties which could win elections on clear class interests.

In the early part of this century there were a number of American socialist parties organized by *language* group: Finnish, German, and so on. When women were working for the vote they often lost referenda because recent immigrants voted against them, partly because of Old World attitudes toward women and partly because the newcomers' votes could be manipulated by the breweries and party machines.

The white/black conflict in America needs only to be mentioned to evoke the picture of worker fighting worker while the owners happily look on. In fact, those who want to hold on to their power and wealth have not had to *divide* and conquer; our society was born divided and the task has only been to keep the groups set against each other lest they combine for justice.

In this century American political life has been dominated by identification with status groups—groups of nationality, race, sex, age, and so on. (Classes spring from the unequal distribution of economic power; status groups spring from the unequal distribution of honor or prestige. I am a member of the working class if I do not own a factory but am paid to work with what others own. I am a member of a status group "youth" if my opinions are taken with a grain of salt and I am reminded that I will be wiser when I am older, or kept out of a meeting because I have not been in the organization long enough.[1])

While American political life has appeared to be the struggle of status groups, its economic life has reflected a subdued class conflict. The trade unions are the active agents of that conflict from the workers' side. The preoccupation with status groups, however, has kept the arenas of "politics" and "economics" remarkably separate in the public mind.

In Western Europe, where class struggle is rightly felt to be a political as well as an economic fact, there is now a large immigration of workers from Africa, Southern and Eastern Europe, and elsewhere. The newcomers take the dirty, low-paying jobs. They are not being recruited aggressively by the unions. Will the American pattern repeat itself there?

The power elite in America has been split on how to treat the non-WASPs, the status groups which over the years have sought a share of political power. The Republican wing has generally refused to share political position while the Democratic wing, often reluctantly, has conceded the necessity of giving the have-nots a piece of the political pie. The difference between the wings has not been on distribution of economic power. There are differences on style of response to status group demands (how much repression, for example), and how much money should be spent (the Republicans tending to be somewhat more tightfisted than the Democrats).

Both wings of the Establishment, however, agree on the basic framework of American society: economic power should be kept by the wealthy, and the government's first priority is to maintain the capitalist system. Whether Anglo-Protestants or Irish Catholics run city politics, the basic structure of injustice remains; only the administration of that injustice varies.

The Democratic Party, because of its differences with the Republicans on response to status group demands, is the major vehicle of co-optation into the American Empire. It was heavily symbolic for John Kennedy, Democrat and the first Irish Catholic President, to declare, "I am determined upon our system's survival and success, regardless of the cost and regardless of the peril."[2]

The process of entry into the Democratic Party may come very slowly. In the party convention of 1948 Hubert Humphrey led an attack on the racism which prevented blacks access to the party, and finally in 1972 there was more than a sprinkling of black delegates. But whether the party assimilates slowly or quickly, it nevertheless functions to bring neglected status groups into the political limelight. There is in this process little consciousness of class conflict. The trade unions accept this because they have largely accepted the capitalist framework and settled for material gains which are supposed to translate into higher status for their members.

THE FUTURE OF CO-OPTATION

I expect that in the next years more status groups will emerge politically: Japanese-Americans, small-town people, the mentally ill, Chinese-Americans, the physically handicapped, and prisoners, for example. As I write, the old, retired people are beginning to find their voice. The common demand is *equality*—that they not be discriminated against because of their membership in a category. The struggle will involve, as it has for the other groups before them, giving up the individual route to honor and dignity in favor of group mobilization. By pushing forward as a group, they expect to lose the stigma of membership in that group, as homosexuals are already doing.

This will happen against a background of continuing erosion of legitimacy of the Old Order. The hollowness of the culture will become more apparent.

At the same time as equality becomes more consciously the motif of the ferment, a class perspective could also grow. The giant corporations are, after all, the common enemy of working ethnics, blacks, women, small-town people, and others of the status groups which have no way to participate in major economic decision-making. I expect the corporations to remain rigid in putting profit first because that is inherent in the capitalist framework; any other course would be financial suicide. Further, the corporations need not feel hemmed in by mounting pressures in the United States for social responsibility; they are already springing loose from the national framework. If all else fails, they can follow the example of New England textile mills which went South when workers demanded justice. The corporations can step up the present trend toward relocation of plants to low-wage areas.

Another pressure which may sharpen class conflict and make it politically conscious is the decline in abundance. Revolts against the American Empire, as in Chile, will make scarce resources scarcer and more expensive. The power elite will be forced to make do with less, pay more, or to embark on more wars to preserve access to their raw materials. Each course would put heavy pressure on the economy. A further dimension is ecological—even if there are no more Chiles, resources are running out. The growth of the Gross National Product may slow or stop, even though modern economics depends upon growth.

Henry C. Wallich, the conservative Yale economist, is worried about what would happen if the GNP stopped growing: "Growth is a substitute for equality of income. So long as there is growth there is hope, and that makes large income differentials tolerable."[3]

In other words, if growth of the national income pie stopped, workers would look at the piece of the pie allocated to them and begin to protest. As Wallich says in the same article, "If GNP per capita stops rising, is everybody to remain at his current income level, like wage-earners during the late, lamented wage-and-price freeze? The low-income classes would hardly put up with that."

Co-optation has depended on having material benefits to distribute in large enough amounts to keep up the hopes of the have-nots. With a stable or shrinking economic pie, the wealth will not be there.

Finally, ecological disasters are disasters for corporate capitalism. The oil spills, air inversions, power breakdowns, water shortages will more and more clearly be linked, I believe, to the major cause: the rapacious nature of our economic institutions. Although people of all classes feel the effects of environmental violence, major stock owners are likely to resist the major changes that will undermine the sources of their wealth. This is another reason why the class structure will become transparent.

I expect that a massive revolutionary consciousness will emerge which will be reflected organizationally in a variety of ways. I see some contradictions between this consciousness and the style of mass politics.

Mass politics is something like a movie theater, in which many individuals react to the film but little to each other. The political parties seek to engineer support through images and slogans meant to attract an audience. Candidates "sell" themselves to a market of consumers rather than engage in genuine dialogue with groups of citizens.

Mass politics reflects a large country dominated by high mobility, mass communications, centralization, swollen cities. The essence of participative democracy—discussion among peers of the great issues of the day—is eclipsed by one-way communication via the press and television.

The growing body of radicals will increasingly see through the Democratic Party as a primary agency of co-optation, I believe. They will discover that you cannot capture a party unless, at a minimum, you *win* the Presidency, and you cannot win the Presidency on a radical platform with the present American distribution of power and wealth. A campaign for President (or Governor or Senator) is enormously expensive. The major contributors to campaign chests are people in whose interests it is to have an accelerating GNP, domination of the Third World, and welfare to the rich.

Working within the party means endless compromise as party leaders shift among the coalitions, looking for votes by means of the lowest common denominator. With occasional exceptions, party workers cannot hope to do much radical education and survive with any influence in the party.

Mass politics is very thin; the search for the common denominator deprives it of cultural richness. The decline of the old culture, felt differently but increasingly in our society, means that a counter-culture is essential. The arena of mass party work is not an environment for the discovery or even the transmission of new, compelling symbols of identity. The youth, especially, are likely to reject that arena.

The increase of ecological disasters, economic pressures, and social disruption may encourage many radicals to find a way to "live the revolution now"—being uncertain that the world will stay together long enough to enable us to live humanely "after the revolution." That means finding communities of celebration and common purpose; many radicals will choose to root their political work in community rather than in the fragmented existence of mass politics.

The sexism which many people find in mass politics—influence going to the aggressive, flamboyant, *macho* type—provides another reason why alternative structures for political work might be sought.

In the light of these tendencies I believe that the future of co-optation is dim. The pragmatists who urge that the party framework is the crucial arena will remain persuasive for a while, but their reasons will lose cogency as the larger dimensions of power and meaning in America break into consciousness. A living revolution requires organizational forms which renew and encourage our lives.

AFFINITY GROUPS

A characteristic of revolutionary conditions is the emergence of small groups or committees. In 1905 and again in 1917 they sprang up in Russia, often spontaneously. In the French insurrection of 1968, Revolutionary Action Committees arose in many areas of society. Hannah Arendt in her book *On Revolution* argues that the council form of organization is a basic democratic tendency found when people are suddenly liberated from the old machinery of the status quo.[4] Unfortunately, in the Russian case Lenin considered this grassroots democracy to be a threat to central planning and direction, and he emasculated the Soviets. In neither France nor Russia were the committees strong enough to carry through a people's revolution; in France reaction set in, and in Russia a new class of bureaucrats emerged to rule in the name of the people.

But what if the mass movement which arises in response to the strains in society grows largely from experienced small groups? What if the committees were started now, in pre-revolutionary America, and gained their experience in democratic movement-building as teams of people committed to the revolution for life?

Nothing could be more indigenous to American culture than teams. Everyone from middle class suburban schoolchildren to poor people in an urban ghetto has experience with team play.

Because the teams are small—from three to twelve—they can be started even where conditions would not support a typical protest organization. Because they can arise from already existing friendships or ties of work-place or religion, they can start from a stronger base of solidarity than strategy alone. Because they can grow as cells grow, by division, they can proliferate rapidly. Since their size prevents exaggerated claims and hopes, they can confidently run the risk of experimenting.

In the early 1970s such teams sprang up in Northern Europe, in a period of political malaise. There the small groups seemed useful because radicals need strong support in the face of general apathy— while in the United States the solidarity may have meant more for support against repression, like that shown by the state-sponsored killing of Black Panthers and of the students at Kent State university in 1970. In Europe the people with a revolutionary perspective were few and far between, and they therefore needed to find ways of acting not dependent on numbers. Because the political atmosphere in much of Nothern Europe was then a study in shades of gray, a number of small groups independently creating and trying out ideas was more likely to yield imaginative and relevant action than the central committee of a more sizable organization. The plan in Europe is nevertheless to work toward a mass movement which will emerge when forces described in Chapter I of this book become visible.

Fortunately, small protest organizations are proliferating in America—ecology action groups, for example. Also needed, however, are groups which are consciously revolutionary in the following ways:

- They aim for fundamental change: redistribution of power and wealth, social equality, transformation of values, elimination of organized violence, creation of world community.
- They insist on the big picture, making connections between concrete issues and the fundamental causes underlying them.
- They emphasize brotherhood and community, not only in the great utopia but also now, in the means used and in the form of organization. This implies giving up the characteristic scatter of liberal activities which results in fragmented selves and soulless

organizations, replacing it with concentration and community. The group would be the number-one means of political activity for each member.

● They prepare for the emergence of a mass movement, rather than acting *for* the people. Self-criticism needs to be directed especially towards sectarianism. A good slogan for the groups would be Mao's "Serve the people, learn from the people."

● They internationalize their program, consciously working now for the *trans*national movement of the future. This implies working outside the framework of electoral politics, since all the major parties are committed to the nation-state system.

We could call them Groups for Living Revolution because they live the revolution now, even though only in seed form[5]. Whatever they are called, the Groups engage in nonviolent direct action and training, exploring alternatives to the traditional methods of violence. Theodor Ebert, a German conflict researcher, has noted that a choice between organized violence and the *idea* of nonviolence is in reality no choice at all.[6] Committed revolutionaries will act in the way which is, in an organizational sense, open to them. Considering the practical advantages of a nonviolent commitment, it is only sensible to pioneer in that direction. Departing from the tradition of violence is not easy; we are creatures of the old order, even though we call ourselves revolutionaries. But the difficulty is all the more reason to do our pioneering collectively, so we support each other while breaking new ground.

The problem of the Groups, then, is largely direct action on concrete issues where the structure of injustice most clearly reveals itself. In the next chapter we will describe in detail this kind of "propaganda of the deed," but it is important to the Groups that they choose issues which easily point up the revolutionary picture. Each Group will have to struggle with this problem (rather than accepting the solution passively from a central committee): How, in the Group's local situation, do basic contradictions of the status quo most clearly show themselves?

In June 1970 I heard the chief city planner of Belfast, Northern Ireland, describe to neighborhood leaders the highway plans for the future. He described with the aid of charts and slides the extensive expressways which are planned. He mentioned as an aside that the planning commission had indeed considered the possibility of developing mass transit, even of subsidizing buses to the point where people could ride without charge. This was feasible. "But," he said, "we decided to put the subsidies into motorways instead."

One does not often hear a planner so clearly admit the alternatives which are chosen and rejected; the workers' bus system would decline (he admitted) while the middle class automobiles would get increasingly good service provided by the public funds, with the by-products of destroyed housing and increased pollution.

Such an issue matters to the people, has obvious connections to the power structure and the ecological crisis, and lends itself to tactics of direct action. The Group can serve the people, teach a revolutionary perspective, and develop its ability to use the revolutionary means of nonviolent direct action. Through its activity it will come into contact with a variety of people: workers, housewives, students, professionals. Some of these might become convinced of the rightness of the Group's approach and themselves organize teams to struggle for revolutionary change. And so the movement spreads on a grassroots level. A Group may discover that one element of the population is particularly open to revolutionary discussion, and concentrate on relating to these people until cells emerge there. Or it may feel that its best work is to reduce the opposition to change of the reactionary elements by carrying its style of action to the very centers of support for the status quo. Like a lightning rod, a Group might conduct safely some of the repressive force which otherwise builds up to a destructive explosion.

In addition to concentrating on a local or national symptom of injustice, the Group should support a liberation movement outside the country. In doing this it will broaden its own consciousness and learn to see its own work in a transnational perspective. It would learn what the American Empire looks like from another angle, would learn more about the nature of revolutionary struggle. It could be of positive aid to the foreign movement through medical aid, propaganda, and so on.

The relative importance of the two centers of attention, local/national and foreign, will vary from Group to Group. Even if little is done on one of them, however, it still seems important that the revolutionary cells develop their capacity to work on more than one thing at a time.

Radical organizations often have a time perspective which lays most emphasis on the immediate and on the distant future. They tend to be enthusiastic about this month's program and the remote glimmer of the new order, and less attentive to the intervening steps. Bengt Höglund, a Swedish sociologist, has studied a variety of organizations and found that those which are most effective are those which emphasize the middle range. This suggests that we must learn to restrain our headline-hopping tendencies and instead develop strategies which make sense in our situation.

The strategic stages in this book can provide a basic model for thinking through a plan. Another tool is the strategy game, in which the Group can test out various possibilities. A strategy game is played by dividing participants into the elements which have a stake in the issue. These elements meet separately and develop moves and counter-moves. In a game of two or three hours followed by evaluation by all the participants, a sense of the dynamics of campaigns begins to grow.

This kind of strategy-gaming has been developed recently in connection with training for direct action.[7] The Group would profit from training in the various methods: role-play (acting out bodily a situation of conflict), extended role-play (taking many hours or even days), situation analysis (blackboard work something like football coaches use), quick decision analysis (small-group practice in fast responses to crisis), and so on. The Group would certainly profit from extensive street-speaking for the sake of both training and developing solidarity.

Teamwork is not always easy. Boys in a neighborhood easily form a team for baseball because the rules of the game are highly structured. Rules for revolution are not nearly so clear-cut. The very process of teamwork itself should be raised to the conscious level, therefore, through training in group dynamics. The methods developed in the past several decades can make anarchy a realistic possibility on a small-group level: no one person needs to be the leader once the Group learns to share the functions of leadership. Group dynamics can help us to unlearn those habits of submission which serve the old order. Groups which receive this training can become more effective in achieving their group goals and at the same time more sensitive to the needs of the individual members. While there has been some legitimate criticism of the group dynamics movement for its emphasis on process almost to the exclusion of content, one need not fear that a group of committed revolutionaries will forget the purpose of their work.

The team as the building block of a mass movement makes sense because it meets the dilemma of collectivism versus individualism. Unlike some of the old communist cells, it is not secret or conspiratorial, therefore it cannot hold individuals to it rigidly with implicit threats. On the other hand, there is sufficient community to help the individual overcome his excessive attachment to self, revealed in conservatism, arrogance, or authoritarianism.

The often criticized tendency in mass movements for a kind of mob hysteria to sweep people away is not likely in a movement made of teams. On the other hand, the positive movement feelings of joy and celebration of community can be captured by teams. The solidarity which enables people to withstand the terror of repression is even more likely in teams than in an unstructured mass facing water hoses or bullets. Studies of combatants in battlefield conditions have shown that the solidarity of the small unit is crucial in conquering fear and withstanding attack. Fear, of course, is the central weapon of repression. In a movement of small groups we may hold hands against repression and continue to resist.

Each organizational form has its limits, and Groups are no exception. Teams are not suitable for all kinds of work under all conditions. A team of twelve would have difficulty organizing a mass civil disobedience campaign, for example, although teams which focus on the same issue might develop common projects from time to time.

RADICAL CAUCUSES

Most of us in the movement have experienced the familiar dilemma of working within or outside of a liberal framework. If we work outside, we can lose touch with those people and have little influence. If we work inside, we can get co-opted and spend most of our time working for goals and analyses which are far more limited than those in which we really believe.

The radical caucus is emerging as one answer to this dilemma. Nearly every professional association now has a radical caucus within it—social workers, scientists, teachers, architects, physicians, sociologists, lawyers—as well as some labor unions. The radicals function as what the British call a "ginger group"; they combine to press the association to take more advanced stands on political and social issues. The pressure can include direct action at the national conventions.

The importance of the radical caucus lies in the close linkage to the non-radicals in the association; this ensures a dialogue and reduces the chance of isolation. Revolutionary ideas can in this way permeate important elements of society, especially if the radicals do not get distracted into mere power games with the leadership of the association.

Radical caucuses can play a useful role in the transition to a new society because of their knowledge and experience. Rather than party ideologues trying to develop a humane medical service system, for example, the radical medical workers themselves would lead the innovating work in close cooperation with consumers. This also provides a check against the militant ignorance which can masquerade as anti-elitism in times of ferment.

A limitation of the radical caucus, however, is that it does not by itself provide the chance to *act* with a full measure of radical expression. The frustration of trying to get large associations to take positions in advance of their readiness may lead to the escalating rhetoric and negative feelings which help no one.

If the association has in its tradition a radical impulse, the caucus might spin off an action group which, while taking direct actions, still identifies itself with the larger body. The Brethren Action

Movement and A Quaker Action Group did essentially that: in sending medical aid to North Vietnam and in other acts of civil disobedience, they acted for themselves, yet openly laid claim to the prophetic tradition of their own churches. This pattern liberates revolutionaries to act on their own perceptions and analyses without losing touch with those who are not like-minded.

An example of a highly developed radical caucus which does take actions is the Medical Committee on Human Rights (MCHR). The organization began in 1964 largely as a response to the civil rights movement's medical needs and the movement's exposure of injustice to the blacks and poor.

Providing emergency medical service for nonviolent direct action campaigns has remained a primary activity of MCHR chapters. For the November 1969 anti-war demonstration, the Washington, D.C., MCHR reported staffing up to 25 medical-aid stations on an around-the-clock basis with about 450 medical workers. Sometimes the mere establishment of a medical presence at a demonstration has reportedly cooled the situation and prevented violence.

Also of great importance has been attacking the American Medical Association (AMA) and other organs of the health care establishment. The MCHR does studies on inadequate medical care and relates the studies to an analysis of the profit-oriented health institutions of our capitalist society. The members expose through demonstrations and publications the complicity of the medical profession in death and disease through misplaced priorities and overweening concern for money.

While most of the MCHR activity has been in its dozens of chapters across the country, it works together on the national level with other concerned groups, gives testimony to legislators, develops alternative approaches to health care, publicizes the free clinics and other counter-institutions, and attends health professionals' conventions to promote progressive resolutions from within the accepted framework.

Through its newspaper, *Health Rights News,* the MCHR fosters debate on controversial issues and helps radical medical workers find their allies in the struggle against disease and against those who profit from it.

PLANTING THE REVOLUTION THROUGH
COUNTER-INSTITUTIONS

Service associations, veterans' groups, churches, unions—these and other organizations are part of the social fabric that supports the status quo in most oppressive systems. They form a subtle net of social control which helps keep the population docile. The churches that serve opiate-religion and the unions that push capitalist propaganda help prevent a situation from arising where the more obvious forms of control are needed.

Sometimes radical caucuses can make a difference in shaping the response of these associations to the erosion of the old order. The unions and other associations may be radicalized, or at least become progressive and fight the right-wing clamor for repression.

But many associations are so dominated by the lieutenants of the power elite that they cannot throw off their function of social control. In this stage of organization-building we can begin to withdraw support from such institutions. As consciousness of injustice grows, more people will feel alienated from these business-as-usual associations. This is especially likely when alternatives exist which fill the legitimate functions of the organizations (worship, social, leadership, etc.). We already see in the United States the growth of an "underground church" which provides an increasing number of Christians an ecumenical religious experience in a context of clear commitment to social change.

This is a very oblique threat to the system. Even in dictatorships people do not get punished for withdrawal from a veterans' group. Nevertheless, it does in a small way deprive the rulers of one means of social control.

An advantage of this to the movement is that it liberates people to participate in movement-building who otherwise are doing "good works" in the context of the organizations of the old order. Many people who are sharply critical of the American Empire are nevertheless active members of associations which have a "non-political" banner. A careful look at the programming and connections of the organizations often shows that they are pillars of the Establishment. Energies and abilities are much better spent in building revolutionary counter-institutions.

Communes, or intentional communities, are flourishing in the United States and Europe today. A few families or individuals live together on a farm or in the city, often pooling incomes or developing a community source of income such as farming or crafts. In rejecting capitalism's emphasis on the individual and the immediate family, the collectives are leaders in the cultural revolution. These pioneering individuals are seeking that integrity which has its roots in community.

Many Americans, especially in the middle class and in the counter-culture, are like psychic hypochondriacs: they constantly have an inner ear cocked to their emotional condition, testing to see where the aches and pains are today. In the name of liberation (from "neurosis" or from "the straight world"), they seem anxiously driven on their search for a continued sense of well-being.[8] Although this "hypochondria" results basically from the dissolution of Western culture, it is intensified by mobility and individualism, both of which drive the person even more back upon him- or herself.

Communes may play a vital role for such persons, developing their ability to become outward-looking, to commit themselves to group tasks, to risk emotional intimacy with others. Revolutionary communes can help their members see that their private alienation is a part of the general condition, and that full personal liberation is linked to the liberation of humankind. These communes can give needed emotional support to individuals who otherwise leave the movement under the strain of work and fear.

Communities can, like the Gandhian *ashrams*, be base camps for the movement. By sharing responsibilities they can release parents for struggle. By developing research and other skills and materials, they can be resource centers. By developing training tools they can be learning centers, transmitting hard-won lessons of organization and struggle to new members of the movement.[9]

Unfortunately, there are many communes which have not found a broader movement context for their work and have become engrossed in serving only themselves. These inward communes do not join demonstrations, do not share their emotional and spiritual togetherness at points of movement confrontation with the state.

The classical historic case of inwardness is the Amish, or Old

Order Mennonites of rural Pennsylvania and Ohio. These people live an intensely communitarian existence. They spurn modern technology and have a rich social life. They are also withdrawn, belying their own pacifist belief in loving everyone by scarcely stirring off their farms to help the world's desperate people.

It could be argued that the inward communes are nevertheless important in the sense that they influence the culture by example. Did not the early Christians make heavy waves in the Roman Empire by practicing their own communist existence apart from the hurly-burly of political life? Did not the early Quakers grow in seventeenth-century England largely by being conspicuous examples of what they preached?

Unfortunately, the strategy of change by example has most of its power muted by tolerance. When governments learn to tolerate peculiar sects a kind of accommodation takes place: the government stops interfering in the business of the sect, and vice versa. The Roman Emperor Constantine enforced toleration, and the Christians started to support the Empire. The English authorities stopped trying to suppress Quakerism, and Quakers there became a small, respectable denomination. The society around the band of cultural revolutionaries may note them as a quaint survival, possibly of importance in attracting tourists, as with artists' colonies. The growth of the new way declines because the example is taken for granted.

Ironically, if the authorities decide that it is un-American to have more than one family in a household, the inward-looking communes will have a major opportunity to influence our social life. They will be key organizational units in the struggle for liberation. But if, as seems to be the case, the Establishment considers them to be fairly harmless, the collectives will remain only centers for individual growth and limited cultural development.

Another suggested means of planting the living revolution is through community self-help projects, like organizing new schools and playgrounds, cooperative stores, and the like. When people learn that they can change things by their own work they learn self-reliance. Discovering that they have untapped power has revolutionary implications.

All too often, however, this is a band-aid approach to a problem which requires massive treatment. Neighborhood cooperative stores cannot challenge the corporate giants that control food production and distribution. Neighborhood-organized playgrounds can relieve the city government of its responsibility but cannot challenge the forces which have allocated so little money to playgrounds in the first place. The small structures are pitifully inappropriate for challenging the increasing size of institutions in Western industrial countries.

But what about the Groups for Living Revolution—what could be more puny than a cell of seven people taking on the American Empire?

The difference is that the teams are units for movement-building, taking their place in a strategy for a massive people's movement. The cooperative store, neighborhood school, and so on are not movement organizations, usually, but on the contrary tend to harden with success to become part of the status quo.

When the self-help efforts take place in the *context* of a revolutionary movement, such as the Black Panthers' breakfast program or medical center, they take on a revolutionary character. To be more precise, counter-institutions become revolutionary when they:

- Carry a revolutionary ideology,
- Build a revolutionary organization,
- Take place within the context of open revolutionary struggle.

If these elements are present the counter-institutions become an important front in our struggle. In the context of these elements we are planting these seeds of the future in a situation which is *becoming* the future, that when the plants are grown they will live in a new environment. Without this context we are planting a fragile greenhouse flower that will require constant attention in an environment not suited for it.

Gandhi made a great deal of this planting process; he called it the constructive program. It was a powerful support for the Indian independence campaign. This emphasis has continued in the Gandhian movement, but without the context of political struggle. The land-gift movement led by Vinoba Bhave has had some impressive results; it is no small thing to redistribute hundreds of thousands of acres. But it cannot attack India's problems on the scale needed even to preserve its gains unless the constructive program is put into the Mahatma's own context of revolutionary struggle.

John Braxton, in his study of the California grape strike and boycott, points to the role of counter-institutions in sustaining the first successful major strike in grape-pickers' history.[10] Cesar Chavez, realizing the precarious position of the farm workers, spent several years organizing before the strike began in 1965. "If you don't have the organization, the strike is going to be broken, don't you worry about that," he said. A drugstore, a cooperative food store, a service station, a newspaper, and a health clinic all helped to knit together the fledgling union. When the strike began there was sufficient solidarity to withstand the repression and five years of resistance by the agricultural corporations. The organizational infrastructure grew threatening enough to prompt one grower to remark, "All Chavez wants to do is to replace my power structure with his."

UNIFYING THE MOVEMENT

How can the counter-institutions, affinity groups, radical caucuses, and other revolutionary groups work together to provide a more powerful thrust than they can by working separately?

Radicals commonly assume that organizing for revolution means organizing a revolutionary party. I am willing to question this assumption too. The fact that socialist parties have so frequently been elitist and statist makes me suspect that their nature may be inconsistent with a really democratic people's revolution.

Political parties, even though radical, suffer a number of afflictions: an oligarchical tendency in the leadership, a compromising tendency in electioneering, an overemphasis on verbal skills and personality at the expense of program, a tendency to down-play popular struggle, and a commitment to the national-state as the critical arena of work.

Robert Michels pointed out long ago the "iron law of ogliarchy" which takes over; party bureaucrats develop vested interests in the organization which take precedence over the needs of the membership and even, frequently, over the opportunities to take revolutionary acts.[11] A recent example appears to be the French Communist Party in May-June 1968; preserving the Party organization seemed much more important to its leadership than joining the insurrection touched off by students and workers. The Party acted as a moderating force and tried to get the struggle off the streets and into Parliament. The parliamentary arena would be a losing one for the cause, but at least (they seemed to reason) the Party apparatus would be saved; the insurrection was much too risky.

Of course in the United States we are a long way from a mass party with revolutionary ideals. Advocates of a radical party therefore say that the party will not contest elections in order to win, since that is plainly impossible, but only as a forum for education. I believe the difficulty will arise in the future, when the party grows in appeal (because of changes in the general society) to the point where some candidates actually win, and others, by compromising, *could* win in their districts. The nature of parties in liberal states is to win elections, and the closer one comes to winning, the more pressure there will be to win.

Precisely at the time when the revolutionary party becomes a mass party is the time when, in more cases than not, "nothing fails like success." The German Social Democratic Party is a conspicuous example of a party which left its radicalism behind as it drew tantalizingly close to the chance of victory. When in power it has presided over a robust capitalist economy with exploitative relations to the Third World and membership of NATO.

In fact, with the onset of World War I nearly every socialist party in the world dropped its socialist internationalism, forgot its own analysis of imperialism, and joined its own national ruling class. Having entered the world of practical electoral politics, the revolutionary impulse was too weak to prevent the greatest sellout since the Christian Church was recognized by Constantine.

True, the American Socialist Party by and large stuck to its principles, and Eugene V. Debs ran for president on the Socialist ticket while in prison for war resistance. The Socialist Party was in a sense fortunate in its smallness; even though it had no chance at electoral victory there were still some in the Party who felt it should compromise on the war issue. If it had been in serious contention for the national political victory, I believe the American Socialist Party would also have given in to the war hysteria.

History suggests the importance of all participants in the movement having a clear picture of the American power structure and the relatively minor importance of the Congress. Movement leaders, gifted as they are in verbal skills, and likely to develop an inflated view of their personal influence after successful experiments in electoral campaigns, may be tempted to seek public office as a base for revolutionary work. Realistic earlier estimates of the futility of the parliamentary road to revolution may be forgotten. "The direct actionists in the party are, after all, irresponsible challengers to our leadership" (one can imagine them saying, wondering if they can compete on the streets with this challenge). "So many people have joined the party in recent years as it achieved influence, and they will support us if we lead the party into Congress."

Electoral campaigns in mass society focus on the person—the candidate—as the bearer of the word, and the campaign machinery projects that person in a very positive light. This is heady for the most humble candidate, and may be disastrous for the ego-trippers more likely to be drawn to the spotlight.

Party leaders gain their influence by verbal and administrative ability rather than by action in the streets and exemplary life styles. It is therefore not surprising that, in dealing with the Establishment, they come to prefer verbal contests and behind-the-scenes politicking to direct action and mass confrontations, despite the fact that the authentic power of revolution lies in popular struggle.

The history of revolutionary organization is littered with the party leaders who, once in the legislature, forgot the need for popular struggle and had their conservative way against a majority in their own party organization. Hugh Gaitskell, leader of the British Labour Party during the height of the Ban-the-Bomb movement, flatly refused to implement the Party's majority vote to oppose

British nuclear weapons. He, backed by other Labour M.P.s, had his way.

The tragic failure of the socialists in Europe to strike against the First World War is more understandable when we remember that most of them had taken the parliamentary road; their leaders had already developed more in common with the bourgeois politicians than with the workers who lost their lives in the ensuing blood bath.

Parties from 1914 to today commit themselves to the nation-state as the arena of work. It is one thing to contest for power on the national *level*—all revolutionary movements must do that because so much power is organized there—but it is another to be working daily in the context of the state. Subtly, over time, the state's assumptions are likely to become one's own and the importance of counter-institutions and decentralist approaches wanes. It is a rare person who can work hard and well in one place while insisting that the real action is somewhere else! The movement must ask: Is the cutting edge of revolutionary work in the lower levels of state decision-making (i.e., the Congress)? If not, should some of the movement's most able and influential people be working there?

This objection to the party style of organizing becomes more important as multi-national corporations grow. The national state will lose some of its power and the arena of electoral politics will become still less significant for lack of political structures which can deal with the corporations. While revolutionary parties can develop relationships across national lines, they are not likely to win elections in their own countries if they can be attacked for neglecting the national interest. The development of a world community does, after all, mean dismantling much of the privilege and power of the nation-state. I do not recall any successful American campaigns for state governor on a platform of giving significant power to Washington; it would be even more amazing if a party could win on a platform for giving power to the trans-national level.

THE QUESTION OF LEADERSHIP

The political party has, of course, been the traditional means of unifying revolutionary movements, where they have been unified at all. If the party is rejected as too centralized, too prone to co-optation, and too statist, what can take its place?

Movements sometimes find their unity in a charismatic figure: Nkrumah, Martin Luther King, Mao, Susan B. Anthony. When Gandhi joined the Indian National Congress it was a small organization of middle class men engaging in ideological debates. With his own charisma Gandhi linked Congress to the masses, and the ideologues learned that they needed Gandhi because Gandhi knew the people.

The assassination of Gandhi, however, shows one of the flaws in this way of organizing. The more dependent the movement is for its unity on one person, the more vulnerable it is to assassination.

Co-optation is another means by which the movement can be stymied; the Establishment in the United States has for years been expert in buying up or weaning away from the people the bright young leaders who are eager for status and influence. The more dependent the movement is for its unity on one person, the more vulnerable it is to co-optation.

We should not wait for our Great Man. He (or she) will not be able to raise the goose flesh on all who need to be reached, any more than Martin Luther King could or Billy Graham can. Our society seems to be creating more and more sub-cultures which respond to different symbols, different styles.

Further, the revolution for life emphasizes growth for everyone, the discovery by each person of his or her own charisma. The spirit exists in each of us, but we can put off forever discovering that by trying to live off the spirit of another. Even if Freud is right about our psychological need for the father and our tendency to look for the father in political and social leaders, growth is still possible. The difference between a five-year-old and a healthy twenty-five-year-old is not trivial. Revolutionary organizations should be structured to stretch our adulthood rather than cater to our childhood.

Leadership is a very difficult issue because of the understandable tendency in the movement to reflect the leadership styles of the dominant culture. The movement hard-driving *macho* male laying his trips on people while speeding around the country is all too sadly like the Hollywood image of "successful" businessmen, cowboys, generals, and politicians. Of course a movement must have room for a variety of temperaments; that is not the issue. The problem is that movement decision-making is easily dominated by these tycoons of idealism. Since the tycoons rarely spend time sharing their genuinely useful skills and knowledge—training is usually scorned in favor of "experience"—a sexist leadership pattern which might initially be defended as necessary continues to perpetuate itself.

Unfortunately, in reaction to the tendency of movement leadership to resemble the styles of the old order, an anti-leadership impulse has appeared which manages to obstruct without offering a radical way forward. The sternest critics of repressive organization are often anarchists, philosophically, although in practice the most articulate ones tend to dominate *their* circles with little evidence of egalitarian decision-making patterns. In my cynical moments I have wondered if anarchism is not chiefly used as a means of disintegrating stable organization in order for, out of the ensuing chaos, the chief anarchist to become the new dominating leader.

The remarkable lack of concern among anarchists for training in *co*-leadership—that is, the sharing of roles which any group must have in order to make decisions in common—only reinforces my suspicion that the movement cannot simply rely on the anarchists to develop their own best insights. We must move ahead from negative critique to alternative patterns by which movement work can get done, such as the patterns suggested in this book.

The Groups for Living Revolution do provide an egalitarian context for movement work. It is demonstrably possible for a small face-to-face group to make decisions, by consensus, without a chairperson or single leader. Groups of a dozen or so can learn how to share the roles which, blended together, add up to a successful decision-making process: roles like harmonizer, initiator, opinion-seeker, philosopher-critic, expediter, and so on. Since mobility is closely related to the super-star syndrome of movement life, the anchoring of individuals to a collective should help them come to terms with their own needs to lay their trips on people and then move on.

If the charismatic figure and the movement tycoon are not sound means of unity, perhaps a coalition of organizations and groups provides the way forward. Coalitions by their nature are not permanent and will form and re-form as appropriate in the flux of social change, yet can coordinate common efforts at a given moment.

In a genuine coalition the power is in the groups themselves and there is little chance of party-like bureaucratic control from the top. If movement organizations themselves shift toward egalitarian styles and rotate their representatives to the coalition, the coalition decision-making may be less dominated by the tycoons who, at an earlier stage, brought the coalition into being.

Because a coalition is usually an alliance for bringing about specific and immediate changes, it is not likely to have in common a coherent analysis of society, a radical alternative vision, or even a long-run strategy. I believe that in the United States, however, the resistance of the Establishment to progressive change and the increasing disruption caused by ecological, economic, and cultural pressures will combine to force the movement coalitions toward a coherent radicalism with unity on strategy. The tendency in any coalition toward the lowest common denominator will still operate, but the denominator will rise.

Hastening this process of radicalizing the mass coalitions will be smaller groupings around particular radical analyses, programs, and strategies which provide a kind of testing ground; if a particular revolutionary alliance proved sound in its smaller way, the mass coalition could more easily adopt its approach.

UNITY THROUGH STRUGGLE

Approaches to organizing come up again in later stages of this strategy, because at each stage new possibilities open up. Even at this point, however, it is possible to resolve a current movement dilemma in the United States: Which is more important—national or local action?

On one level that dilemma is like asking: Which is more important in a book—the paper or the ink? Obviously there will be no revolutionary movement in this country without strong grassroots organization *and* national struggle. No city can be transformed unless the nation changes drastically. Our society cannot be changed neighborhood-by-neighborhood.

The false dilemma results from shortsighted strategy, which either projects a confrontation somewhere (e.g., Washington, D.C.) and then urges everyone to drop everything for that, or digs into a neighborhood somewhere and forgets about national impact.

Sound strategy links the levels in a multi-level movement. The strategy underlying the idea of Groups for Living Revolution connects national struggle to grassroots organizing.

A local Group probably begins its campaign with preparatory activities like research, fact-finding, and negotiations, then moves up to public education, organization, and the drawing in of allies. If its specific campaign goals have not yet been reached, it moves into direct bodily confrontation with injustice and oppression.

As a Group nears the crunch on a significant issue, resources from the network of groups and communities can join the struggle to make it successful. Since other Groups are likely to be at a variety of points in their own developing campaigns, and the counter-institutions and radical caucuses are likewise not constantly in crisis, it is reasonable to expect that they will respond to the call by releasing a member or two to aid the Group which is in difficulty. Nor is altruism the major motivating force in the response, for it is in each Group's interest to aid the others so that it will in turn be aided when the crunch comes.

The Southern Christian Leadership Conference (SCLC) successfully used this pattern in the 1960s. When local work came to a boil in Albany, in Birmingham, in Selma, the resources from other areas flowed to the conflict points; in this way the struggles reached national proportions. This is the organic way of relating local organizing to national confrontation.

At this early stage in the revolutionary process, tight structures of coordination are unnecessary and, I believe, undesirable. Coalitions forming and re-forming on particular issues and action projects are important. Decentralized networks of mutual aid for struggle, with a high common denominator of world view and strategy, are also important. Both these coordinating structures leave plenty of room for local initiative and adaptation to local conditions, but also provide as much unity as necessary. Coalitions and networks are resilient and highly resistant to repression; when the government chooses to strike, it cannot destroy a movement by destroying the center.

In the fourth and fifth stages of this strategy—mass non-cooperation and parallel institutions—more coordination is necessary for solidarity against the power of the state. That discussion of organization is postponed, therefore, until Chapters VI and VII.

ORGANIZING IN A POLICE STATE

"We Mexicans here in the United States, as well as other farm laborers, are engaged in another struggle for the freedom and dignity which poverty denies us," Chavez said in 1965. "But it must not be a violent struggle, even if violence is used against us. Violence can only hurt us and our cause. The law is for us as well as for the ranchers. We have certain constitutional guarantees—for example, freedom of assembly, which enables us to assemble here tonight. . . ."[12]

But what if there are no constitutional guarantees? How can people organize in a police state? The question is asked by revolutionaries in many parts of the world today.

The question is relevant for us in the United States because the civil liberties we now enjoy may be eroded as the power elite finds the population more and more restive, the ecological pressures greater and greater, the social movements increasingly militant. The peace and social justice efforts of the late 1960s, mild as they were, stirred a panicky power elite to political trials, massive FBI infiltration and surveillance, and a "crime bill" making inroads on human rights.

When a radical tries to walk between paranoia on the one hand and smug denials of reality on the other, it is useful to have perspec-

tive. A little-known case of struggle for national independence offers useful perspective; under the oppression of the Austrian Empire, Hungarians developed an organizing style which enabled the
movement to grow even in a police state.

Franz Josef had problems. In the 1840s he was head of an Austrian
Empire which was beginning to shake from the combined assaults
of liberalism and Bismarck's ambitions to make Prussia the leader
of Central Europe. The world of international politics was then, as
now, dog-eat-dog. Austria had been the biggest dog, but was threatened by a persistent movement for autonomy by Hungary, a movement which boiled into major violence in 1849 when Hungary
declared independence from Austria and defended it with an
army.[13]

With help from Russian military forces and skillful divide-and-
conquer tactics, Emperor Franz Josef beat down the rebellion. But
how long would the Hungarians remain quiet before unrest again
weakened his Empire from within?

Ferencz Deák, too, had problems. As the primary leader of Hungarian nationalists after the ill-fated rebellion, Deák faced worse
repression than had existed in the era before 1849. There were
executions, police spies were everywhere, the Constitution was
withdrawn, the county assemblies were dissolved. As Deák began
to prepare for the coming struggle, he had a very large asset, however: the brutal suppression of 1849 had unified the people, and it
would be very hard for the Emperor to get cooperation on projects
where he needed Hungarian participation.

"Boldness in politics is suitable only when it is supported by
considerable power. If not, it is of no use and ends for the most part
in tragedy," said Deák. He therefore spent his time in the 1850s
developing agreement on essentials among the leadership of the
country through conversations in his room in Budapest, and encouraging the organization of the people through voluntary associations. The country became interlaced with associations promoting
Magyar language and music, and self-help in business and agriculture. Through this the people began to regain their shaken self-
confidence.

The moment of truth for the Emperor came in 1859, when he

needed Hungarian help in fighting Napoleon III and found an un-
cooperative leadership and unreliable troops awaiting him. The
Imperial "pacification plan" had failed, and Franz Josef took a new
tack. He restored the county assemblies and made a popular Hungarian general the governor of the country. Only some Hungarian
aristocrats were taken in by these partial measures. The Emperor
went further, setting up a federal Parliament in Vienna with representation from all the provincial assemblies, including that of Hungary. Most Hungarians were not impressed and there was no
wavering.

In fact, the county assemblies took the offensive and refused to
vote for the raising of recruits for the army or the collection of taxes.
Demonstrations took place.

The Emperor then tried another variation on the theme of sub-
stituting the form of parliamentary representation for the sub-
stance of freedom. In February 1861, the new plan was issued from
Vienna, this time for a bicameral legislature for the entire Empire.
The Imperial Parliament would have more power, but Hungary's
own Parliament still was given little. The Parliament met, and
agreed on a message to the Emperor which left him no illusions
about the chances of cooperation: "We cannot recognize the
right of the said Imperial Parliament to legislate on the affairs of
Hungary. . . ."

The key was the Constitution: if the Emperor would submit
himself to the ancient Constitution of Hungary, and become its
constitutional monarch, the Hungarians would end their political
noncooperation.

The Emperor replied by dissolving the Hungarian Parliament.
When the leading county assembly protested, Franz Josef ordered
the assembly itself to be dissolved. The assembly went on meeting
until Austrian soldiers entered the chamber and carried them out
bodily.

This was the signal for a dramatic nationwide campaign of resistance. The other county assemblies followed the example of the
first. The Hungarians in the bureaucracy refused to transfer their
functions to the Austrians, leaving administration in chaos. Hungarians stopped paying taxes. The Austrians imposed martial law
and began the work of repression.

Deák urged the people not to engage in violence, but to base their action on the constitutional conception of legality: "This is the safe ground on which, ourselves unarmed, we can hold our own against armed force. If suffering be necessary, suffer with dignity."

When the Austrian tax collector came, the people told him he was acting illegally, and refused to pay. When police were called in to seize the goods, the Hungarian auctioneers refused to auction them. When Austrian auctioneers were brought in to turn the assets into cash, they found that Hungarians refused to bid, and the Austrian government found it was costing more to try to collect the taxes than the taxes were worth.

To break the spirit of the resistance, the Austrian soldiers were billeted among the Hungarian households. This lowered morale among the soldiers more than among the Hungarians.

When a boycott of Austrian goods began to hurt, the government declared the boycott illegal. Austrian soldiers began to fill the jails with the boycott organizers. After a few months the Emperor tried to mollify the Hungarians by granting amnesty to all the political prisoners. Hungarians responded by adding another verse to their satirical song, "The Austrian Thieves."

The voluntary associations which Deák had encouraged became the informal government of the country, for deposed members of Parliament operated through them and the people followed their lead. The spirit of resistance carried them through a time of economic recession in 1863, and nationalism in literature flourished.

Pressure from Prussia broke the stalemate. The Emperor had to pacify the home front in view of the rising menace of Prussia. He restored the Hungarian Parliament, which met and resumed its old practice of sending demands to the Emperor for restoration of the full Constitution and county assemblies. A full-scale war with Prussia helped weaken the position of Franz Josef still further. After a vain attempt to get Hungarian participation in the war by promising autonomy and an even vainer attempt to decree military conscription of Hungarians for service against the Prussians, the Emperor gave up.

On June 8, 1867, Franz Josef was crowned King of Hungary, with full agreement to rule as a constitutional monarch with the restored authority of the Hungarian Parliament over Hungarian affairs.

Ferencz Deák refused the offer to become prime minister in the new Hungarian government, and planned for a quieter life, still in the service of his country.

What sustained the Hungarians during their long, hard fight?[14] How did their organizing style make it possible to move even in a police state?

A major force in the struggle was the network of Hungarian voluntary associations. The associations developed leadership skills and trust among the people and became, informally, the organization of the resistance when the Parliament was suppressed. If Deák had been arrested there were many other knowledgeable people to take his place, or to take collective leadership. They had gained their experience not only in clear-cut political work (difficult and dangerous in a police state), but also in the community organizations around them.

Why was Ferencz Deák not arrested? It is often argued that if Gandhi had been working in a full-scale police state, he would have spent all his time in jail. Certainly the Austrian Emperor did not have the restraints of parliamentary democracy at home to prevent him from being quite ruthless with opposition abroad. He proved that in his response to the 1849 rising.

It may be that Deák was not suppressed precisely because he worked so consistently in the 1850s on the constructive program and other quiet activities. One account of his work mentions that secret police were baffled by his daily strolls, playing with the children of Budapest, not looking very dangerous. Arresting this well-known encourager of community life would be hard to justify to the people; the government would simply be making a martyr of him. He might be more dangerous dead than living.

Journalist Régis Debray emphasizes the necessity of a *foco*—a mountain or jungle hideaway where relative safety from the police can be obtained.[15] Perhaps the constructive program, plus a commitment to nonviolent action, is the living revolution's equivalent to the guerrilla's *foco*. The *foco* provides, of course, only relative safety. Che Guevara is only the best known of the many guerrilla leaders who have been killed despite their precautions. The constructive program provides only relative safety as well, as the jailing and killing of nonviolent workers in Guatemala and Brazil show. Safety cannot be a high priority for a revolutionist. (A veteran of many dangerous struggles in America's Deep South, Andrew Young, has said, the people most interested in self-defense are usually cowards.)

Nevertheless, enough freedom from repression must be found to enable the organizing work to go on. In Sicily the organizers who began to be successful in organizing the poor were customarily killed, presumably by the Mafia. Danilo Dolci survived (although he had a close call) and has even campaigned against the Mafia. But again, Dolci is a man who worked through constructive program and had a clear-cut commitment to nonviolence.[16] Khan Abdul Gaffir Khan, the nonviolent leader of the Pathans on the northwest frontier of colonial India, was able to stay out of jail long enough to organize a formidable group. He first worked through community development projects, as did his brother, who was, however, imprisoned for most of his life until independence. (The British were noticeably harsher with the "uncivilized nomads" than with the rest of the Indians.)

The major alternative to the constructive program as a means of protecting organizers is underground organization. At first glance this certainly seems less dangerous than functioning openly. It is also useful for planning some kinds of activities which cannot be carried out if the police know in advance.

Underground organization has a number of serious disadvantages, however. It skews the organization toward elitism in decision-making and participation. The constant worry about infiltrators means the number of persons making the decisions must be kept to a minimum. If we want to build a mass movement we must realize the dynamic in secret organization which works against mass participation.

Secrecy brings divisiveness into movement life because there must always be those who know and those who do not know. Those who are outside feel resentful; those who are inside develop feelings of superiority. Knowledge is a form of power, and secrecy ensures that there be a power structure with a distinction between the haves and have-nots.

One way of curbing these tendencies to some degree is by a system of rotation. The jobs which are best done covertly could be rotated among various people so no one stays out of sight for long.

A plan of rotation would not eliminate all the problems, however. Underground organization is an incentive for infiltration of spies, who in turn may gain influence in the organization. I described earlier the dangers of the *agents provocateurs*. Their ruinous suggestions are likely to be countered in open discussion but accepted in the hothouse atmosphere of small secret meetings. No one wants spies to be influential in making decisions, but this must pretty well be accepted in an underground organization. Even the Bolsheviks had a Czarist spy on their Central Committee.

Knowing that spies are probably in the organization also spurs a suspiciousness which can poison solidarity. While spies may also be planted in open organizations, suspiciousness is beside the point when there are no secrets. Nor is it only the likely presence of police agents which gives rise to a certain reserve among the organizers; we also vary among ourselves in our resistance to the temptations of betrayal. Is it you who would sell our secrets for a certain price? What if the price were stopping your torture? The ready use of torture by the French in the Algerian War, or the Brazilian government today, reminds us that secret organization brings with it the likely use of torture to ferret out the facts.

Going underground may not actually reduce the amount of repression. Mexican student leaders decided in the aftermath of their strikes in 1968 that going underground would provoke still more repression because it would confirm the worst image held of them by the government (or the worst image that the government could paint for the people).

Eugene Debs recognized the importance of this image problem when he led the Pullman railway strike. Meetings were open to the press, so all could see the forthright and democratic way of the workers.[17] The usual attacks of "outside agitators," shady finances, and so on lose their credibility in the spotlight of openness.

While it may seem necessary in some places in the world to operate a minimum underground organization, the list of disadvantages is very long: it breeds elitism, divisiveness, spies, suspiciousness, and torture. It may under some circumstances actually increase the amount of repression. It is likely to be less and less effective in maintaining secrecy anyway, given the rapid technological advances in long-range espionage.

I realize that there may nevertheless seem no alternative in some totalitarian situations, where even the constructive program has been rejected for one reason or another. In a situation like that of the United States, with its present degree of freedom, underground organizing is a strategic disaster. It is understandable that some will begin to work covertly as a reluctant necessity to organize a certain action. But if they will begin to look at their work in long-range, strategic terms, they will see that one can pay too high a price for a tactic. One can win battles and still lose wars.

ORGANIZING TRANSNATIONALLY

The world is shrinking and capitalism is organizing itself more elaborately across national lines. Even fifty years ago the Russian Revolution suffered intervention by several capitalist countries. Gunboat diplomacy is still possible, as in 1965 in the Dominican Republic, and the web of social control becomes more extensive even while armed force remains the last resort.

The movement, too, must organize across national lines. The old *inter*national structures, which bring together national organizations for mutual support, must be supplemented by *trans*national structures, those which relate individuals and local groups to each other across national lines.

The task remains community organization, but the communities are those which transcend national boundaries. Scientists increasingly form a transnational community, artists and writers another, religious workers a third, students a fourth. Workers will begin soon to see that a multi-national corporation must be tackled on a transnational level: workers in several countries may need to strike simultaneously to force major changes.

The simplest form of transnational organization at this time may be by occupational groupings. Similar working conditions, interests, and opponents may bring rapid acknowledgment of mutuality. The Brazilian government is trying to reshape universities in the Yankee style, which will increase its control over the students. This may help students in the United States and Brazil to see the advantages of collaboration.

Another form of transnational organization is Groups for Living Revolution in border areas composed of the nationals of two or more countries. They could explore the possibilities of transnational action, and perhaps become the cells of the mass world movement of the future.

Just as in neighborhood organizing, a transnational organization will be only a shell if it does not reflect a genuine community spirit. Facilitating that spirit are exchanges of personnel, student exchanges, and the like, and transnational training projects in which participants become involved with each other as they learn to confront injustice through direct action.

Agitators become organizers in this second stage of revolution. Radical caucuses press for change within occupations and religious associations; sometimes they take action which draws on the heritage of the group. They differ from counter-institutions in that they do not try to match the legitimate functions of the institution out of which they operate. The counter-institutions become crucial to our strategy when they develop revolutionary ideology, build revolutionary organization, or are base camps in a period of revolutionary struggle. Teams such as Groups for Living Revolution provide solidarity and skills which are essential to the next stage of action. These building blocks of the movement develop unity among themselves not through a charismatic figure or a bureaucratic party, but through a common strategy and discipline. Coalitions of interest groups and parties will rise and fall throughout this period, sometimes playing a valuable role in developing unity. Later, conscious and enduring coordination will be possible.

Although the growth of a police state makes underground organization tempting, there are strong arguments against it. The constructive program provides a way of beginning to meet people's needs while developing skills and solidarity even in difficult circumstances. An explicit commitment to nonviolent action also widens the options for organizers, while secrecy breeds elitism and other dangerous tendencies in movement life.

While some circles in the United States are only beginning to hear the message about the injustice of the American Empire, other elements are well enough organized to move into action, even very risky action. The third stage finds these people making propaganda of the deed.

V
PROPAGANDA
OF THE DEED

During the stage of cultural preparation, injustice is attacked again and again by discussion, leaflets, guerrilla theater, newspapers, and so on. Although the seeds are planted in many minds, they must receive the water of events to blossom into full-grown indignation.

During cultural preparation agitators try to describe the alternatives to living with fear and alienation, but the alternatives become widely credible when they are acted out in a public arena for all to see.

In short, propaganda of the word is not enough. The message must also be spread through action. In the drama of action and counter-action the people can see more clearly the brutality of the old order and the virility of the new.

Students of guerrilla war also see the importance of this process:

> Popular support for the guerrillas is predicated upon the moral alienation of the masses from the existing government. The revolutionaries' chief aim is to activate and perpetuate the moral isolation of the enemy regime until such isolation has become total and irreversible.[1]

DILEMMA DEMONSTRATIONS

The best kind of action is one which puts the opponent in a dilemma: whichever response he makes helps the movement. If he allows the demonstration to proceed, the movement gains that opportunity to educate the people. If he represses the demonstration, the people are awakened further to the underlying nature of the regime.

The *Phoenix* voyage to North Vietnam with medical supplies in 1967 put the United States government in a dilemma about how to respond. The decision was finally made in the White House. The *Phoenix* was not physically prevented from reaching Haiphong; the successful voyage strengthened the anti-war movement. If the government had actually stopped the *Phoenix* on the high seas, it would have shown still more clearly the inhuman policy of its Vietnam policy.

The "Wobblies" were effective in putting the authorities in a dilemma which demonstrated the underlying injustice of the economic system:

A campaign for the right to organize, to assemble, and to hold street meetings was conducted during the winter of 1914–15 in Sioux City, Iowa, the strategic center for controlling the harvest hands who move into that region. Without this "freedom of speech," no organizer could be placed in the city. As the point of attack, the officers of the Industrial Workers of the World agitated for better working conditions in ice-harvesting, appealed to the public for redress, and staged protest meetings in the streets. The city officials forbade these gatherings, but the organizers defied the order. One assembly was dispersed by the police, but no arrests were made. For two months thereafter the meetings were held daily, when one of the promoters was arrested on suspicion. The union accepted the challenge and went to the police station in a body, demanding his release. They were arrested on the charge of disturbing the peace and were put in jail. The battle was on. An appeal was sent by letter from the jail to IWW members, explaining the strategic location of Sioux City, and naming the "prime movers in this procedure of persecution," and urging all "foot-loose rebels" to come to that city.

In a few weeks eighty-three members were behind the bars, but the street meetings went on. The prisoners refused to crack stone, and went on a hunger strike. A citizen protested against the arrest of men who were making these "harmless speeches" from soapboxes. This turned the tide. The prisoners were released with the understanding that they would stop the immigration which was bringing scores of recruits every day from San Francisco, Chicago, and almost every other large city of the land. The promoters got permission at the city hall to hold a banquet on the rock pile, and the members assembled in hundreds for an evening feast. Then they began to steal out of town as silently as they came, leaving behind a little group of men to carry on the work of organization.[2]

If the authorities of Sioux City allowed the IWW organizers to make their street speeches, they would be encouraging the labor movement. By making arrests, however, they also helped the movement. The repression actually aided the cause by gaining favorable publicity for the union and dramatizing to the workers the actual extent of liberty in the heartland of American democracy.

The IWW was a revolutionary organization which was organizing for mass noncooperation. The Woman's Party during the same period gained woman suffrage by means of protest demonstrations and grassroots organization. The skill and heroism of the militant suffragists are exemplary; they found a vulnerable spot in the American self-image which virtually forced the concession of the vote.

The leader of the militants, Alice Paul, explained her strategy simply: "If a creditor stands before a man's house all day long, demanding payment of his bill, the man must either remove the creditor or pay the bill."[3]

Despite the patriotic hysteria evoked by the First World War, the women began to picket the White House in 1917. They were arrested and sometimes attacked by hostile men before the arresting began. The prison sentences grew in length despite the tendency of the women to go on hunger strikes. When the President refused to work for the suffrage amendment the women attacked him as a hypocrite by burning publicly the speeches in which he said he was for freedom.

The early reaction to the civil disobedience of the women was largely hostile. "The opinion seems to be almost universal in New York that the White House pickets have blocked equal suffrage in the state for from five to ten years," noted the *Washington Post* soberly.[4] The large National American Woman Suffrage Association, which confined itself to polite forms of agitation, found that even its own work was made more difficult by the militancy of the small Woman's Party.

Underneath the hostility, however, there began to grow a sympathy for the courageous suffering of the women. When former prisoners toured the country relating their harrowing experiences, newspaper editorials began to change their tone. As it finally became clear to Congressmen that only the passage of the suffrage amendment would make the women stop their escalating protest, lawmakers revised their position. (One admitted after the vote that he still opposed suffrage for women, but he opposed even more the rough treatment they were getting. To stop the repression, he voted against his opinion.) Even stubborn President Woodrow Wilson included suffrage as one of his war aims!

Julia Emory, arrested thirty-four times, and dedicated women like her, posed dilemma after dilemma to the authorities. Wilson could not tolerate the demonstrations during the mobilization required by the war, but the repression of the women brought him to an even more difficult position. The more women Wilson jailed, the more awkward he sounded when he said that the war aimed to make the world safe for democracy. Finally the brewers' and industrialists' opposition to suffrage became less important than the mounting support for the women and indignation at their treatment.

The Woman's Party, fortunately, was able to sustain itself during a period when the demonstrations seemed counter-productive. The Party refused to change its strategy even when some of the women defected. Some months passed before the reality of the suffering began to get through to opinion-makers across the country, but in the end public sympathy backed up the nuisance value of the demonstrations to hasten the passage of the suffrage amendment.

Of course there are many protest actions which do not take the form of the dilemma demonstration, but are simply expressions of a point of view: the usual marches, parades, pickets, and so on. Where civil liberties exist, these actions can often become ritualized to the point where they educate almost no one. When imagination is used, however, demonstrations can be effective even where they are legal. They can communicate beyond words by being dramatically relevant to political life at the time or because of the hardship involved in doing them (for example, an extended vigil and fast).

Clearly, the authorities often respond to dilemma demonstrations with violence of some kind. What prevents such demonstrations from becoming mere provocation? This is an important issue, because provocation may alienate the revolutionaries from the people, brutalize the police, and even brutalize the demonstrators.

In New York demonstrations in the 1930s, one tactic was to stick hat pins into the rumps of policemen's horses, to precipitate violence in which demonstrators would be hurt. For a revolutionary who affirms life, this is unhealthy. The provocation helps the policeman to justify his violence to himself. The movement is in an awkward position in the public eye when the provocation is exposed. Further, provocation makes manipulators out of organizers. The leaders find themselves setting up situations of violence without telling the demonstrators. The sheep will no doubt be grateful to the organizers who thus "radicalized" (read: manipulated) them.

The organizers of dilemma demonstrations avoid these negative effects by being honest about the situation and by intending to accomplish the goal of the demonstration. In the case of the *Phoenix*, we in A Quaker Action Group really wanted the medicines to reach Haiphong. We were pleased that the U.S. Navy did not seize the ship, although if it had, the movement also would have gained. The organizers should never be in a position of *depending* on the authorities to react violently in order to make their point. Among other things, that policy would play into the hands of the sophisticated government people who, like the London police officials, can simply reduce the overt violence to a minimum while countering the activists. The resulting frustration can tempt people into desperate action to goad the police into using violence.

On May 9, 1970, I participated in a mass protest in London against

United States intervention in Cambodia. The London police are well-trained for demonstrations and are usually very restrained, certainly by American standards. Some of the demonstrators had planned to provoke the police to violence in order to "show the British people the brutality which lies under the surface of the state," as one student in the crowd told me. Some of the demonstrators taunted, lunged, and finally used fists to goad the police into fighting.

The press and television reports were utterly predictable: "Sixty Policemen Hurt" blared the top headline in the liberal paper *The Observer,* while other media stated that more police were hurt than demonstrators. The demonstrators managed to place the police in a sympathetic position and themselves in a bad light, and did nothing for the cause of the Cambodian people.

By contrast, a few months later a campaign against chemical warfare was launched in the United States with a pine tree, a symbol of the American colonial struggle as well as life and ecological sanity. The campaigners found opposition at Edgewood Arsenal, a chemical weapons factory in Maryland. The commandant refused permission to plant the pine tree on the Arsenal grounds. In a series of confrontations twenty-nine demonstrators and several pine trees were arrested. After a week of embarrassing reports in the mass media, the commander of the Arsenal told the press, "We'll accept the tree as a tree."

The *Baltimore Evening Sun* wrote in an editorial on July 16, 1970: The wonder is that it took Edgewood a week of confrontations with peace marchers, twenty-nine arrests, endless humiliating pictures of husky M.P.s [military police] glaring at the offensive seedling to get the point. The point is that, if rival symbols were to be juggled, the tree had them licked before they started. In symbol language, when the tree said life, all Edgewood could say back was death, no matter how daintily it picked its phrases.

The campaigners both in Maryland and in London wanted to reduce the legitimacy of the defenders of the status quo. In London the police actually used violence as well as arrests, while in Maryland there were only arrests. Yet the demonstrators in Maryland projected their message much more successfully, because the violence of the London police seemed to most people justified while the behavior of the military in Maryland seemed ridiculous. Of course there were also other factors which made the situations dissimilar, but the basic point remains: propaganda of the deed is much more creative than provoking a policeman to use his club.

Guerrilla warriors sometimes engage in acts of terror early in the struggle in order to provoke harsh reprisals from the regime. The reprisals, out of all proportion to the violence used by the guerrillas themselves, often stimulate more support for the guerrilla cause while undermining the position of the government. In Algeria a bomb explosion in a café brought massive retaliation by the French, such as the destruction of a whole block of residential housing. The people could in this drama see for themselves who are the "goodies" and who are the "baddies." The essence is in the *contrast* between the forces of justice and the status quo. If the revolutionary movement were to be indiscriminately violent, as is the regime, its popular support would melt away.

Since the heart of the dynamic is in the contrast, it makes sense to increase that contrast by initiating the encounter with nonviolent action. Nonviolent struggle is so clearly consistent with the goals of the revolution that the movement using them is likely to achieve not only most of the support which the guerrillas gain but also the support of elements which remain uncommitted in a violent struggle.

Is destruction of property a form of propaganda of the deed? It has been used historically in later stages of struggle as an accompaniment to mass noncooperation. In this stage we are concerned with symbolic communication. Is sabotage useful here?

This discussion has surfaced in the United States regarding the destruction of draft files and the like. Admirable and courageous pacifists such as Daniel and Philip Berrigan have been sent to prison for destroying that property which, they say, "has no right to exist." I very much agree that draft files should not exist, along with concentration camps, anti-ballistic missiles, and slums. Whether trying to destroy them communicates our message clearly, however, is something else. (I realize that some advocates suggest that draft-file destruction goes "beyond symbolism," but the movement is not strong enough to coerce the government into giving up conscription via file destriction. On a sheer physical level, the government obviously has far more power and resources than the movement has. The action should, I think, be evaluated on a symbolic level.)

Destroying a widely hated piece of material shows determination and courage, especially when the demonstrators are openly available for arrest. When the object is not widely disliked, however, the character of the act itself (destruction) is likely to be the dominant impression made on the people. When property destruction is defined in a society as violence (however irrational that may seem to a revolutionist), the act is again likely to be very ambiguous if not negative in its communication. Our revolution affirms life, but that commitment is clouded by acts defined by the people as violence.

Complicating this question is the matter of *degree* of destructiveness in the symbolism, and the staying power of those who use the tactic. Sometimes the general public sees a tactic initially as negative, but during a long campaign they change their perceptions of it; this happened in the woman suffrage case. But this process depends partly on whether there is a long campaign, or whether the initiators were mistaken in their estimation of the follow-through ability of the movement on a controversial tactic.

There may be compelling reasons for property destruction which outweigh its ambiguity as a form of symbolic communication to the people, such as the need to bolster the morale of the movement or spur it to acts of greater courage. But when we add to the symbolic difficulty the organizational problems of secret activity described in Chapter IV, we will search very hard for alternatives to material destruction.

REPRESSION

Fear is the central issue. If the government can create enough fear, it can divide the movement, isolate the leaders, and relax again into routine administration of the system. As Tom Hayden put it following the confrontation in Chicago during the Democratic National Convention of 1968:

The experience of refusing to be intimidated by the police state set up in Chicago was very important for people to go through because I think one of our chief problems within the movement is fear. Fear of repression, fear of violence, fear of walking into hazardous and unpredictable situations and overcoming that fear is the first step in breaking down the police state which thrives on fear and depends on it.[5]

Repression has broken many revolts in the past. Struggles for justice both violent and nonviolent have been beaten by the fear of the participants. Sometimes, however, the repression boomerangs, and the oppressor finds that its use of violence aids the movement instead of itself.

Eugene Nelson described an incident in the California grape strike in which a grower drove close to the picket line which was trying to persuade grape harvesters to come out on strike:

The newcomer apparently has parked, and I turn back to the field and hold up my Huelga sign, anxious to press the attack now that the men in the field seem to be seriously considering what we are saying. The next thing I know I am flat on the ground—this new maniac has backed up and knocked me for a loop! I find myself in a half-sitting position, the bumper of the now-stopped car protruding a foot or so over my left leg, as I shake my head and try to grasp what has happened. . . . The crowd gathers around me. And the man in the car has gotten out and comes strutting around the rear of the car (in the usual cowboy boots) not to ask if I am hurt, but to snort contemptuously, "What an actor! Look at that faker! . . .

Suddenly there is a murmur of excitement a few feet away, and "They're coming out!" someone yells. I twist my head to see the whole crew of workers walking out of the field, led by the man with the intelligent eyes, and I am tempted to believe that God has already punished this brutal man for his reckless and murderous actions. Again violence has backfired on the growers; they continually underestimate the intelligence and sensitivity of the workers, and fail to realize they are capable of being revolted by their coarse actions. When will they realize that fear won't work on these people? I am overjoyed, I forget the pain in my knee for a moment as I watch the faces of these humble working people as they come to peer at me and sign authorization cards.

"He knocked him down, just like that!" one of them is saying.
"The strike is really getting violent! What will they do next?"
"This is too much for me—this decided me once and for all—I'm
with the union!"[6]

The boomerang effect of repressive violence worked on a national scale in 1919 in India. In Amritsar on April 18 a large meeting
was held to protest the arrest of Gandhi and two local leaders of the
movement for national independence.

> Some 20,000 unsuspecting men, women, and children gathered to-
> gether in the Jallianwalla Bag, a walled-in garden with only one exit.
> All were peaceful and pledged to nonviolence, and none among
> them was armed with even so much as a stick. Suddenly, General
> Dyer, a British military officer, arrived on the scene with fifty picked
> soldiers armed with machine guns. He posted his troops at the only
> exit of the walled-in garden so that no one could escape. Without a
> word of warning, he gave orders to fire. About 1,650 rounds of ammu-
> nition were leveled at the peaceful gathering of men, women, and
> children at close range. The holocaust was over in a few minutes.
> When Dyer withdrew, some 1,200 dead and 3,600 wounded were
> lying in the garden.[7]

This event triggered a nationwide campaign of noncooperation
as the masses, outraged by this evidence of the brutality of British
imperialism, joined the movement.

What is the difference? Why do some movements actually grow
under the impact of violent opposition while others lose heart and
decline? In the discussion of the South African struggle I sometimes
hear the claim that the Africans had to give up nonviolent resistance because they encountered government violence, but the
shootings at Sharpeville pale in comparison to Amritsar. Yet in one
case repression dampened the movement while in the other it
spurred the movement on. It is not repression that destroys a movement. It is repression plus lack of preparation.

At least two conditions seem essential if the violence of the Old
Order is to be turned to the movement's advantage.

First, people must realize that repression is expected and in no
way means defeat. It is a kind of recognition from the government

that movement action is a serious threat. The only way to avoid repression is to avoid struggle; just as guerrillas are not surprised by army retaliation, so people should not be surprised when the police and army are used against a nonviolent movement. Just as people must steel themselves for casualties and dislocation during a war, so they must in nonviolent revolution. One purpose of training for direct action is precisely this kind of preparation.

Part of the problem of expectation may have been caused by advocates of nonviolent struggle; some describe it in such glowing terms as to suggest magic. The way of nonviolent revolution is not painless; freedom is not free. There will be little suffering if the status quo is only a brittle façade behind which the dry rot of corruption has been at work for decades. There will be a lot of suffering if the regime is still vital and has the loyalty of efficient and clever men. All I will say is that, other things being equal, there will be *less* suffering to be endured by the people when a nonviolent strategy is used than when a violent strategy is used. While that is a serious claim for humane persons to consider, it is not the same as talking magic.

Knowing that there would be a price to pay for opposing the British, Gandhi turned the repression into a tangible measure of success. When the government struck back, the Indians knew they were being effective. When Gandhi was arrested during the 1930 civil disobedience campaign, for example, a mass meeting was organized to *congratulate* the government for the arrest! Gandhi's own attitude toward prison was that he should enter it as a bridegroom enters his bride's chamber; the exaggeration made the point to everyone that the government had no power over him because it could not make him fear its punishment.

The first condition for overcoming the violence of the regime is expecting it. The second condition is social organization.

Totalitarians such as Hitler try to eliminate voluntary associations and all forms of organization which stand between the state and the solitary individual. They know that the best-known antidote to terror is community. This is one reason why the organization-building stage comes before propaganda of the deed in this strategy. Recall the Hungarians' successful nonviolent resistance to Austrian repression: it seemed that each new measure of Austrian violence brought a stiffening of determination from the Hungarians. The basis for Hungarian solidarity lay in their organizations as well as in their nationalism. The participants in civilian insurrections in El Salvador, Guatemala, and France withstood repression well for a short period, but I doubt that they could have sustained their revolts much longer without extensive organization. A great deal of organizing lay behind the U.S. farm workers' ability to stand against abuse from the grape-growers and the suffering of a long strike.

The necessity of organization and realistic expectations explains why the African National Congress did not become an effective mass movement in its 1952 campaign against South Africa's pass laws. There certainly were a number of people willing to struggle for a decent society, as this glimpse from the campaign will demonstrate:

> On Sunday night, Dr. Conco with his batch of twenty-three men and women defied the curfew law, informing the police well in advance, but the police delined to effect an arrest on the ground that they were "busy with more important matters." . . . Monday night, Dr. Conco and his batch "marched past the Charge Office under the very nose of the District Commandant's Headquarters. Policemen saw the resisters, looked the other way (one bowed his head down shamefully), and they passed on their way." On Tuesday morning, "Dr. Conco and his gallant band were not to be denied the pleasure of arrest and imprisonment for long!" They entered the railway cloak-room and booking-hall reserved for Europeans, were arrested by the police, and "pushed and prodded into the van, though they were most willing. . . ."[8]

However, they did not have realistic expectations about the amount of repression in store for them. Resistance leaders told participants to expect three to six weeks in prison for civil disobedience; naturally, when the courts increased the sentences, enthusiasm waned. Emotionally appealing reasons for accepting suffering were not given, and the leaders themselves rarely set an example by going into the streets in defiance of the regime.[9]

The organizational problem was equally great. When the ANC

began its 1952 campaign it had only 7,000 members. During the campaign the membership shot to 100,000, but that is not many troops with which to tackle the South African government! The Congress had only gained a full-time secretary in 1945 and had never developed a newspaper. Finances and records were inadequate. When experienced leaders were banned or imprisoned, untrained men had to try to cope.[10] In short, the ANC did not have the organizational strength to withstand the repression unleashed by the government in its defense of white privilege.

Organizers are often tempted to respond to repression by reducing the intensity of the struggle, especially when well-meaning third parties urge a "cooling-off period." There may indeed be good reason to be flexible and change the form of the demonstrations, for example, to small groups rather than large groups, or fasting rather than marching. But reducing the level of combat may actually encourage more repression as the opponent learns that violence is effective. As political scientist Gene Sharp puts it: "The shortest way to end brutalities is to demonstrate that they do not help to achieve the opponent's objectives."[11]

That was certainly the instinct of Student Non-Violent Coordinating Committee (SNCC) organizers in 1961 when a bus carrying Freedom Riders was burned in Anniston, Alabama, and the occupants beaten severely. According to Bernard Lafayette, then on the SNCC staff, the organizers decided the Freedom Rides must continue "because the best way to respond to violence is to *continue the movement*, the best way to meet profound violence is with profound love." So the rides continued and the campaign grew into mass jail-ins in Jackson, Mississippi.

Theoretical support for this approach comes from a study of power in prisons by sociologist Richard McCleery. McCleery found that a key element in the officials' use of terror was withholding information about the future; this provoked anxiety about what might happen which was worse than knowledge would have been. "Uncertainty, even more than exemplary punishment, is a keystone of 'terror' as a technique of government, and it was a major factor in control in the traditional prison."[12]

Movement organizers who reduce the level of their action may increase anxiety among the people about what will happen now that the ball is in the opponent's court; by giving up the initiative the organizers are providing the government with a means of terror. It may be better to continue filling the jails.

These are matters which must of course be decided in the situation, but well-wishing allies should consider an alternative to urging the movement people to "cool it." Such an alternative was taken by the physicians of Santiago, Chile, in 1931. Students at the National University declared a four-day strike to protest the oppressive regime of Carlos Ibáñez del Campo. They occupied the main building and hung out banners marked *Libertad.* The medical association, realizing that the students were in danger, threatened Ibáñez with a strike if troops fired on or injured any of the students.[13]

More recently, Brazilian priests managed to reduce police repression of students. During the June 1968 demonstrations in Rio de Janeiro, 130 priests formed a living chain to push themselves between the police and the students. They were organized by Archbishop Dom Helder Camara, who has been developing a nonviolent revolutionary approach to the oppression and poverty in Brazil.[14]

Facing repression is never easy, and there are bound to be people in our movement who feel it impossible not to hit back when they or their comrades are attacked. Training for direct action needs to be stepped up in this period. Training was an important ingredient in the ability of black people in the United States to maintain self-control under fire.

Military technique also has this problem of self-control, of course. Che Guevara pointed out in his book on guerrilla warfare that there are times when the fighter feels very strongly like staying and fighting when he really ought to melt back into the jungle. He has to overcome his inclinations in order to fulfill the requirements of his method.[15]

Every technique has its requirements, and these may be hard to honor. Training is one important way for people to find within themselves the strength to do what needs to be done.

It would be a mistake to dwell too much, however, on the difficulties of struggling in the face of reprisals. A century of often-bitter struck by workers should remind us how much the people can stand for a just cause, as in this garment workers' strike:

> The suffering among the strikers was so great that the officers of the international would not assume responsibility for rejecting the proposal for settlement. But the strikers outdid the leaders. "Mothers of half-starved children fairly drowned the voices of officers and organizers as they strove to speak. Girls of sixteen and seventeen developed remarkable powers of oratory as they sprang to the platform to urge their sisters to stand out for full union recognition."[16]

SOLDIERS AND POLICE

In the Washington, D.C., jail I once met a soldier who had been used against peace demonstrators. "We have something in common," he told me. "We both hate the army." He was against the Vietnam War, which he described as "killing a lot of us off." He was among the troops which surrounded the Pentagon on October 21, 1967, when a massive anti-war demonstration took place.

But this soldier, against the war and alienated from the army, was proud of being the first on his side of the Pentagon to start beating the demonstrators. "A girl started to piss on my boots and I got mad —I worked hard to polish those boots—so I clubbed her."

Obviously, the way to increase repression is to insult the men who, often unwillingly, are being used as tools of the government. A policy of generosity toward the agents of repression was stated by Mao Tse-tung during the Second World War:

> Our policy toward prisoners captured from the Japanese, puppet, or anti-Communist troops is to set them all free, except for those who have incurred the bitter hatred of the masses and must receive capital punishment and whose death sentence has been approved by the higher authorities. Among the prisoners, those who were coerced into joining the reactionary forces but who are more or less inclined toward the revolution should be won over in large numbers to work for our army. The rest should be released and, if they fight us and are

captured again, should again be set free. We should not insult them, take away their personal effects, or try to exact recantations from them, but without exception should treat them sincerely and kindly. This should be our policy, however reactionary they may be. It is a very effective way of isolating the camp of reaction.[17]

If this policy can be made during a war, when large-scale violence tends to dehumanize all sides in the conflict, it certainly can be useful in civilian resistance. The Czechoslovakian people found it so; their fraternization with Warsaw Pact troops during the invasion of August 21, 1968, was so effective that the officers had to begin to rotate the troops out of population centers on the fourth day! (When Czechoslovak leader Alexander Dubček returned from Moscow he called off the national resistance action, so it is difficult to know what the results would have been of a sustained struggle. In Chapter VIII I will describe this case in more detail.)

Sympathetic soldiers and police can help the movement in a number of ways: inefficiency, tips, protesting in the ranks, deserting, joining the movement, mutiny.

There are endless examples of inefficiency among police and soldiers because of sympathy with the cause. Indian police were sometimes very lax except when directly supervised by officers in the effort to suppress the 1930 civil disobedience campaign. Tips from Occupation authorities helped the Danes in 1942 to organize an extensive getaway operation to Sweden, which saved the lives of nearly all the Danish Jews marked for Nazi destruction. In Occupied Norway, both Norwegian police and German soldiers gave tips to the resistance movement which saved lives.

Protesting within the ranks is becoming common within the United States armed forces; if the government gives up conscription it may be partly because conscripts are more likely to protest against war than volunteers.

Desertion created a major problem for the Czar during the February 1917 revolution in Russia. In Petrograd the Volynsky Regiment fired under orders on nonviolent demonstrators and the next day the whole unit deserted. They lost their cohesion and mingled with the crowd of demonstrators.[18]

Desertion is growing among American soldiers. Deserters do not always want to identify with the protest movement, but some have publicly joined the movement in a "sanctuary" in a church or Friends meetinghouse.

Mutiny is not frequent for the punishment is severe, yet there are a number of cases in which soldiers have refused to fire on nonviolent demonstrators. In the German Democratic Republic there was a civilian insurrection in 1953. The top bureaucrats of the workers' state were unable to defend themselves against the workers and called in the Soviet troops to help.

Everywhere the tanks moved very slowly into the crowds, and where the soldiers met no armed resistance they discharged their firearms into the air. Some Russian and German officers and other ranks were later shot for refusing to obey orders. The Federal Ministry for All-German Affairs has put the number of Russian officers and other ranks at seventeen.[19]

In the Hungarian revolt in 1956 the Russian troops proved so unreliable when ordered to suppress unarmed crowds that new troops were brought in from Soviet Asia who could not speak the language and were told lies about the nature of their mission.

Because mutiny has such serious consequences, it is unlikely, certainly at this stage of propaganda of the deed. Mutiny is more likely during a time of general insurrection. Even in the period of propaganda of the deed, however, we must keep in mind the *range* of sympathetic responses from inefficiency to mutiny. In this stage the tone is being set by the movement on how to act toward soldiers and police. If the prevailing trend is toward dehumanizing the agents of repression (calling them "pig" is one way of dehumanizing), the harvest of tips and desertions will be meager. People have a way of living up—or down—to their image.

One of the lessons Lenin gained from the 1905 experience in Russia was that it is foolish to attack the government forces in an insurrectionary situation. The Bolsheviks were active in February 1917 in reducing the amount of violence by the crowds; they knew that soldiers do not become sympathetic while under attack.

The American movement may not have two chances. It can start right now to make a distinction in action between the *role* of the repressor and the *person* occupying that role. By that spirit we in the movement give the person a chance to make the same distinction between himself and his role; he can then find a way to help us.

In this stage of the struggle we therefore make efforts to contact the police and soldiers of the regime in a friendly way, to explain the aims of the revolutionary movement and the injustice of the oppressive regime. We emphasize the nonviolent character of the struggle (and therefore the lack of threat to their persons).

In other words, the dilemma demonstrations which we mount should pose a dilemma not only to the decision-makers, but also to the men on whom they depend to carry out their policy of reprisals.

TRANSNATIONAL ACTION

On a transnational level there have not been many experiments with propaganda of the deed, largely because the awareness and organization are only now emerging. The Sahara protest against French nuclear testing in 1959–60 was organized by activists on three continents and gained participation from Africans, Europeans, and North Americans. Unfortunately, lack of follow-up made the project less effective than it might have been.

The invasion of Czechoslovakia spurred a transnational project in 1968 which required a good deal of organizational sophistication. The War Resisters International sent small multi-national teams to Moscow, Warsaw, Sofia, and Budapest to demonstrate on the same day in public squares. The governments of the Warsaw Pact suspected CIA sponsorship because of the smooth coordination of participants from half a dozen countries! They were soon convinced otherwise by the record of WRI opposition to NATO and the Vietnam War, and the protesters were let out of prison.[20]

The growth of transnational consciousness and organization will encourage many more projects which express revolutionary aspirations through action. Such projects are essential if the people are to realize the world scale of injustice, to see the connections behind local poverty and, for example, the $215 billion spent each year for arms.

DEEDS AS WELL AS WORDS

People are worrying about nihilism. Rapid change encourages such anxiety, and the Establishment exploits the fear in its effort to stop the movement for change. Radicals are attacked as "anarchists" who want to destroy the present order but have nothing positive to replace it with.

Of course we can try to counter the attacks via pamphlets and speeches, but we must admit that the most dramatic and visible things we do are often the protests rather than the positive alternatives.

In this situation the combination of constructive program with protest may be more telling than any number of words. In the spring of 1970, for example, A Quaker Action Group devised action which combined medical programs for the poor, solidarity with the Black Panthers, and war-tax resistance. In the weeks preceding the April 15 income tax deadline, AQAG collected over $2,000 from the Philadelphia area in taxes which were refused the federal government. This sum was given to a medical clinic sponsored by the Black Panthers in a poverty area, to the accompaniment of a work-camp in the clinic, street meetings, and publicity. AQAG was showing in action that the withdrawal of financial support for the war-makers is not merely negative, but is a response to a philosophy which values life over death. While attacking the warfare state, the project was helping to build a community medical institution. The public could see for itself what these protesters have in mind.

Another advantage of a constructive project side-by-side with a protest campaign is that it can provide tangible progress even when the campaign is going poorly. Most campaigns have their ups and downs, after all, and morale can sink dangerously. Building a community facility, cleaning up a polluted area, serving breakfasts to poor children can boost morale even when the direct action front is in trouble.

A characteristic of the best direct action in this stage is that it reveals people acting out the future in the present. With the *Phoenix* project of medical supplies to the North Vietnamese, for example, activists did not wait until the day when governments will acknowledge that people have the right to help their brothers and sisters no matter where they live. The activists brought the future into the present, by carrying out the forbidden voyage. Black college students did not wait until some remote day when lunch counters would be integrated; they brought it into the present of 1960 by sitting-in. Their very form of protest showed the immediate end they had in view.

A few years ago I was asked by a group of academics what they could do to press more strongly for social change. I mentioned the usual things—organize movement activities, give more financial support, urge the professional associations to stand against racism, war, and so on. The suggestions did not fully satisfy these men and women because the actions are not directly related to their vocations. I should have seen that there is a way of very direct confrontation of the status quo within the ideals of the profession itself, and that is through acting out the future in the present.

For social workers this may mean bringing into the welfare system all who are eligible and writing checks of the sort the recipients *ought* to be getting. For lawyers this may mean refusing to waive jury trials and insisting on all the rights of the accused, even in situations of large-scale repression (such as during mass demonstrations). For physicians this may mean admitting to hospitals all those who need medical help regardless of ability to pay. (When interns did a similar action in California they called it a "heal-in." The corridors were jammed wih patients who needed help.) For teachers this may mean introducing revolutionary content into the curriculum, refusing to grade students, and so on.

The point is clear: by putting into practice now the ideals of one's profession, one would be putting a test to the status quo—does it *count on* hypocrisy and myopia to survive? Can it tolerate professionals "doing their thing" as it ought to be done? Perhaps even those who think of themselves as free will discover in new ways that the system prevents them from doing their job in its fullest expression.

Journalist Milton Mayer interviewed a good many Germans after the Second World War to discover their experience during the Nazi period. He found a surprising number who thought they were free, who were not conscious of the many ways they were hemmed in. Content to play their roles as defined for them, they did not discover the boundaries of their "freedom."[21]

In America today there are many who have a subjective sense of freedom but who never test it out, never live their lives fully enough or do their work well enough to crash against the inhibitions of the system.

An increasing number of young people, on the other hand, are determined to live life fully even though this means confrontation with the mechanisms of control. Thousands of young men are acting as if they are liberated even from short-term slavery to the state; they turn in their selective service cards. The conscription-less future is brought into the present for we who have done this. The society which tests us is now put to the test by us: Can it stand for a sense of human responsibility that denies the state even two years of involuntary servitude?

As the movement develops its capacity to confront the oppressive institutions with the truth, it will grow. When the government strikes back in an effort to hide the truth, the people will see more clearly what is at stake. If the movement is prepared in its expectations and organization, it will maintain a nonviolent spirit which even more strongly contrasts with the brutality of the repression.

In such a situation the movement can develop a mass basis, and move to the fourth stage of its revolutionary strategy: political and economic noncooperation.

VI

POLITICAL
AND ECONOMIC
NONCOOPERATION

> The only chain that a man can stand
> Is the chain of hand in hand. . . .
> —Black freedom song

The people advance their struggle for life by massive acts of non-cooperation. Where the government found compliance it now finds defiance. The earlier boycott of social institutions, which reflected growing alienation from the status quo, now spreads into political and economic areas. Even repression can help the movement as it enters the stage of mass struggle.

In this book I have emphasized organization. The strength of noncooperation in labor history hs been tied very much to organization. This chapter borrows heavily from the experience of workers and from coordinated strikes and boycotts, but I do not wish to minimize the spontaneous forms which arise. The wise organization learns from the spontaneous experiments of the people, whether Johannesburg Africans who boycott their buses or Swedes who stop supporting their commercial Christmas.

In eastern Angola in 1966, tax-refusal occurred among a group of villages. Twelve chiefs refused to cooperate with the Portuguese in collecting taxes; they explained that there was widespread unemployment and no tangible benefits from the taxes. The twelve were arrested and taken by plane to another part of Angola. While en route the Portuguese officers pointed out that they had planes and weapons while the Angolans had nothing. The chiefs replied that the Portuguese still could not force the people to do what they had decided not to do. The chiefs were put in jail and questioned further, then threatened, but still they refused to give the order to the people for tax-payment. Finally the officers said the chiefs could return to their villages on condition that there be no more subversive action. The chiefs replied that they would continue to oppose the payment of unjust taxes and other injustices.

After a time the Portuguese released the chiefs and returned them to their villages. The Angolan nationalist leader who described this incident said that the Portuguese knew how to handle the guerrillas but not how to deal with this sort of united resistance by the villagers themselves.[1]

The frustrating thing to the authorities about noncooperation is that the threats, even the beatings and killings, do not of themselves do the needed work or produce the needed goods. As the worker in the 1919 Lawrence textile strike said, "Let them try to weave cloth with their machine guns." The repression can only try to scare the people into cooperating, and if the people still will not cooperate, the regime is in deep trouble.

A note about method is needed. All along I have been in the awkward position of outlining a strategy which has not yet been tried, of describing a revolution which has never happened.

On the other hand, I use illustrations drawn from history and current events because they help me to keep my feet on the ground and to show the reader better than abstractions will what I mean. The illustrations suggest possibilities. They do not prove anything, of course, and all examples are unique in some of their circumstances. They simply show that some proposals which sound farfetched have connections to historical reality. The illustrations show, moreover, that we new radicals have a rich heritage of direct action against injustice; if we care to, we can stand on the shoulders of giants. There is no need to be provincial in time or space when so many people are working around the world for peace and freedom.

In the United States, parts of the movement are in the stage of propaganda of the deed, although there is still a lot of politicizing and organizing to do. American readers of this book may not, therefore, mind the use of illustrations from the past for these first three stages. The awkwardness grows, however, when I describe the fourth and fifth stages, since for the United States these lie in the future. The flexibility of Western capitalism so far prevents the conditions for mass noncooperation linked to revolutionary programs and organization. Since these stages are in the future I hesitate to use tactical illustrations drawn from the past and present. Yet a description without illustration will lack life. It might also suggest that we have nothing to learn from workers and others who have used on a mass scale some tactics we will need in the final stages.

The reader can resolve the dilemma. You can accept the illustrations in the spirit intended: neither as proofs nor as examples of revolutions for life, but simply as ways of advancing our common exploration of strategy.

POLITICAL NONCOOPERATION

Often a legislature exists as a public relations gesture toward democratic participation of the people, but without substantial power. As long ago as the late 1950s Harrison Brown claimed publicly that the Pentagon had more power over the Congress than vice versa.[2] That once-shocking statement is hardly controversial any more. Certainly the executive branch reigns supreme, having the means at its disposal (including the provocation of incidents such as the Tonkin Gulf attacks on the U.S. Navy) to leave the Congress hopelessly outflanked. When Lyndon Johnson ordered the bombing of Hanoi and Haiphong I was told by one Senator's office that I had as much power in the situation as the Senator did! President Richard Nixon showed no more regard for the Congress than his predecessor did; the invasion of Cambodia in 1970 in the face of strenuous prior objection in the Senate showed that rather clearly. Despite the Founding Fathers' clear intentions, the Congress seems to be going the way of the Roman Senate during the Caesars' rule.

The relative impotence of the Legislative branch and growing power of the Executive, also found in countries other than the United States, will become clearer as the propaganda of the deed stage develops. Already in 1969, seven U.S. Congressmen committed civil disobedience with A Quaker Action Group on the steps of the Capitol. One of them frankly told us that he realized how little power he had from within the system as a Congressman. He also told us later that he gained increased respect from his colleagues for his illegal protest.

Lawmakers will increasingly become lawbreakers (in a nonviolent way) as they lose patience with the way law is used to mask immorality. Some may resign in protest or boycott the sessions. Some may attend but disrupt the proceedings, as John Hume did in 1969 in the Stormont Parliament of Northern Ireland. Hume, a civil rights M.P. from Londonderry, conducted a sit-down in the House to protest the suppression of debate on a civil rights issue.

While Adlai Stevenson was representing the United States at the United Nations there were efforts to get him to resign to protest against U.S. foreign policy. He was reported to be unhappy with his position. (He once found himself denying in the U.N. that the United States was involved in the Bay of Pigs invasion of Cuba.) Still, he reportedly thought he would have more influence from within the government than outside it. There is also a certain imperative among members of the political Establishment that they not be ungentlemanly toward others in the club.

Stevenson could have been a powerful voice at one point in the development of American social change movements—if he had left the framework and liberated himself to speak. He did not, however, perceive it as his *duty,* and men in public affairs are not likely to see it so until the propaganda of the deed stage is well advanced, until the violence of the system is beyond question.

Noncooperation by administrative personnel can also be a powerful force. No government can survive long without its bureaucrats, as Wolfgang Kapp discovered when he staged a coup d'état in Germany. On March 13, 1920, a group of military officers established the extreme nationalist Kapp as the new ruler. In Berlin and other parts of Germany there was a complete general strike, and the civil service united in its opposition to the new regime. In fact, the erstwhile head of government found himself wandering up and down the corridors of power looking in vain for a secretary to type his proclamations! Despite his efforts to repress the resistance by shooting unarmed demonstrators, Kapp found himself without the means of governing and fled to Sweden on March 17.[3]

That degree of unity comes only under special circumstances, of course, and in this strategy for revolution we will not count on such unanimous noncooperation. But even segments of the civil service going on strike can have an effect. Certainly the developing political organization of federal employees in the United States is an encouraging factor.

Mass political noncooperation is more important than the protest of government officeholders, however. No one can give freedom: people have to win it for themselves. Only through popular struggle can the people gain a freedom they can keep. Mass civil disobedience, tax-refusal, boycott of elections, and draft resistance help people unlearn their submissiveness. The tactics of noncooperation can be accessible to the bulk of the population. We saw how in the El Salvador insurrection even the children joined the action by passing out leaflets.

A problem in the noncooperation in El Salvador, Guatemala, and France was that the resistance was too short-lived to alter the people's habits of submission. For this stage in the strategy the movement should plan organized, long-term, and selective forms of noncooperation. All-out campaigns for total change are unrealistic because they cannot be sustained, even after careful organizational and cultural preparation. It is much better to develop our strength through noncooperation focused on clearly defined, limited goals. This principle is reinforced by the unhappy experience of the African National Congress in 1952. The ANC threw all its limited resources of organization into a nationwide campaign for unlimited goals. It optimistically hoped to overwhelm the government by filling the jails and breaking down the means of law-enforcement.

Is there a contradiction between revolutionary aspiration and limited goals? There can be, but need not be. The movement should make clear in its program its revolutionary intentions, but this does not prevent it from making specific, limited demands at a given stage or connected to a specific campaign. The specific demands help to rally the people (not everyone is moved by goals which seem vague and far away). Further, when the immediate goals are achieved, morale is heightened. Those who thought they were powerless find that they have achieved something. The skeptics who thought that struggle is useless may see their mistake.

"Reformism!" I can hear someone mutter with contempt. The contempt is misplaced, unless we readily condemn Marx for agitating for an eight-hour day. Revolutionaries often work for reforms, but they do not always become reformers in the process.

Che Guevara, not likely to be dismissed as a liberal reformer, emphasized the difficulties of revolution while the government is still able to give reforms. "Where a government has come into power through some popular vote, fraudulent or not, and maintains at least an appearance of constitutional legality, the guerrilla outbreak cannot be promoted, since the possibilities of peaceful struggle have not yet been exhausted," he wrote.[4] The essential popular support for revolution will not come while the government still has legitimacy, that is, responds to "peaceful struggle" (read: "conventional pressure tactics").

In his important book *The Urban Guerrilla*, Martin Oppenheimer argues that society has a kind of reform potential. Its ability to produce a particular reform in the face of pressure creates for it an outpost, as it were, against revolution. If there are no outposts, it is either because the system has not yet been tested or because the outposts have fallen, in which case the fortress is open to attack, and the system is ripe for revolution.

> As long as reform is demanded, and the system *can* give it, it will be given, provided enough pressure is applied. But if the system *cannot* give a particular reform (because it strikes too closely at some *fundamental* aspect of the system, as its leadership sees it at the time), then we know its point of weakness. The revolutionist looks for those limits of a system to press an attack.[5]

Revolutionists campaign for specific reforms, then, because there will be no revolution while reforms can be given. Of course the reforms are worth having for their own sake as well. A revolution for life does not sneer at improving the lot of miserable people right now, and does this through the constructive program as well as through its pressures on the state.

André Gorz in his book *Strategy for Labor* points out that limited changes can have specifically revolutionary meaning when they involve an actual shift in power of decision-making. He uses the example of an Italian Fiat factory where production workers went on strike rather than make the luxury car which Fiat management planned. Instead, the workers insisted they make a low-price car. When management loses some of its decision-making power in such a basic area as this, the workers have indeed won what Gorz calls a "revolutionary reform."[6]

Two important differences mark a revolutionary organization working for reforms from those who are merely reformers: revolutionists have a radical analysis and program, and use means which are inherently revolutionary. Unlike those who soft-pedal their basis of action until it gets lost in a welter of pragmatism, revolutionists emphasize their analysis and long-term goals even while working for a specific change. Second, the means of noncooperation is inherently revolutionary because it is extra-constitutional, nonviolent, and dependent on the people's active participation.

ECONOMIC NONCOOPERATION

The civilian insurrections in France, El Salvador, and Guatemala suggest the coercive power of economic noncooperation, especially the general strike. For this stage, however, we stress the value of *selective* strikes and boycotts which can be sustained for a longer period, or general strikes for limited aims. The Hungarians in the nineteenth century boycotted Austrian goods over a period and developed their own industries at the same time. Since Austria operated Hungary as a colony, for markets and raw materials, this boycott aided the struggle.

American schoolchildren learn about the economic noncooperation of the colonials in the struggle against Britain. The Continental Congress actually had an elaborate strategy worked out in which the colonials eventually would stop import trade with Britain. We do not learn in school the degree to which these measures were having an effect and how far along the road of nonviolent struggle the colonists went before 1776. The governor of Massachusetts Bay Colony by 1772–73 found himself almost irrelevant to the life of the colony; he wrote at one point that he was in effective control only of his own house![7]

The swelling popular movement in the Colonies found a response in growing agitation for the American cause within Britain itself. Unfortunately, these developments were partly checked by the military struggle begun at Lexington and Concord: the struggle lost adherents in the Colonies and the pro-American forces in Britain lost their zeal.

Strikes and boycotts often take time to achieve results. "We have no time to wait," the ardent organizer may say to justify an ambitious short cut. Sadly, the usual sequel to an unsuccessful adventure is no action at all. After the exhilarating crunch comes a letdown in which people appear to have all the time in the world, for they are not busy organizing actions.

Labor organizers have contended with this problem of keeping morale high when no immediate results are forthcoming. We can count on the regime to try to define the situation in a discouraging way, too, and we cannot count on the press for accurate assessments. During the great American steel strike in the early part of this century, "Full page advertisements begged the men to go back to work, while flaming headlines told us 'men go back to mills,' 'steel strike waning!' and 'mills operating stronger'; 'more men back to work,' and so forth."[8] Organizers must have their own means of communication to counter this; it is foolish to rely on the capitalist press.

Noncooperation can more likely be sustained when it is backed by understanding of the issues, by organization, and by dramatic demonstrations of the injustice of the present order. The organizers of the Southern Christian Leadership Conference counted on demonstrations for preparing boycotts on white-owned stores in Southern cities. The marches in the shopping areas often resulted in beatings and water-hosings, which in turn sparked the boycott campaign.

Cesar Chavez developed strong organization to back the grape strikers. The strike itself, and the efforts to repress it, provided the drama necessary to launch a widespread boycott against California grapes. And the participation in the boycott by liberal forces across the United States encouraged the strikers to continue to victory. It is worth looking at this situation more closely even though it is not by itself revolutionary; it shows an important political process at work which is likely to operate even in the stage of widespread noncooperation.

When the grape strike began in 1965, the civil rights coalition of the early 1960s was in disarray. In fact, it was commonly pronounced dead with a mixture of regret and sometimes bitterness. The coalition of liberals, churchmen, and labor, sparked by the dramatic actions of black people, had been a major progressive force in American life. The coalition had made possible solid institutional change in the South, which was the focus of the nonviolent campaigns led by the SCLC, CORE, and SNCC.

For several years a compelling mechanism of social change had been operating. Black people sat-in, marched, picketed, and went to jail. Their actions illuminated the contradictions in society. Their emphasis on nonviolence allayed the apprehensions of the people in the middle and created an atmosphere of moral courage that emboldened their allies. The allies put additional pressure on mass media, the Legislature, and the Executive branch of government. High officials huddled to agree on reforms which would take off the heat. With a reluctant shudder, America changed.

But in 1965 the coalition was disunited. Various reasons were given: "Black Power frightened the white liberals." "Watts and other riots set up a reactionary atmosphere." "White liberals deserted domestic change by chasing after the Vietnam War." "The 1964 Lyndon Johnson landslide buried many leaders' capacity for independent action."

While the New York–Washington radical circles were full of head-shaking and discouragement, some chicanos on the opposite side of the continent were engaged in the direct action which spurred the coalition back into informal existence. The grape stike began to reveal the injustice of the farm-labor situation. Church and labor responded: the Migrant Ministry, there from the beginning, interpreted the strike to church social action agencies, and Walter Reuther of the United Auto Workers helped financially at an early point. The farm workers' union became a part of the AFL-CIO, and got help from experienced civil rights activists.

When the boycott tactic was begun, the liberals found a role. Across the country the farm workers discovered the unions, churches, and liberals of the old civil rights coalition swinging into supporting action. The response was more on a grassroots level than on a legislative level, since the form of the struggle was different. By 1968 the boycott had forced some growers to concede while others took refuge behind the Pentagon, which bought the tons of grapes unwanted on the American market.

While the grape strike was not as dramatic as, say, the 1963 Birmingham campaign—a major city was not dislocated—it nevertheless was strong enough to start the mechanism of change. Stirred by the courageous, nonviolent spirit of the workers, the coalition responded. This response shows that the death of the civil rights coalition may have been proclaimed too hastily, that the allies of black people can again be mobilized when mass nonviolent campaigning begins.

A mass revolutionary movement has in common with the farm workers a need to mobilize allies, neutralize the forces in the middle, and make it difficult for the opponent to use its repressive capacity.

The French insurrection of 1968 mobilized allies and put in doubt the reliability of the army for repression; De Gaulle was obviously shaken. Unfortunately, the middle classes were not neutralized. For a time they were sympathetic with the students, then undecided, but they swung over to the government at last. There were many causes for this, but one was certainly the violence of the students. The government made the most of this. The movement had no revolutionary program, so people in the middle could not choose on the basis of the programs of the government and the movement. They took their cues from the styles of the two, and the movement style increasingly was perceived as chaotic and violent. Middle classes are not made neutral by such a style.

But that was an insurrection; in such a time people improvise as

best they can with little time for discussion. The use of noncooperation over a longer period of time as an organized means of forcing
change is something else. A movement then can discuss its experience and learn from it. The Belgian workers in their struggle for the
vote experimented with violence as a supplement to noncooperation and over a period of years drew some lessons from the experiments. A study of their struggle by Patricia Parkman illuminates
this important question.[9]

VIOLENCE AND NONCOOPERATION: A MIX?

Belgian socialists in the 1880s were deeply attached to the heroic
dream of a sudden, violent action to remake a society which had
been with Europeans ever since the French Revolution. Yet this
kind of revolution seemed less and less a practical possibility, as
modern technology concentrated increasing power in the hands of
the state.

Further, labor unions were by then legal, and through them
industrial workers were making important bread-and-butter gains.
The gradual spread down the social scale of the right-to-vote
seemed to open the possibility of a take-over through constitutional
means by the working class.

The Belgian Labor Party, founded in 1885, was born into this
period of ambivalence and change in socialist thinking. The founders were convinced that giant strides toward the improvement of
the workingman's lot and the ultimate creation of a socialist society
could be taken with the political muscle exerted at the polls. There
was only one problem: Belgian workers still could not vote. The
party therefore focused on the struggle for universal suffrage.

Some form of direct action was needed to budge the Parliament,
which was dominated by the conservative Catholic Party. Here the
fundamental ambivalence within the Labor Party came to light. Its
leaders often stated a preference for peaceful methods of direct
action. But for nineteenth-century socialists, the very concept of
direct action merged into the old revolutionary dream, conjuring
up visions of street fights and barricades.

In 1890, 40,000 socialists paraded peacefully in Brussels to push their Liberal parliamentary allies and impress the opposition. But no action followed in that year, nor in 1891 or 1892, despite continued agitation. The Labor Party decided to call a general strike if the suffrage bill was not passed in spring 1893. The bill was defeated and the strike began the next day.

At its height the strike involved 200,000 people and it lasted a week. The demonstrations began to turn to violence as days went by with no action in Parliament. There were fights between demonstrators and police in Brussels and a few other cities, and Brussels even saw a short-lived barricade. Workers in Ghent were running out of money to continue the strike and were about to try to seize arms from the local military base.

The Parliament began to discuss the railroad budget to avoid giving the crowd gathered outside the impression that it was fearful. When word came that police in Joliment and Mons had opened fire and killed twelve people, the chamber decided to consider the suffrage proposal again. When the Labor Party assured the deputies that the strike would be called off if the bill passed, the deputies voted for suffrage 199–14.

The struggle was not over. The bill provided for one vote for every man twenty-five or over, but certain classes of people received one or two additional votes depending on income or education. The Party was determined to get equal suffrage, and after the next election it had socialists in Parliament to speak for it.

The electoral way was of course not sufficient and six years went by without gaining equal suffrage. The government introduced a bill in 1899 that would have increased the power of the conservative Catholic Party. There were protest demonstrations in the cities and riots in Brussels. The mayors of several cities informed the king that they would not be responsible for public order if the bill were not withdrawn. The government began to make concessions, and a month later the Cabinet fell.

The Labor Party rightly claimed victory for direct action in the 1899 agitation. In 1893 and 1899 the strike and peaceful demonstrations had been mixed with incidents of violence, yet in both cases the socialists' immediate aims were achieved. By 1901 the Party was badly split on strategy. A proposal for a national demonstration was rejected by delegates who declared themselves tired of peaceful demonstrations and insisted that "it was time to act," by which some meant violent action.

The Party finally united on continuing struggle "if necessary by the general strike and agitation in the street." By February 1902, two bills relating to suffrage were before the Parliament, and constant demonstrations were being organized throughout the country.

In March, a Catholic Party mayor's home was dynamited, then a post office. In Ghent four hundred demonstrators fought with police. The National Bank in Brussels was almost blown up, and a series of violent demonstrations occurred, including the breaking up of a meeting in a Catholic church.

In Brussels, during a demonstration, a group of Labor Party youth attacked the policemen and then moved on to a day-and-a-half spree of window-breaking. Policemen were injured in a number of street fights in other cities, one fatally, and there were more explosions as well as attempts to derail trains.

The government responded with repression. Demonstrators were fired on and some were killed. Meetings of more than five people were forbidden in Brussels, the Party headquarters was surrounded by police, and soldiers began to guard the Parliament.

The Party called a general strike, to which about 300,000 people (about half of Belgium's industrial workers) responded at its height. Just as the strike reached its peak the second bill for suffrage was defeated in Parliament. Workers lost heart and began to return to work. The Party acknowledged it was beaten for the moment and called off the strike.

It seems clear that some people in positions of leadership in the Party had thought that a little violence, or at least the threat of it, might be useful in gaining equal suffrage. This was partly because violence had been present in the direct action which produced the victories of 1893 and 1899, and partly because those victories seemed to demonstrate the weakness of the government before an aroused working class. The Party was generally convinced that it could end the unequal vote with a show of force, and those who were not so sure of its invincibility were almost accused of treason.

The official Party newspaper had gone so far as to offer revolvers and cartridges to its readers "as a species of coupon prize," and the principal Flemish-language organ of the Party published directions for making and using dynamite. While there was division on this question, with some socialists believing that the cause would be best served by peaceable behavior, there was an atmosphere of easy tolerance of violence—until the "Brussels massacre" of April 12 when two workers were killed and some twenty wounded. The shock of general firing on the crowd led the Party leadership to a realization that street-fighting would only invite repression, and from then on Party workers made every effort to prevent further violence. By then it was too late to stop the violence of the workers entirely. Perhaps more importantly, the Party was in no position to disavow the violence even if it was committed by police agents, because of its earlier ambivalent position on the issue.

In the inevitable post-mortems following the defeat, socialist writers found major causes of the failure to be poor organization, insufficient finances, and unwise tactics. There was evidence on every side that the violence had alienated public opinion and made it easier for opponents of the socialist movement to carry the day. The whole experience produced an immediate, decisive, and permanent reaction against violence within the Labor Party.

The years which followed the defeat of 1902 were gray. In 1912 the Catholic Party, which had been declining in strength, made a comeback. This spurred renewed agitation among the workers for a general strike. A major Labor Party conference was called to consider the matter, and the resolution which was adopted contained the following words: "We want the general strike; we shall prepare it formidable and irresistible, but we want it to be peaceful in spite of all provocation and all possible incidents."

The atmosphere in the country had improved since 1902, and there was some hope that the government would give in with only the threat of a strike. But the right wing blocked parliamentary efforts, and in April 1913 approximately 400,000 workers put down their tools. Even the most contemptuous commentator admitted that "the Socialists must be congratulated on the order which they maintain." It was well organized and completely nonviolent.

The strike ended after eight days when a government commission was given the power to work out the details of equal suffrage, and although the work of the commission was overtaken by the First World War, the actual reform of the franchise was the work of the first post-war Parliament in 1919.

Unfortunately, the Belgian movement lost its revolutionary vision and became trapped in parliamentary reformism. The war was a reactionary influence on the working class movements in a number of countries, of course. The Belgian upper class was also successful in setting up "outposts of reform" which protected the basis of the capitalist system.

Belgian socialists at the time were nevertheless right to see the victory of 1913 as a milestone in the development of the working class. The maturing of the movement had shown the contrast between "the considered action of a proletariat organized and conscious from the desperate convulsion of a mass in revolt."[10]

The movement had learned from its own experience to distinguish between violent and nonviolent direct action, and to commit itself explicitly to the latter. When the government in 1902 made it clear that it had superior means of violence and was willing to use them, socialists stopped being ambivalent about the use of violence in their struggle. In rethinking their nineteenth-century heritage, they became pioneers in the twentieth-century concept with which Gandhi was experimenting in far-away South Africa. An enthusiastic (and perhaps clairvoyant) American commentator on the 1913 general strike wrote that the Belgian socialists had pointed the way for the women then fighting for the right to vote, for the Negroes of the American South, and for the peace movement.

I have sometimes heard that nonviolent action is aided in achieving results by the implicit threat of violence in the wings. The government or industry makes concessions to the nonviolent movement because it is worried that by holding out it may have to deal instead with a violent movement. The Belgian case does not support this claim, for in the long run even the small amount of violence by the people provided an opportunity for hardening the conservatives' position. We discussed in Chapter III the frequent government use of *agents provocateurs* to try to shift the movement to violence. Far from being worried about the possibility of violence in the wings, governments sometimes try to bring it onto center stage in order to discredit the movement and justify repression.

The Hungarian insurrection of 1956–57 suggests a striking comparison of the *persistence* of violent resistance and noncooperation. Quite a variety of tactics was used in that situation, of course: general strike, massive demonstrations, workers' councils, sabotage, attacks on the Russian army, execution of Hungarian secret police, and so on. The general strike was able to continue in Budapest for some time after the Russians were able to crush the military resistance.[11]

In my reference to the American struggle for independence from Britain I mentioned the effects of opening the military front at Lexington and Concord: the coalition in the Colonies diminished and the pro-American forces within Britain also declined. It is notable that a nonviolent strategy is often accepted by political realists because it can gain the broadest support and has a good chance of splitting the opposition.

In the preceding chapter on propaganda of the deed, we explored the reactions of soldiers and police, and saw that they can give concrete aid to the movement in ways ranging from inefficiency to mutiny. This aid is less likely in a mix of violence with noncooperation, as Lenin saw from the 1905 civilian insurrection in Russia. The evacuation of Jews from Denmark in 1942 was possible partly because of the character of the Danish resistance. Until then there was no violence by the Danes. The variety of contacts with the opposition resulted in useful leads and inefficiency.

Sir Basil Liddell-Hart, one of the leading military strategists of our time and a specialist in guerrilla warfare, studied intensively the effects of the resistance movements in Europe. He brought to light a further disadvantage of armed resistance:

> The armed resistance movement attracted many "bad hats." It gave them licence to indulge their vices and work off their grudges under the cloak of patriotism—thus giving fresh point to Dr. Johnson's historic remark that "patriotism is the last refuge of a scoun-

drel." Worse still was its wider amoral effect on the younger generation as a whole. It taught them to defy authority and break the rules
of civic morality in the fight against the occupying forces. This left a
disrespect for "law and order" that inevitably continued after the
invaders had gone.

The habit of violence takes much deeper root in irregular warfare
than it does in regular warfare. In the latter it is counter-acted by the
habit of obedience to constituted authority, whereas the former
makes a virtue of defying authority and violating rules. It becomes
very difficult to rebuild a country and a stable state on such an undermined foundation. . . .

While the practice of nonviolent resistance is not entirely devoid
of such after-effects, they are far less damaging, materially and morally. The practice may foster a continuing habit of evasion, but it does
not sow the seeds of civil war, nor breed terrorists.[12]

In most historical situations there has been a mixture of violent
and nonviolent methods. In Cuba the prolonged struggle against
Batista had an important dimension of nonviolent tactics, so much
so that one Latin American specialist describes the Cuban revolution as essentially a "civilian political revolt."[13] In India there was
a terrorist movement which worked throughout the struggle for
independence from Britain. Whether the struggle is labeled "violent" or "nonviolent" depends partly on whether a Castro or a
Gandhi is the charismatic leader.

The question for our strategy is: Does the mix actually help the
struggle, or is the use of violence alongside noncooperation a draw-
back? No scientific precision is possible here, for as in other important practical issues I have raised, there is not enough research to
justify final conclusions. But the tendencies of violence already
mentioned make the case against a mix very strong:

- Violence pushes the middle-of-the-roaders toward the reactionary forces.
- Violence is harder to sustain over a period of time and
  when it is defeated there may be a loss of morale among the
  noncooperators.

- Violence is welcomed by government because it justifies massive repression.
- Violence makes less likely sympathy for the movement from soldiers and police.
- Violence tends to reduce the size of the movement.
- Violence reduces the chance of a split in the opposition.

DEFENDING THE PEOPLE

The question remains: How can the people defend themselves against the violence which comes from the oppressors? Repression will surely be great as mass noncooperation takes the outposts of reform and moves to the fortress of the system itself. It is very well to organize a strike, but if the soldiers press their rifles against the backs of workers and say, "Now work!" what are we to do?

We refuse to fight them on *their* terms, but instead rely on *our* choice of weapons. "Let them try to weave cloth with machine guns and see how far they get." They cannot put a gun at the back of every man—a bit of arithmetic makes that clear. They may try to scare us into submission with exemplary punishment, but that may make us even more stubborn, as it did the Salvadorians and Guatemalans. Wolfgang Kapp tried to break the general strike against his coup by repression; unarmed crowds were shot into and people were killed. Kapp even made picketing a capital offense, but it had no effect.

The truth is that our own fears lead us to exaggerate the power of the oppressors and down-play the effect of ordinary, aroused people. Who would guess that the following could happen during the height of Nazi power?

In Berlin in 1943, during one of the last roundups of the Jews for deportation to death camps, the Gestapo sorted out those with "Aryan kin" and put them in a separate prison in the Rosenstrasse. No one knew what was to be done with them.

At this point the wives stepped in. Already in the early hours of the following day they had discovered the whereabouts of their husbands and as by common consent, as if they had been summoned, a crowd of them appeared at the gate of the improvised detention center. In vain the security police tried to turn away the demonstrators, some 6,000 of them, and to disperse them. Again and again they massed together, advanced, called for their husbands, who despite strict instructions to the contrary showed themselves at the windows, and demanded their release.

For a few hours the routine of a working day interrupted the demonstration, but in the afternoon the square was again crammed with people, and the demanding, accusing cries of the women rose above the noise of the traffic like passionate avowals of a love strengthened by the bitterness of life.

Gestapo headquarters was situated in the Burgstrasse, not far from the square where the demonstration was taking place. A few salvoes from a machine gun could have wiped the women off the square, but the SS did not fire, not this time. Scared by an incident which had no equal in the history of the Third Reich, headquarters consented to negotiate. They spoke soothingly, gave assurances, and finally released the prisoners.[14]

In some cases the best defense is an offense, and demonstrations alongside noncooperation can put the *regime* on the defensive. We must show dramatically that the repression cannot achieve its object, that it cannot scare us into submission. In Argentina in 1902 the labor movement was suffering repression; even strikes were outlawed.

On one occasion, the Buenos Aires police chief ordered the arrest of jobless workers on grounds that jobs were available for all who would work. In retaliation, the unions published an announcement calling for workers who wished jobs to apply at the police chief's home. Suddenly, overwhelmed by throngs of applicants, the police chief dispersed the crowd in disgust and withdrew his order.[15]

Carrying the struggle to the opponent will be a surprise to him (should not these people be afraid of my guns?) and shatter the most important assumption of his work. *He* respects the gun so much that he expects others to do the same. He has lived behind the shield of violence for so long that he imagines everyone is obsessed with shields.

On a tactical level, SCLC organizers have discovered this in civil disobedience in the streets. The police are less brutal to those who stay where they are than to those who try to run away. Running away can touch off a police riot as during the Democratic National Convention in Chicago in 1968, when the police chased madly after the frightened demonstrators. "One reason why we urge thousands in the streets to kneel and pray," an SCLC organizer once said, "is because it is very hard to run on your knees."

The unofficial guardians of the status quo can be as violent as the police, of course. We can expect that, as our movement grows, the opposition of groups like the Minutemen will become more vigorous. How can we deal with these vigilantes?

The black people of St. Augustine, Florida, once neutralized the Ku Klux Klan by a daring nonviolent offensive. The KKK rode through the black community as a means of intimidation. Some blacks killed a member of the Klan, which heightened the danger until no one was safe. When the SCLC came to help a civil rights campaign, the people attended mass meetings with guns. A system of armed escorts operated to get people home again safely. Tiring of the situation, the people agreed to confront the Klan. They marched to a crowd of Klansmen who were armed with guns and bricks. The Klansmen were so surprised that nothing happened except shouts. The second night a smilar march was more stormy, and in the third, one of the leaders, Andrew Young, was knocked down. No one retaliated. The cycle of violence was ended, according to Young.

When I was in Saigon in 1967 I had the chance, unusual for an American, to talk frankly with a group of militant Buddhist students. The events of the revolt of 1966 were still fresh in their minds. In the spring of 1966 the Buddhists posed the strongest challenge to the junta of Colonel Ky that had been made, by a combination of civil disobedience and winning over part of the Vietnamese armed forces. The revolt was suppressed with the aid of the U.S. Air Force. The Buddhist students naturally raised the question of self-defense in a revolutionary situation, but in discussion they revealed that fewer Buddhists had been killed where the struggle was clearly nonviolent than where it was mixed with violence. Even when facing the ruthless Ky, the best defense seemed to lie in the tactics and tone of nonviolent action.

The urban revolt of 1966 is important, too, in showing the increased sophistication of the Saigon government. When the Buddhists launched what became a civilian insurrection in 1963, they met a rigid and violent response from dictator Ngo Dinh Diem. The Buddhists marched, conducted sit-downs, fasted, and some burned themselves to death. The aristocratic Diem treated the opposition as a monolith and, egged on by his fanatical brother and sister-in-law, unleashed a violent repression which culminated on the night of August 20–21 with simultaneous raids on pagodas throughout the country. The repression widened the anti-government coalition to the point where even Diem's personal friend, the Catholic rector of Hué University, threw in his lot with the Buddhists. The publicity undermined support for the regime in the United States; the campaign generated far more popular sympathy for the Vietnamese than did the military struggle by the National Liberation Front. Finally the instability, government resignations, and declining U.S. support required that the unyielding Diem be forced out. An army coup took place on November 1–2.[16]

All the limitations of civilian insurrection which I described in Chapter II apply here. The 1963 rising was certainly no revolution. The important thing to see here is the contrast between Diem's behavior in 1963, which led to his overthrow, and Ky's response to a similar challenge in 1966.

The resistance surfaced in Hué in March 1966, pivoting on the figure of the commander of the army in that region, General Thi. When Thi was dismissed on March 10 demonstrations began in Hué and nearby Danang. Ky declared that he would take strong measures against them, but weeks went by before he took action, and even that was minimal. On March 28 he punished seven junior military officers who had participated in the demonstrations. As many as a thousand soldiers had participated in one demonstration in Danang, so we can hardly view Ky's action as repressive. Throughout the campaign Ky tried to keep violence at a minimum, to avoid martyrs. An exception was in the invasion and occupation of Danang in May (until this time Danang was under the control of the dissidents). Even there, however, Ky's troops avoided direct confrontation with the Buddhists as much as possible, directing most of their violence against dissident soldiers.

Not until Danang was completely under government control and the resistance in Hué was weakening did the government risk shooting at rioters in Saigon. Until then the troops had relied on tear gas, which is unpleasant but does not leave bodies in the streets as martyrs.

Other factors were also different in 1966 from 1963: Ky worked hard to divide the Buddhist camp and succeeded; the sympathy of military officers in Hué and anang led to a struggle for physical control of cities that played into the hands of Ky and the U.S.; much more violence was used by the people than in 1963, providing Ky with opportunities for strong mopping-up operations.[17]

Ky seemed to have learned from the 1963 experience that massive violence against a nonviolent movement can recoil against the government. American writer Richard Gregg once compared this process to jiujitsu: the physical power of the opponent is used against him, and the bigger he is, the harder he falls.

TRANSNATIONAL NONCOOPERATION

The forces of privilege are organizing themselves more and more across national lines. The Common Market is expanding, NATO is reportedly developing plans for suppression of revolts within member nations, and multi-national corporations are growing stronger. These trends provide increasing opportunities for noncooperation across national lines, although the organization and political understanding hardly exist to take advantage of these opportunities.

We are not entirely without examples of transnational acts of noncooperation. In 1920 English, French, and Irish longshoremen refused to load arms onto ships destined for Poland and other states intervening against Soviet Russia. The British miners and transport workers joined together to fight the interventionist policy of their government. This work of solidarity helped to force withdrawal of British troops from Russia.[18]

A hopeful recent sign is the aid that the California farm workers received in the boycott against table grapes. *El Malcriado,* the newspaper of the strikers, reported on February 15, 1969, that British dock workers refused to unload more than 70,000 pounds of table grapes. The Finnish, Swedish, and Norwegian transport workers' unions also refused to unload the grapes. The Swedish Consumer Cooperative boycotted the grapes as well.

American longshoremen refused in 1971 to load military equipment bound for Pakistan because of that government's ruthless suppression of the people of East Pakistan. The Philadelphia local of the union went so far as to refuse to load even civilian materials for the U.S.-supported dictatorship of Yaya Khan.

In the stage of political and economic noncooperation the movement challenges the government to meet concrete demands for change. Through mass participation in tax-refusal, rent-refusal, strikes, boycotts, civil disobedience, and so on, the movement enforces its demands. Tactics are chosen for their relevance to the demand, for widespread application, and for their ability to be sustained over a period of time. By saying "no" when the regime depends on our saying "yes," we unlearn the habits of submission that have made possible the injustice of the status quo. By refusing in a collective and organized way, we learn from experience and we grow to be sociable inhabitants of the new society. By developing the organization of our movement, we find ways of carrying out social functions that supplant the institutions of the old order.

Although the powerful, wrenching process which destroys the ability of the rulers to rule is started in this stage, the new life will not be firmly rooted until the fifth stage. In the next chapter we will explore the development of parallel institutions.

VII
INTERVENTION
AND PARALLEL
INSTITUTIONS

As the government and corporations lash out against the mounting problems caused by ecological crisis, Third World liberation movements, declining legitimacy, and the growing people's movement, they will discredit themselves still further. Our struggle cannot end with mass noncooperation; we need a revolution. The warfare states which hold small nations down and prepare ecological disaster must be radically changed, not only shaken up. The giant enterprises which alienate people from their work and accumulate more power and wealth to themselves must be decentralized and made sociable. The institutions which educate us in the false values of materialism and nationalism must be supplanted.

After working through the overlapping stages of cultural preparation, of organization-building, of propaganda of the deed, and of noncooperation, the people have the chance to root new institutions and values firmly in the soil of the new society. The institutions will have grown from the seeds of the organizing stage: the teams, counter-institutions, and radical caucuses. Now, in the wrenching process of all-out struggle, the institutions can demonstrate their vigor.

I write this chapter as a working paper only; it will obviously be substantially revised as the movement broadens and discussions of strategy become popular. Planning for the future, as sociologist Alvin Toffler says, should be an exercise in "anticipatory democracy." I am fully aware of the dangers of blueprinting; our planning must be open to constant revision. This chapter may, however, stimulate thinking about what we mean by drastic change in power relations. I believe we need a populist way of accomplishing the transfer of power, a way of change that does not mortgage the revolution to the top-down, state-centered society which has resulted from past revolutions. I am uneasy when I hear "All Power to the People" chanted by a prospective bureaucrat in an all-powerful state.

COUNTER-INSTITUTIONS, RADICAL CAUCUSES, AND TEAMS

Some of the counter-institutions are already planted in the organization-building stage: free universities, underground churches, free presses, community medical centers, freedom schools. Others emerge during propaganda of the deed: worker-owned enterprises, neighborhood-controlled police forces, poverty lawyers' cooperatives.

The pressures of the noncooperation campaigns provide opportunities for growth in numbers and strength. A school boycott generates new freedom schools, boycotts of chain stores encourage the growth of cooperatives, strikes of hospital employees stimulate community medical centers.

The counter-institutions need to grow in unity throughout the. struggle, to avoid being played off against each other. They also need to experiment with structures to discover how each institution can best express participatory democracy. The various stages of movement-building are opportunities for "many flowers to bloom" in organizational form. There is no reason why a freedom school should make decisions in the same way as an underground church;

the emphasis is on innovation and experimentation with structures by the participants themselves.

As these institutions grow they become part of the unfolding new society. The people transfer allegiance from the discredited institutions of the past to these new institutions.

The radical caucuses will also have grown in strength and members in this period. These radical organizations will show through analysis and action why revolution is needed. Their respective constituencies may be persuaded and, by the time the fifth stage is reached, some of the occupational associations and unions will in fact be revolutionary.

In the wake of widespread noncooperation, these radical caucuses can practice intervention at the points of their own special competence. By intervention I mean that people place their bodies where the business of the old order takes place, so as to disrupt it. Sit-ins and occupations are well-known forms of intervention.

Radical political scientists can occupy and begin to dismantle the State Department; radical workers can occupy factories and set up workers' councils to reorganize and operate them; social workers can occupy the offices of finance companies that fleece the poor, and so on.

Some interventions in this final stage of the strategy can be carried out by matching the counter-institutions to the institutions: aided by the appropriate radical caucuses, the underground church can occupy the cathedral, the free press can occupy the capitalist press, and so on. The occupation might sometimes be a temporary measure leading to the orderly dismantling of the institution itself: an inter-tribal revolutionary league of native Americans would probably want to dissolve the U.S. Bureau of Indian Affairs. In other cases the occupying group would immediately start to work in the new way they had prepared to act "come the revolution."

These transfers of power to revolutionary organizations will gain their legitimacy from mass acceptance and participation. If the people accept them, they are legitimate. Neither the caucuses nor the counter-institutions have violent means of coercing the people; they can only win the people through service.

The teams, or Groups for Living Revolution, will have been growing phenomenally in number. The ease of organizing them, the cultural background which facilitates teamwork, and the tendency already noted for revolutionary committees to spring up during an insurrection combine to make teams the basic building blocks of revolution.

The Groups for Living Revolution will grow in experience with direct action, for many of the actions in the propaganda of the deed stage are organized by the teams. Further, the teams should play a major role in the mass civil disobedience of the noncooperation stage, since their structure helps them to resist the inevitable repression. That kind of "battlefield" experience will lead to an ability to make democratic decisions quickly which will be essential as the pace of change accelerates.

While many people will spontaneously form teams in the course of this final phase, there could be a conscious effort to reproduce the Groups for Living Revolution as rapidly as possible. Reproduction of the Groups would increase the change of passing along valuable knowledge and experience to the many persons who join the revolutionary movement late. Group-dynamics theory, sensitivity training, and direct-action training should be applied with an eye toward developing a capacity for rapid reproduction during a crunch. The cell structure lends itself to rapid growth.

The Groups, because of their training and solidarity, could take on many of the more dangerous tasks of this final stage. They could play the lightning-rod role regarding reactionary groups, confronting the Minutemen and others with discipline and courage. They would continue to participate in mass civil disobedience. They could help the radical caucuses occupy difficult sites, and could themselves occupy government offices of a repressive nature like the FBI and the military. It will be more difficult for the government to administer repression if its own centers are plagued by defiant teams of revolutionaries.

Dismantling military institutions and providing life-affirming work for their personnel will involve careful planning by radical veterans and other movement groups. Re-education will no doubt be helpful for many officers accustomed to authoritarian styles and violent purposes. The quantity of land and other resources owned by the military should be transferred to civilian activities; this represents a huge increment of wealth available for redistribution.

An important factor in reducing the resistance of the rank-and-file soldiers to revolution will be a program which guarantees work and retraining in the new society. Civilian life in the new society will be much more attractive than military life in the old order, and this should be stressed by the movement.

COORDINATION OF THE MOVEMENT

The reader can see that this proposal has a much different basis from the usual thinking about revolution. I am not proposing that a mass party, governed by a central committee, confront the rulers in a final tussle for control of the apparatus of the state. Even less am I suggesting that a small elite of professional revolutionaries stage a coup d'état. My concept is that the old order be attacked and changed on *many* levels by *many* groups, that is, that the people themselves take control of the institutions which shape their lives.

This runs counter to those strategies which want to protect the state apparatus, even while they throw out the class which steers it. The state apparatus is protected so the revolutionaries can use it for their own ends. I will say more later about the role of the state in the continuing revolution, but already at this point it is clear that I have been describing an intrinsically populist revolution. One cannot encourage people to discover their own nonviolent power without hoping that they will keep that power for themselves rather than hand it back to the new class of bureaucrats which runs the state.

Coordination, however, is necessary. The movement must become united, and essential services must be provided. Communication must be maintained and judgments made about the best use of resources. Coordinated actions are likely to be more powerful, especially where noncooperation still plays a role.

The need for coordination, in fact, will have shown itself long before stage five. Already in the organization-building stage there might be festivals of life, a newspaper, and travelers to facilitate loose coordination. In the propaganda of the deed stage it may be possible for coordinating councils to grow out of the festivals. Receiving their mandate from the assembly of people at the festival, the councils could be made up of representatives of the counter-institutions, radical caucuses, and teams. In this way we would increase the chance that the council would be a service to the Groups rather than the center of initiative.

Coordinating bodies have a tendency to accumulate authority to themselves, and this is not wholly bad. As we come into the non-cooperation stage, a high degree of unity is in fact required; strikes are easily broken when they are not backed by unity. The councils remain, however, creatures of the counter-institutions, teams, and radical caucuses which compose them, and can build in the usual precautions of rotation of staff, etc., to reduce the tendency toward oligarchy. In the advanced stages of struggle, coordinating councils will be needed on local, regional, national, and transnational levels.

The councils are the bodies which form, in the last stage, the parallel governments. The people pay their taxes to the councils instead of to the governments of the old order. The councils organize essential services such as traffic regulation, garbage collection, and the like. The national council works with the other councils to dismantle the national government by distributing its legitimate functions to local, regional, and transnational levels. The councils can also work with the workers' caucuses, cooperatives, and teams to dismantle in an orderly way those corporations which can be decentralized.

The repression is likely to be very mixed in character at this stage. In a popular, nonviolent revolution, there would be the full range of sympathetic response from the soldiers—from inefficiency to mutiny. (In 1905 in St. Petersburg even the *Cossacks* mutinied!) Prior fraternization would also be producing mutiny among the police. On the other hand, some of the police and army might remain loyal to the old regime and reactionary groups would certainly act on their own as they saw the government's ability to maintain order crumbling. There might, therefore, be pockets of extreme brutality while large areas experienced a peaceful transfer of power.

In such a situation the brutality would only discredit the government further, especially since the revolutionaries are nonviolent. When the repression failed to achieve the desired result, the waverers would come over to the revolution and the reactionaries would be isolated. There would be suffering as bombs were planted by the hard-liners, but the suffering would not be in vain when even the most stubborn reactionaries realize that their cause is fading.

What action is taken by the man in the White House at that point would be of little consequence. If he has any sense he will gracefully endorse the movement and suggest that he *has* been the President "of all the people." If he insists on his authority, despite the fact that the life of the people has made him irrelevant, we could conduct schoolchildren on tours to see the man who used to be Chief Executive of the United States.

IS THIS ONLY FANTASY?

The reader may by now think I am entirely in the realm of fantasy, without connections to reality at all. It is certainly true that this has never happened as a stage in a prolonged, nonviolent revolutionary struggle following the kind of preparatory stages already described. But *fragments* of this picture have occurred in history; it may help us descend from the stratosphere if we look at a series of incidents which have actually happened. The incidents occurred in very different contexts and do not prove anything about this strategy; they only show that soviets, occupations, parallel institutions are real phenomena!

In the French civilian insurrection of 1968, sit-ins and occupations were the order of the day. Students occupied universities and the Odéon theater, workers occupied factories, professional dancers took over the Folies Bergères, and gravediggers occupied the Paris cemeteries.

When the students occupied the Sorbonne they organized a general assembly, which included any and all participants of the movement. Each night the assembly chose a fifteen-person team to act as a steering committee for twenty-four hours. (The nightly election was eventually given up because it was impractical.) After a month the students emptied the Sorbonne of its occupiers for forty-eight hours to clean it thoroughly.

Throughout France action committees were formed spontaneously at all levels of the movement—in schools, offices, and in neighborhoods. Two hundred and fifty committees met in Paris on May 19 to coordinate action. By the end of May there were about 450 action committees. A coordinating committee in Paris met daily during most of the struggle. Some of the committees did practical work, such as collecting money for relief and garbage collection; others led street meetings and educational forums.

From May 26 to 31 the city of Nantes became virtually an autonomous soviet. A central strike committee was formed by the unions of workers, peasants, and students. Transport workers set up roadblocks around the town.

> The Prefect, representing the central government in Paris, was left with no staff except a doorman and a small force of police which he dared not use. . . . The first task the Committee assumed was the control of traffic entering and leaving the town. . . . It started issuing gasoline coupons as well as travel permits to truck workers carrying essential supplies for the strikers or for the farms. . . . In the working class area of Les Batignolles . . . the wives of the striking workers decided to take in hand food deliveries to local shops. . . . The district committees made contact with the Central Strike Committee which on May 29 opened six retail outlets in schools. . . . Teams of workers and students went out to help the farmers pick the new potatoes. By cutting out middlemen, the new revolutionary authorities slashed retail prices: a liter of milk fell from 80 centimes to 50; a kilo of potatoes from 70 to 12. . . . The big grocery stores were forced to close. Some small shops were allowed to open, but trade union officials checked the price every morning. The unions helped the poor families of strikers by distributing food chits. . . [1]

On the night of June 1 the roadblocks were taken down because it was feared that Paris would send armed convoys to the town. It was not a consciously nonviolent movement, and no preparations had been made for nonviolent resistance to repression as such.

In the Salvadorian civilian insurrection of 1944 similar incidents were reported. Students volunteered to bake bread when the supply was running low. When the police freed criminals to foment disorder, the people began to enforce the law. For example, when a leather goods store was broken into, the thieves were punished and the goods returned to the owner. Relief funds were collected for the families of the strikers.

Parallel government was developed to a large extent in the American colonies before the military struggle began. Patriots considered the actions of the First Continental Congress to be the supreme law of the land.[2] By means of social pressure the patriots often made it difficult for people in the middle to go on obeying only the King via his colonial governors. The governors, who legally were supposed to be in control of their colonies, found the situation frustrating.

Governor Wright of Georgia complained in the autumn of 1775 that government had entirely been assumed by "Congresses, Councils and Committees." "The poison has Infected the whole Province, and neither law, Government, or Regular Authority have any Weight or are at all attended to."[3]

Illustrations of the inconsistency of repression also abound in the literature of struggle. During the 1953 civilian insurrection in East Germany, thousands of German demonstrators greeted Polish tanks that were sent across the border at Görlitz to disperse them.

> The senior Polish officer stepped out of his tank, faced the Germans —and saluted. "I don't fire on German workers," he said. The Germans returned his salute.
>
> When the Russians saw the Poles were not going to resist the Germans, they ordered the Polish troops back across the border and sent in Russian tanks.[4]

The unreliability of the troops—even the Cossacks—was a constant worry to the czarist government of Russia both in 1905 and in 1917. At one point in 1917 it appears that police agents threw bombs at the troops to stiffen their morale. The soldiers seemed particularly unreliable when facing unarmed demonstrators.[5]

White firemen in Birmingham, Alabama, refused Bull Connor's orders to turn on the water hoses on the black demonstrators during the 1963 campaign. For days the hoses had been used, but the black people were determinedly nonviolent and the firemen finally buckled.[6]

I could give illustrations from other times and places for parallel government, unreliability of the agents of repression, and intervention. These will probably suffice to give the reader some relief from the futuristic and seemingly fanciful description of the fifth stage of the strategy for a living revolution.

THE STATE AND CONTINUING REVOLUTION

The transfer of state power from one group to another is a shorthand way of marking when the revolution has "occurred," but there is a broader view of the sweep of radical change. We can look at revolution as a continuing process, a process which occurs quickly compared to other change but nevertheless is not finished when the people's organizations take authority. Whether the task then becomes "nation-building," as for the newly emerging, or de-nationalizing, as for the United States or the Soviet Union, the transfer of office becomes only a milestone on the road.

On the day the official transfer of power from Britain to India was taking place in Delhi, Gandhi was elsewhere working on the revolution. Gandhi's attitude toward this whole question of the continuing revolution was astonishing. From George Washington to Mao to Ho Chi Minh, the leaders of national struggle have taken the helm of the new state. Gandhi did not take office and even urged the Indian National Congress to stay out of the government, returning instead to the villages to continue the grassroots struggle for economic and social equality.

One might well argue that Gandhi made a tragic mistake. If he had become head of the state and endowed it with his charisma, he might have made enormous strides toward equality. The conditions in India now are the opposite of Gandhi's hopes. Economist Gunnar Myrdal has recently completed a major study of India:

The social and economic revolution [Gandhi] had looked forward to had been, first, postponed and, later, shelved altogether—except for some continued rhetorical exuberances in public speaking. Instead of the economic equalization he had seen coming, inequalities have been widening. The concentration of financial power has increased. Against the clear condemnation in the Constitution and special legislation, which had been adopted under the influence of the legacy from Gandhi, caste as a social institution has shown an obstinate persistency and may even have gained in importance. The rise in the freedom and status of women which he had propagated has, for the most part, remained a rather empty prescription—except in the top upper classes. The land and tenancy reforms have been little more than a sham. There has been no fundamental reform of education, which still serves to preserve and mark the gulf between those who work with their hands and those who, having acquired the badge of education, do not have to do so. The effort to lift up and move rural life—agricultural extension, credit, and other cooperatives, community development, *panchayat raj*, and so on—have, contrary to proclaimed objectives, mainly favored the better-off.

And so the masses of people in the villages, where now, as in Gandhi's time, more than 80 percent of the people live, have mostly remained in relative stagnation.[7]

Gandhi's way of continuing the revolution was rejected by Nehru and most other leaders of the Congress in favor of a liberal democratic state which would build nationalized industries and administer a mixed economy. Nehru's way (sometimes mistakenly ascribed to Gandhi) has been a failure. Compared with it, Mao's way has been a stunning success.

Unfortunately, it is difficult to be very certain about the actual conditions in China today, since so few observers on the scene are as willing as Gunnar Myrdal was in India to be critical. One cannot deny, however, that even with a burgeoning population the Chinese government has been able to provide for the material well-being of the masses of people. Unlike the corrupt Chiang Kai-shek regime or the contemporary Indian government, Mao's government has refused to tolerate starvation; it has provided schools, medical care, and basic financial security to the millions. It has suppressed exploitation by capitalists and developed an impressive spirit of cooperation among the people.

Mao's way has, of course, not been a total success. Not only has a price in human suffering been paid for these achievements, but also the state apparatus itself has developed interests that are in conflict with the people's interests. Mao presumably catalyzed the cultural revolution because he saw so clearly the state's trend away from serving the people. He stimulated that vast upsurge of people's action, for the most part nonviolent, so the state might be purged of its alienation from the people.

Mao admitted this problem of tension between the people and the state long before the start of the cultural revolution:

> Our People's Government is one that genuinely represents the people's interest, it is a government that serves the people. Nevertheless, there are still certain contradictions between the government and the people. These include contradictions among the interests of the state, the interests of the collective, and the interests of the individual; between democracy and centralism; between the leadership and the led; and the contradiction arising from the bureaucratic style of work of certain government workers in their relations with the masses. All these are also contradictions among people. Generally speaking, the people's basic identity of interests underlies the contradictions among the people.[8]

We now see one means by which a growing gulf is to be handled —the cultural revolution blessed by the charismatic father. (One is reminded of Thomas Jefferson's hope that there might be a revolution in the United States from time to time!) The problem is that the father will not be around forever. When he dies, what defense will the people have against the state? In theory, very little. Mao tells us that the members of the Communist Party are subordinate to the Central Committee. Within society at large, people are to distinguish right from wrong by criteria that include whether one's statements help to strengthen the leadership of the Communist Party. The Party, of course, runs the state. Further, Mao says that political power grows out of the barrel of a gun; the government has a monopoly on violence.[9]

In short, the people are left without the power to defend their interests where those interests conflict with the interests of the party leadership. To oversimplify: Mao's way is better than Nehru's way, but it still leaves a populist revolutionary uneasy. Gandhi would probably prefer present-day China to present-day India, but the stubborn Mahatma would nevertheless insist there is a third way.

Whether there is in fact a third way in a given historical context is nearly impossible to say; the plans of human beings are terribly at the mercy of huge forces inside and outside of their societies. A major ingredient of Gandhi's expectation for post-independence India—himself as the bearer of his charisma—was dissolved by an assassin's bullet.

If we think of *models* of social change, however, we can usefully think of these three approaches to the state as alternative orientations. For Nehru the state leads social change, but is a weak leader. For Mao the state leads strongly. For Gandhi the leadership lies elsewhere.

Gandhi said that "Economic equality is the master key to nonviolent independence. . . . A nonviolent system of government is clearly an impossibility so long as the wide gulf between the rich and the hungry millions persist."[10] Equality was to be achieved by the most intense participation of the people themselves, through the continuation of a movement for struggle and development. The continuing revolution would be marked by the same means as the independence struggle: direct action and the constructive program.

Gandhi was too optimistic about the chance of the rich voluntarily giving up their wealth for the sake of a just Mother India. But he had a check against his own optimism: if the rich did not join willingly in the task of building a just society, the poor would take direct action. If landowners did not accept their responsibility as trustees of land which is really owned by God for all his children, the landowners would be the target of powerful nonviolent campaigns. Gandhi had already organized agricultural laborers and industrial workers in noncooperation campaigns, so he knew it could be done. With his willingness to experiment with new forms, he might also have adopted the tactic, common in Latin America, of occupation of estates.

Imagine a situation, then, in which a mass movement enforces equality in various sectors of society through direct action and a constructive program while the state (now in friendly hands rather than belonging to an empire thousands of miles away) ratifies the changes through legislation and coordination. The apparatus of the state, because it has inherent in it some interests antagonistic to the people, is relegated to a minor role in social change. The initiative and dynamic are retained by the people at the grassroots. Because the state is in friendly hands, it will not help the landlords by sending police to repress the people. On the other hand, the state will insist that all struggle be conducted nonviolently and will step in to check any violence which gets out of hand.

The imagination boggles. It seems so chaotic, all these people conflicting with each other with minimal recourse to law courts and legislation. Does not a developing country need *order* to be able to get things done? Yes, but Nehru's way has hardly produced order and Mao had to initiate a nationwide convulsion less than twenty years after taking power. What a developing nation needs more than the order dreamed of by planners is the *participation* dreamed of by democrats. When people struggle for land they are more likely to develop it and keep it; they have invested themselves in it in the very process of struggle. This contrasts both with the state parceling out the land and the gifts of conscientious landlords touched by Vinoba Bhave's appeal in India. When workers struggle nonviolently for control of a factory, they already have the organization and solidarity to help them operate it. Since a part of the nonviolent ethos is that the combatants look for a solution which includes them all, the landlords and factory owners might find themselves working side by side with the men, sharing knowledge and skills.

But conflict remains conflict, and the picture of contending parties using nonviolent methods against each other may seem incongruous. Still, one must admit that a good deal is learned in the course of struggle, including how to fight with the weapons of the opposition. At one point in the Indian salt *satyagraha* of 1930, the government grew so despairing of its ability to contain the Indians by violence that it decided to try a nonviolent tactic.

> A few days after the martyrdom of Ganu, a huge procession of Satya-grahis [campaigners for truth] was stopped by armed police on one of Bombay's main streets. About 30,000 men, women, and children sat down wherever they were on the street. Facing them sat the police. Hours passed but neither party would give in. Soon it was night and it began to rain. The onlooking citizens organized them-selves into volunteer units to supply the Satyagrahis with food, water, and blankets. The Satyagrahis, instead of keeping the supplies for themselves, passed them on to the obstructing policemen as a token of their goodwill. Finally, the police gave in and the procession cul-minated in a triumphant midnight march.[11]

Confronted by a nonviolent tactic of the police, the Gandhians *escalated* their degree of nonviolence by a positive expression of goodwill!

What could be more in contrast with war, where each side esca-lates its destruction in a vicious cycle of death? Here is a form of direct action which provides a beneficent cycle of life. When the people have learned fully the method and spirit of nonviolent strug-gle in their revolutionary work, they hardly need the state to con-tinue their revolution for them.

NEW POLITICS

The implications are far-reaching, so much so that to explore them in depth would require more than a strategy book. One obvi-ous implication of the widespread practice of nonviolent action is that it makes possible an advance on representative democracy.

I am not one of those radicals who are contemptuous of repre-sentative democracy. I consider free elections, universal suffrage, and freedom of political association to be tremendous advances, dearly bought by workers, black people, women, and other op-pressed groups.

Representative democracy is, however, failing in a number of large nations, in some cases (such as the U.S.) failing spectacularly. There are many reasons for this, but three which are immediately relevant here are:

- Too much is expected of it.
- It fails to energize the people.
- Its units are too large in proportion to expectations and involvement.

Americans have been taught since childhood that our salvation lies in parliamentary or other representative institutions. We learn that the very word "politics" is tied up with the action of the state. Even the corporations urge us to gain redress for our grievances from the Congress (perhaps because they know we will not get help there which threatens corporate interests).

Obviously the Marxist critique is extremely relevant here, but it is not complete. The representative assemblies are too weak to handle the size of the problems which are presented to them. In their nature they are so preoccupied with power games far removed from the needs of the people that "constituents" become "people to be manipulated to gain my re-election." I believe that we need representative bodies to make decisions, since many matters are more conveniently dealt with there than by plebiscites. But they should be places for making the lesser, not the greater, decisions. They certainly should not be considered the places for deciding such survival questions as whether to engage in arms races, whether to develop the capacity to destroy whole populations, and so on.

Parliaments are less and less successful in involving the people in debate. Perhaps the citizens are getting wise, are realizing that the parliaments are not what they pretend to be. Of course this is partly because of the growing cynicism of the parties. In Britain in 1960 and in the United States in 1968 the Labour and Democratic parties made it crystal-clear that the will of their memberships was not to be respected. Hugh Gaitskell in Britain and the Johnson-

Humphrey-Daley axis in the United States ran roughshod over the protesters who had gained a majority in their parties.

In relation to their weakness as agencies of social change and their lack of success in involving the people in important debates, the parliaments are often presiding over too many people. It may be that a parliament which considered a very few issues of interest to all could legitimately represent huge numbers of people, even all of humankind. In the next chapter this will be examined. At any rate, it is likely that a drastic decentralization would give new life to representative democracy. As in Scandinavia, the high visibility of and easy access to the representatives give a more solid ground for their existence.

In the United States (among other countries) representative democracy is deeply embedded in mass politics; the individual is a mere consumer of rhetoric delivered one-way through the media. Actual face-to-face discussion in public decreases in mass society while the media increase in importance. Obviously these trends encourage manipulation by elites and give little chance for the condition assumed by the Founding Fathers: communities in which people who know each other debate major issues.

The new society may need forms of political decision-making which provide a clean break with the current situation. The council model is worth considering. The basic unit of political life might be a group of twenty to forty people. This unit would meet frequently to consider issues and instruct its representative (who might be rotated) how to act on the second level of councils.

The second level, composed of representatives of a number of basic units, would consider the situation and instruct *its* representatives to the third level, and so on until the whole population is included. Five tiers of councils would be enough, using a multiplier of thirty for each level, to include a population of 24 million, which is actually more than would be desirable in "national" political units.

The enormous advantage of the council model is that it is rooted in face-to-face discussion of issues by ongoing communities of people. Even though there are disadvantages to this model, the chance to break with the mass politics associated with our electoral institutions is worth study and experimentation.

But even with decentralization and the possibility of the council system, the first point still holds: we are mistaken to equate all political action with activities focused on the state. The value of self-reliance is pursued when we enliven the people's own capacity for waging conflicts and finding solutions for the issues which matter most.

Is this anarchy? I think not, for I continue to see a role for the state in making middle-level decisions and for maintaining the rules in social conflicts. Conflict researcher Arthur Waskow has worked on this problem in terms of police power, and he argues very strongly for a concept of the police which limits intervention to the situations where conflicts have become violent. The police restrain the combatants until they agree to return to nonviolent forms of struggle, and then let them go at it.[12] This does not rule out arbitration, mediation, or even the courts, though it does diminish the role of courts considerably. (Judging from the state of American court calendars, this might be a popular step if it could be implemented right now!)

I have been speculating about a more sensitive and populist political system which could be the outcome of a Gandhian approach to the continuing revolution. Gandhi's way failed in India for a number of reasons, one of which was its dependence on his charisma; he was assassinated soon after independence. In this strategy for revolution I have tried to find alternatives to charisma as an organizing force. We may never be able to do without the father (Freud was pessimistic about it), but degrees are not trivial; there is a difference between a boy and a man. I believe that we can learn in the process of organizing our movement, especially through the Groups for Living Revolution, to manage without a Mahatma or a Castro at the head of the procession.

Gandhi's way also failed because his approach did not become the approach of his movement. Like many men ahead of their time, he was able to hold within himself, creatively, forces which seemed like contradictions to the others around him: shrewd politician and saintly mystic, cosmopolitan and rooted to the soil of Mother India, stubborn fighter and patient spinner of cloth. Small wonder that after his death the bulk of his followers chose one side or the other of these seeming contradictions. Nehru, the politician, cosmopolitan, and fighter worked in another world from Vinoba Bhave, the saint, worker in the constructive program who has never been outside of India.

This discussion of China and India is bound to leave the reader uneasy. How relevant is all this discussion to continuing the revolution in a Western, industrialized country? Are we in another variation of the Western radical's love of the exotic figure in a distant struggle, whether Mao, Gandhi, or Che?

While there are certainly vast differences among China, India, and the Western industrial states, in at least one important sense we are similar. In the United States today there are disparities in knowledge nearly as great as in India. The differences in symbol manipulation and conceptual understanding between a sharecropper and a White House staff member are as great, I would guess, as between an Indian peasant and an Indian technocrat. Consider the exploding fund of knowledge, difficult to appreciate even when we remember that most of the scientists who ever lived in the world are living now. How much of a forty-year-old's high school physics is useful to him now? How can even college graduates of thirty years ago cope with the computer age?

The unevenness of development breeds technocratic elites who work hand-in-glove with political leaders (in their own way, now masters of technique—the skillful television appearance, etc.). The disparities in the degree of knowledge make the statist way just as tempting and just as undemocratic in its way as in China or India. We do not need a political system which substitutes knowledge for wealth as the basis of power. Instead, we need a system which insists that the men and women of knowledge produce a range of alternatives which can be chosen among by the people according to their convictions. The people may not always choose the most rational or efficient solution; humans are fortunately more than rational. People can choose solutions which express their values most completely. The solutions can be tried to see if in practice individuals become more human and humankind, more sociable.

In the fourth stage, the alternatives which the people design can provide the basis for demands backed up by noncooperation. Where the alternatives are not simply outposts of reform, but actually form part of the fortress of the status quo itself, the alternatives can wait until the fifth stage, when they are programs implemented after the transfer of power. The very groups which were agitating for years for a particular change will have the chance to implement it. The inevitable conflicts among designs can be coordinated and mediated by the coordinating councils.

The continuing revolution is not, in this strategy, led by the state. Neither Nehru's way of mixed economy guided by a liberal democratic state nor Mao's way of a socialist economy dominated by an all-powerful state is revolutionary enough. The people themselves should lead the continuing revolution through popular movements, using direct action and a constructive program to gain equality. The state is not abolished, but is restricted to a few essential functions: it coordinates and ratifies change rather than initiates it. In this way "All Power to the People" can become more than a slogan.

The basic economic and political life of a society is heavily conditioned by the international scene. The most obvious form of influence is military intervention: the United States in the Dominican Republic, the Soviet Union in Czechoslovakia. But these interventions are the tip of the iceberg. Building steel plants, ravaging the countryside with strip-mining, ignoring the needs of the poor, expanding the army—these are all spurred by the larger world situation.

It is too simple to lay all this at the door of capitalism. The history of Soviet-Chinese relations is ample proof that eliminating the corporations does not eliminate international power struggles. In a variety of countries industrialization is pushed at a breakneck and inhuman pace to build power for the nation in the international arena. Callous disregard for natural resources can spring from higher priority to national might. Uplift for the poor waits while money is put into "security" via arms and space races. The swollen military establishment becomes able to veto key decisions and even to carry out coups d'état.

Pressures from the international system operate on the newly independent nations as well as on the old ones, on the noncapitalist as well as on the capitalist. The pressures prevent the creation of a humane, democratic, and egalitarian society in *one* country. The revolution must cross national borders—it must be *trans*national.

VIII
THE WORLD
IN REVOLUTION

The growth of revolutionary ferment in the Third World is a powerful force for justice. Not only do societies free themselves from outside domination, but they also help to undermine the world system of inequality. The Vietnamese struggle helped the American people as well as the Vietnamese, for it taught us the real nature of our economic and political order.

In the context of the Vietnam War a former commander of the U.S. Marine Corps admitted: "America has become a militaristic and aggressive nation."[1] General David M. Shoup has also pointed out the close ties between the generals and the corporations which another soldier, Dwight D. Eisenhower, called the "military-industrial complex."

The defense industries are, however, only a part of the driving force behind American expansionism. American soldiers are found in 135 countries because American corporations are heavily dependent on foreign markets and raw materials. Sales abroad are increasing more than they are at home for a number of large corporations. Foreign investments are more profitable than domestic, in general. Since U.S. sources of raw materials are beginning to run out, corporations are more anxious than ever to ensure a continuing supply from abroad.[2]

If a nation in the Third World has a socialist revolution, it is largely closed to penetration by corporations. When a people can determine their own economic life, they are not eager to see massive profits flowing out of their country to New York or London.

When we realize this we can understand the real meaning of the "free world." The dictatorships in South Korea, Taiwan, Greece, Spain, Portugal, Guatemala, Brazil, and South Vietnam claim their membership in the free world because their countries are free to the corporations. "Free" means "capitalist" and has nothing whatever to do with freedom.

The liberation movements are resisting the crusade to make the world safe for the dollar by waging struggle in their own nations. They are fighting one front of a many-front war; we, from the heart of the American Empire, are waging another. The fact that we are engaged in what is at bottom the same struggle raises the natural question: How can the different aspects help each other?

I believe that more change will come faster by using the general approach described in this book adapted to local circumstances. Although the strategy here aims to continue the American revolution, it is based on general principles which I believe are sound. Where movements of national liberation develop nonviolent strategies, they will help us all move more quickly toward a just world community.

Arguments for and against the use of this general strategy in the Third World have no doubt occurred to the reader as the stages were described. I would like to stress some reasons why nonviolent revolution may make sense for the liberation movements.

In the first place, nonviolent struggle is more effective than violence in splitting the opposition, other things being equal. I sat one night in Saigon with a group which included both a leader in the Buddhist struggle movement and an adherent of the National Liberation Front. The NLF advocate was arguing very strongly for the effectiveness of guerrilla war as a means of combating the Americans. After a time, the Buddhist said quietly, "Think for a minute about all the Vietnamese who have lost their lives in struggling the violent way."

In the pause I wondered how many hundreds of thousands it has been. The Buddhist asked, "If those people had died in the course of nonviolent struggle, would half a million American soldiers be here now?"

No one replied. Everyone at the table knew that the Pentagon could never fool the United States into maintaining massive repression year after year against a nonviolent struggle. The division of the U.S. that emerged in 1968 would have come years earlier if there had not been the propaganda about "Communist atrocities." Time after time Congressmen who were against the war were maneuvered into voting money for it by the accusation that they were "failing to support our boys who are dying over there." The public justification for bombing the North was protection of American lives. Richard Nixon used the argument, with others, to justify the invasion of Cambodia.[3]

We radicals want to split the country when it is engaged in evildoing; we want to build a powerful movement against the repressive violence of the American Empire. The violence of the liberation army, however, does not help us do it.

One might think that the increasing toll of American casualties provides a powerful argument against a war; of itself, however, the casualty list does not mean much if the war is defined as legitimate. There was little American opposition to the Second World War, which involved many more casualties than the Vietnam War. For a variety of reasons, the Vietnam War has lost its legitimacy, and the consciousness of casualties correspondingly has grown. Even this tragic suffering of the soldiers can be taken, irrationally, as a reason to support the war. I have been working against the war since 1963 and have heard people argue that the U.S. cannot turn away from a cause for which so many good men have sacrificed themselves. People hesitate to admit that their sons, husbands, or friends have died in vain.

I mentioned earlier the success of the American colonists in splitting the British Establishment during their nonviolent campaigning prior to 1776. The military outbreak which began at Lexington and Concord reversed that splitting process.

One effect of the splitting is to reduce the amount of violence the oppressor uses. If his power base gets shaky (his political support, reliability of troops, and so on), he has to be restrained in his violence against a nonviolent movement. The government sometimes plants spies in the movement to try to persuade it to give up nonviolence; if the government's ploy works and the movement turns to violence, the government's waverers will rally and support massive repression.

Every humane revolutionary wants to limit the amount of repressive violence. When facing the United States, he can learn something from the black people's experience. During the decade 1955–65 nonviolence was the slogan of the movement. As many as a million people participated in demonstrations, boycotts, sit-ins, civil disobedience. The white Establishment began to come apart under the pressure and was forced, reluctantly, to agree to black suffrage in the South and a series of other reforms. The reforms were almost entirely in the South, since the goals and mass participation were Southern. The wave of protest brought America out of the deep-freeze of the Joseph McCarthy period and stimulated the movements of the late sixties—anti-war, anti-poverty, and so on. The opinion polls showed a shift in white opinions toward a position of equality; even if white people remained as prejudiced as before, the changed atmosphere made them more reluctant to admit it.

The 1955–65 decade was hardly a revolution, and no one would claim that it was. But it helped immensely to change the atmosphere in favor of social change, to confuse and split the Establishment, to mobilize allies and spur other movements, and to gain some concrete reforms. The cost in lives was, I estimate, less than one hundred.

Can anyone seriously argue that a guerrilla movement could gain that much with so few casualties?

Since 1965 the country has largely been in a state of reaction. The series of riots changed the atmosphere and reversed the process of opinion change among white people. During the Detroit riot a bill for rat control in the slums gave rise to laughter on the floor of Congress—a drastic change from the seriousness with which the nonviolent dislocation of Birmingham and Selma was taken.

Police departments are arming themselves with military weapons, white people are arming themselves, "law and order" is a major campaign issue, both major parties have breathed a sigh of relief that the momentum of the movement is broken. A few changes have been made in cities where riots took place (in Chicago, for example, water sprinklers are put on ghetto fire hydrants in the summer). Industry continues to upgrade middle class blacks while ignoring the poor, deepening the class division among blacks.

Some enlightened whites have continued to read the violence of the blacks in the way they read the sit-ins—an expression of outrage against the racism and economic injustice of America. But these enlightened whites have much harder sledding since 1965; even the celebrated liberal Daniel Moynihan suggested in 1970 that the problems of blacks should have a period of "benign neglect."

When the Black Panthers began to insist on their right to self-defense by violence, a right with some constitutional basis, they became the target of nationwide repression. The Panthers have not been practicing violence as a means of social *change*, but only as a means of defending themselves against the occupation armies called police. Even this defensive position, however, has unleashed a series of killings without benefit of judge and jury, not to mention the shocking judicial discrimination.

Fortunately, the 1955–65 decade of struggle and the revelations about American militarism have prepared a substantial body of liberals and radicals to defend the Panthers; if this were 1955 there would hardly be a murmur from white people as Panthers were gunned down. Nevertheless, the price paid by a small group of people who have yet to organize mass confrontations with white power has been very high; and the general public considers them nothing more than criminals.

Of course the picture is more complicated than this, but the main features are clear. In dealing with the American Establishment from within the United States, even a minimally violent movement unleashes a racist and brutal response. The riots since 1965, largely consisting of property destruction, have brought more deaths to black people than the mass civil disobedience of fifteen years. The measures of self-defense by the Panthers have brought death, exile, or long prison sentences to many of their leaders.

Some blacks facing the nightmare of Mississippi in the early sixties, however, found a way of working that reduced the violence even of the nightriders, the Ku Klux Klan, the brutal sheriffs. Robert Parris Moses, the leading Mississippi SNCC organizer in those days, put it very simply to a group of prospective co-workers: "The only reason we've survived is because we don't have guns in our Freedom Houses, and everyone knows it."

The movement cannot doubt the capacity of the United States to be genocidal in Brazil any more than we doubted the brutality of the nightriders of Mississippi. A revolutionist in Brazil or Gautemala or the Philippines is bound to ask himself: "Do I want my country to become another Vietnam? Do I want my people to be subjected to campaigns of annihilation, my land poisoned, my families so broken apart that a whole generation of scarred persons is bred?"

Clearly the cost of violent revolution can be terrifyingly high. The creative revolutionist will at least *try* to devise a nonviolent strategy for his people.

A second advantage of nonviolent struggle for the liberation movements is that it weighs in decisively on the side of life in a world where the sheer continuation of the human species is a question mark. The ecological challenges are accumulating so rapidly that ecologist Barry Commoner estimates that we have a thirty-year period to change fundamentally our traditional ways of doing things.

The very margin of life is becoming thinner, more precarious. Mass organized violence is one of those institutions that people will have to give up if we are to have grandchildren at all.

Revolutionists usually justify the suffering of struggle in terms of the future—our children, or at least *their* children, will benefit from our sacrifice. It is a statement of faith, and a noble one. The faith is shaken, however, by the contradictions of technology and mass society. Human evolution has brought us to the kind of divide which the dinosaurs might have once faced: either we change our ways drastically and live, or fail to change and die. If we want to assure a better future for our grandchildren, we must act on the side of life now. Our strategies should reflect this basic commitment to life.

The third advantage of nonviolent struggle is that the movements can avoid dependence on the suppliers of weapons. It is awkward to be dependent on the big military states and/or capitalist manufacturers. These sources are themselves part of the problem rather than of the solution. Granted, guerrillas often proceed in the beginning with simple weapons and they get those from the enemy. But the intention is that the guerrilla army will grow to the point where it can engage in positional warfare. This requires modern heavy weapons, and plenty of them. The suppliers of weapons have different goals from the revolutionists; they seek influence for their larger strategies in the big power rivalries. No revolutionary seeks to become free of the American Empire only to become dependent on the Soviets, but he would be naïve not to remember that big powers have price tags on their "gifts."

A military struggle also makes more likely getting into the military power game with the big states. Vietnam changed from being oppressed by one medium power, France, to being the subject of a tug of war of three super powers.

One slogan is that the people should have power, and the strategy described in this book may make a populist revolution possible. Military struggle has inherent in its organizational requirements a centralizing hierarchy of power; this is less true in guerrilla war then regular war, but it remains true even for the guerrillas. The very process of military revolution shapes the future politics of the new order.[4] Those politics, in all the revolutions I know of, are elitist. The state has a monopoly of power with even the trade unions brought to heel. The initiative comes from the center and the decisions are finally made at the center.

Certainly the argument for a Leninist approach (a powerful state led by a vanguard party) is strong for the Third World. Briefly, the aim is rapid industrial development. For this, great quantities of capital are needed. Part of that can come from nationalization of mines and other resources owned by foreign corporations, but a rocky period can then be expected as the international capitalist institutions retaliate. Most governments do not loan money without strings of one sort or another, and even such loans are not enough.

The result of that equation is getting the capital internally. The fixed assets of the upper class can be used, but most of the liquid assets are likely to be in Swiss banks and other unreachable places. This leaves the bulk of the population, who must work harder and spend less. These forced savings have in most countries come largely from the peasantry. The organizational means is mainly collectivization, usually against the will of the peasants. (In the Soviet Union this led to the terrible repression of millions of peasants.)

Forced collectivization is the Communist equivalent of the enclosure mechanism in industrializing England, or exploitation of small farmers by banks and railroads in nineteenth-century America.

Clearly, mobilizing the population to work very hard, yet not, as individuals, to consume the increased fruits of their labor, requires great state power plus a heroic ideology.

In the previous chapter I described three models of social change in terms of the role of the state. In the liberal democratic society with a mixed economy, the state leads, but weakly. In the centralized socialist society, the state leads very strongly. In Gandhi's view, a third alternative was needed: a society in which the continuing revolution was led by the people's movements, ratified by a friendly but weak state. The means for destroying the remnants of the old feudal and capitalist orders and building new institutions is by the self-reliant power of the people.

But can people's movements which do not use the systematically coercive power of the state sustain a high rate of capital accumulation? (Clearly, the people can, through nonviolent struggle, coerce the landlords to give up their land, but *systematic*, protracted coercion requires bureaucracies, courts, and police.)

Left to their own devices, would the people tax themselves at virtually a punishing rate? I think not, even granting the existence of a heroic ideology and dedicated revolutionary cadres.

Gandhi could imagine a populist path of change because he questioned the primary aim of rapid industrial development. Behind that aim he saw, in addition to the goal of eventual better welfare of the people, the goals of building a respectable "factory civilization" and joining the international power game.

These latter goals have been the sacred cows of the West, and most of Gandhi's westernized colleagues could not accept his rejection of them. Only recently are the military state and factory civilization being questioned by more than a tiny minority of thinkers.

The sweep of military technology, especially with the advent of nuclear weapons, is forcing a re-evaluation of the meaning of "security." The more that governments press for security by arms, the less secure the people become. The people may rightly resist forced-march industrialization when it leads to participation in arms races whose outcome is likely to be disaster. Added to the power competition is the plague of conscription, which often hits the peasantry especially hard and is a force for militarism and against democracy no matter what the guiding ideology.

Gandhi did not oppose the application of technology per se, but his period in England as a young man persuaded him that industrialization there was dehumanizing. He emphatically rejected that as a model for Indian society, as, a couple of generations later, Frantz Fanon was to plead for the new nations to avoid mimicking the patterns of their former imperialist masters.

Gandhi did not, of course, have a scientific concept of ecology any more than Lenin did. (Gandhi opposed birth control methods, for example.) But his intuition put his economic ideas in tune with the integrity of peasant life, with village uplift, and with decentralized technology at the service of the people.

My reading of the ecological perspective suggests that Gandhian economics is remarkably consistent with global environmental imperatives. The factory civilizations which Gandhi rejected must *de*-develop, which probably means decentralized political and economic life and intermediate technology as the norm. That does not mean going back to the European Middle Ages; it is impossible and undesirable to turn back the clock. It means using the knowledge gained in many parts of the world, over many centuries, to develop means of production and distribution which are ecologically sound.

The breakup of large cities into villages and towns seems essential for conservation and recycling of resources. Cities are not viable from an ecological point of view; in towns, less energy and material are needed per capita, and waste, including human waste, is more easily recycled.[5] A vegetarian diet may be imperative, since protein is more efficiently produced on the plant level than higher on the food chain through meat.[6]

Scientists and engineers should develop designs for long-lasting products which can be easily repaired, and finally, recycled. While some complex technology, like kidney machines, will be justifiable, the norm will be simple or small-scale technology. Bicycles, for example, would be the normal private transportation instead of cars, with free and rapid mass transport the normal means of going any distance.

At the same time as ecological sense requires de-development in the industrialized world, the Third World peoples are demanding equality. If equality meant imitation, in this context, it would be like a poor youngster hoping some day to be like a grossly fat, corrupt rich person who is about to die of a heart attack.

What equality means now must take into account the ecology knowledge that was unavailable to Lenin and is hardly realized by his followers today. It is ironic indeed to see Soviet economists anxiously comparing the size of their GNP with that of the United States. Can one justify a police state and forced savings in order to arrive at such a goal?

INTERNAL AND EXTERNAL MILITARY THREATS

A tragic aspect of violent revolution is that it leaves the people defenseless against a coup d'état. The people have been taught to respect the gun and to believe that political power flows from it. Since the liberation army is associated not only with effective use of violence but also with the heroism of the struggle, there is little incentive or ability to combat an army coup d'état. One can create a people's militia to guard against this threat; the militia could launch civil war if a take-over occurs; but a civil war is not going to appeal to people who have just been through a violent struggle and are tired of it, or to people who are concerned with building the economy of the new society.

The people did little to resist the 1967 coup in Greece. This was due partly to the fear of another civil war, for the people apparently did not know of the nonviolent way in which the workers of Germany defeated would-be dictator Wolfgang Kapp. The Greeks were in practical terms helpless against the colonels, left defenseless, I suspect, by the combination of their respect for the gun and their fear of the destructive effect of a civil war. The increasing frequency of coups in the new nations makes this problem critical.[7]

But these internal questions of a centralized state and a liberation army are heavily conditioned by the external environment of the new society. After all, Lenin had other matters to think about besides encouraging a grassroots democracy of soviets; how much decentralization could be allowed when the revolution was threatened by armies from capitalist countries?

Mao also emphasized in 1949 the defense of the revolution as a major reason for postponing the withering away of the state:

> Don't you want to abolish state power? Yes, we do, but not right now: we cannot do it yet. Why? Because imperialism still exists, because domestic reaction still exists, because classes still exist in our country. Our present task is to strengthen the people's state apparatus— mainly the people's army, the people's police, and the people's courts —in order to consolidate national defense and protect the people's interests.[8]

Revolution does not take place in a vacuum, and the threats from the outside may continue long after the internal change is secure. Not only does the China of today face a continuing military threat from the United States, but also from its rival within the Communist world, the Soviet Union.

The rising challenges which create revolutionary ferment in the Western industrial countries intersect with the growing integration of these countries. This integration is led by multi-national corporations, the Common Market, and NATO. These integrating forces are rightly fought by revolutionists, but we must admit the helpful side of their development as well: the integration makes for more simultaneous revolutionary development in the various countries. The *trans*national revolution becomes more likely.

Other forces are at work promoting concurrent revolutionary development. Urbanization, increased travel, the mass media, growing university populations, the emergence of transnational communities such as scientists and artists: these forces breed similar responses to common problems. Advance indications of the trend were the anti-nuclear bomb movements of the early 1960s and the student rebellions of 1968.

The better the prospects for a *trans*national revolution, the less forbidding are the problems of trying to build a humane and egalitarian society in *one* country. The farther along other countries are in their revolutionary process, the less able their governments will be to make war against the liberated society.

From the perspective of someone struggling in the heart of the American Empire, then, I see five major reasons why my sisters and brothers in the Third World might take a new look at the possibilities of what the Puerto Rican Independence Party calls "pacific militancy" as a means of revolution.

First, noncooperation and other methods of pacific militancy are more effective in splitting the opposition, demoralizing the troops, and so on. Insofar as the Third World country is hoping for a strong response within the industrialized country (as the Vietnamese have counted on while fighting the French and the Americans), then it makes sense to use the means which are most helpful in bringing that response.

Second, ecocide is now a dimension of warfare available to the industrialized powers. The growth of technology which has made wholesale eradication of people possible has also provided the means of destroying the environment of whole countries. When we shudder at what has already happened in Vietnam (in 1967 when I flew over the Mekong Delta it already looked like a lunar landscape), we should realize that the American Empire does *not* have its back to the wall in Indochina. Many Establishment people consider U.S. interests there less than crucial. What will happen when a violent revolution strikes at the vital nerve of the Empire? Ecocide . . . genocide . . . with or without nuclear weapons.

Precisely at a time when the margin of life for all of humankind is shrinking, the leaders of a humanist revolution should search tirelessly for a nonviolent strategy.

Third, violence makes more likely an elitist revolutionary organization and a new society afflicted with statism. A strategy based on people-power rather than gun-power, with a means of power transfer which is intrinsically populist, may at least make possible a democratic new society. The Leninist argument that a strong state is needed to impose sufficient discipline to accumulate capital for industrial takeoff is only valid if one accepts a pre-ecological view of the new society and a pre-nuclear view of security.

Fourth, a protracted struggle using the tactics of pacific militancy provides protection against a later coup d'état by reactionary forces. When gun-power is down-played in favor of people-power, the people can gain confidence in their own ability to struggle no matter who has the guns.

Fifth, the next decade or two will be a time of rising ferment in the industrialized countries and parallel development of struggle across national lines. The international web of imperialism has caught the majority of people in the industrialized countries as well as in the Third World; liberation movements will find allies increasing in the industrial centers.

Nonviolent struggle is probably the moral preference of all humanist revolutionists. That is, given alternative strategies for liberation, they would prefer the nonviolent one. However, few revolutionists seem to take the trouble to develop a nonviolent strategy so that they are actually in a position to choose among alternatives. In fact, I know of no liberation movement which has actually developed a coherent strategy for radical change based on pacific militancy and then compared it with armed struggle. When a movement claims "We found no alternative" to armed struggle, it should say how hard it looked.

When armed struggle movements say they tried nonviolence, they usually mean that it was tried in their early, reformist days, or that a few nonviolent tactics were tried without a strategy or without knowledge of the other 190 nonviolent tactics which have been used historically,[9] or that they expected that the government would not respond with violence when it was threatened nonviolently and therefore the methods were given up when repression came.

Certainly the advocates of nonviolent action are partly to blame for this situation. There has not been nearly enough research or hardheaded thinking in strategic terms; frequently the effectiveness of nonviolent action has been overstated, leading to disillusionment and abandonment of the technique.

Despite the inadequacy of many of the nonviolent experiments, and the comparative newness of the technique as a conscious source of power, revolutionists aware of the exploding potential for good and evil in today's situation can scarcely turn their backs on a new possibility. They should at least do the research and experimentation necessary to work up a serious strategy for nonviolent revolution in their situation. Only then will they actually be in a position to choose realistically among genuine options.

DEFENDING THE REVOLUTION

People can defend a revolution for life the way they achieve it. The social invention called nonviolent struggle can be developed to maintain revolutionary institutions. The strikes and civil disobedience which confounded the old oppressors will comfort any would-be oppressors even less.

In fact, it is easier to gain unity for defense of a society than it is to gain unity for revolution. In revolutionary work, organizers are constantly confronted by conservatism. Many people seem to lack the imagination to see that things could be much better, and they keep the bird in hand rather than go after the two in the bush. In defense of a society, that force of conservatism works *for* the resistance.

Another difference is that community feeling can be a barrier to social change but a help to social defense. The natural affection which we Americans feel for our country sometimes prevents us from seeing the enormous blots on it and weakens our desire to make it the home of justice and community. This same affection, however, is an aid to defense. Even people sharply critical of their country will resent the coercion of an interloper.

United resistance to invasion is illustrated by the Czechoslovakian response to Warsaw Pact invasion on August 21, 1968.
There were severe limitations to the resistance, which was handicapped by lack of preparation and training. Nevertheless, the
resistance deserves our attention for its courage and suggestive
improvisation.[10]

In 1938, when Czechoslovakia was about to be sacrificed to Nazi
Germany by the diplomats in Munich, Gandhi made a suggestion.
Despite the fact that you Czechs are heavily armed, he said, you do
not have a chance against the overwhelming might of Germany
when dueling with the Germans' choice of weapons. Why not
choose a different weapon, and struggle with nonviolent means?

No one could doubt the sincerity which lay behind that advice.
Gandhi had fashioned an instrument of struggle that was giving no
end of trouble to another imperial power with overwhelming military strength. But a vision, even when made practicable in one
setting, often remains visionary in another. Gandhi's ideas did not
match the current assumptions about the nature of power and the
possibilities of politics.

Three decades later, in August 1968, the Czechs and Slovaks
daringly made the fullest attempt in history to use nonviolent resistance to aggression.

It was not the first such attempt. The German government used
a policy of massive noncooperation in the Ruhr to oppose French
invasion there in 1923. The Germans refused to mine coal, make
steel, even to serve food or man the trains for the occupation, and
received harsh reprisals from the frustrated French.[11] But the Ruhr
was just one part of Germany, albeit critical for its economy. The
Czechoslovaks found their whole country occupied by 650,000
troups with a demand for a new government more to the liking of
other Warsaw Pact powers. It is not surprising that, as the London
Observer noted, some in military strategy circles watched the
events with professional interest as a test case for the concept of
civilian resistance.

Although the full development of the Czech resistance was
aborted by decision of Communist Party chief Alexander Dubček
and other leaders, the successes and limitations of the heroic action
may provide lessons for future occasions. We will explore the rea-

sons why it was broken off—the resistance did not move into full instensity. It was confined largely to demonstrations of protest, with some important tactics of noncooperation and civil disobedience. It did *not* include sustained economic noncooperation tactics, despite the fact that the clandestine party congress which met August 21-22 issued an ultimatum to the invaders to leave the country or face a general strike. The impressive unity of the one-hour work stoppage the next day tells us something about the possibilities of sustained strikes and other unused nonviolent tactics.

The leadership group in the first hours of the invasion moved to deny legitimacy to the invasion and provide the groundwork for diplomatic showdowns. They did not, however, have a plan for popular resistance, leaving the initial response of the masses largely to improvisation.

The Czechs and Slovaks improvised magnificently. On the first day of the invasion there was a brief standstill in Prague reportedly observed by hundreds of thousands. Airport officials at Ruzyno refused to supply Soviet planes with fuel. At a number of places, crowds sat in the path of oncoming tanks; in one village, citizens formed a human chain across a bridge over the river Upa for nine hours, inducing the Russian tanks eventually to turn tail.

Swastikas were painted on tanks. Leaflets in Russian, German, and Polish were distributed explaining to the invaders that they were in the wrong, and countless discussions were held between bewildered and defensive soldiers and angry Czech youths. Army units were given wrong directions, street signs and even village signs were changed, and there were refusals of cooperation and food. Clandestine radio stations broadcast advice and resistance news to the population.

On the second day of the invasion a reported 20,000 people demonstrated in Wenceslas Square in Prague; on the third day a one-hour work stoppage left the Square eerily still. On the fourth day young students and workers defied the Soviet curfew by a round-the-clock sit-down at the statue of St. Wenceslas. Nine out of ten people on the streets of Prague were wearing Czech flags in their lapels. Whenever the Russians tried to announce something the people raised such a din that the Russians could not be heard.

As one might expect, violence by the Czechs seemed to be greatest in the first day of the invasion. Uncertain, furious, without clear alternative means of resistance, some Czechs improvised with gasoline-soaked rags for tank-burning, sniping from buildings, and stone-throwing. Even though an alternative course to violence was not outlined by the government, there were still only scattered incidents of violent resistance.

Much of the energy of the resistance was spent weakening the will and increasing the confusion of the invading forces.

> This is a picture which will always stay in my mind: a blond Prague girl crawling under the fixed bayonets of a tank crew, standing up and chalking a swastika on the monster's bows. Then she spat, and crawled back again. The soldiers looked on helplessly. In their faces was written bewilderment and shame. They had not expected this sort of thing here.[12]

By the third day Soviet military authorities were putting out leaflets to their own troops with counter-arguments to those of the Czechs. The next day rotation began, with new units coming into the cities to replace Russian forces. The troops, constantly confronted but without the threat of personal injury, melted rapidly.

For the Kremlin as well as for the Czechoslovaks, the stakes were high. To attain its objective of deposing the Dubček regime, the Soviet Union was reportedly willing to convert Slovakia into a Soviet republic and Bohemia and Moravia into autonomous regions under Soviet control. Premier Cernik said, "My life and that of my comrades was in great danger." What Moscow preferred, presumably, was a new government still under the Presidency and legitimacy of Ludvik Svóboda. But it was forced in those first weeks by the resistance to accept a continuation of Dubček and some of his liberal colleagues at the center of the government.

For Czechoslovakia, eight months of an independent road to democratic socialism—with the flowering of culture, political activity, and economic innovation—was at stake. The compromise settlement made in Moscow on August 26 was initially repudiated by the National Assembly of Czechoslovakia; many Czechs could see that their leaders had conceded much to the Soviets. Although the curtailment of liberties would be more softly and inefficiently done by a sympathetic Czech regime than by the kind of government Moscow would prefer, it was still a bitter pill to swallow for the thousands who took to the streets to show their anxiety about the settlement.

With nonviolent struggle as with military struggle, one rarely gains at the bargaining table what one has not already gained in the field. Why not escalate the conflict by declaring sustained strikes in industries the invaders depended on, by continuing the political noncooperation at all levels, by beginning boycotts of the invading countries' goods, and even by organizing a general strike? The economic interdependence of the countries involved would ensure a very high price inflicted on the occupying powers. The additional expense of occupation, including troop rotation, would probably sabotage the Soviet Five Year Plan.

Dubček might have been answering this line of thought when he said, "We must prevent new suffering and further losses as this would not change the situation and would prolong the abnormal conditions in our country." The suffering would be enormous, it is safe to say, for even though nonviolent resistance is less costly than violent resistance, it is nevertheless not without its price. And would it change the situation?

The answer to that depends on an analysis of the whole Eastern European situation. If Kremlin leaders believed, as Stalin had, that any democratic Eastern European government would be anti-Soviet, and if they saw the strategic position of Czechoslovakia as crucial, and if they were determined to stifle dissent inside the Soviet Union, and if Gomulka, Kádár, and Ulbricht were worried about the desire for "socialism with a human face" in their own countries—then gaining independence even within the Warsaw Pact might have been possible only by shaking up the whole Communist political configuration in Europe. Further resistance in that context would indeed be a radical matter, for it goes to the root of the Soviet security system. If the leaders of a nation of 14 million people shrink before that task, it is understandable.

No one can know what would have happened if the Czechs and

Slovaks had gone on to a second week of open national resistance, and a third, and a fourth. The odds against them were no doubt overwhelming; military resistance was futile and even civilian resistance was uncertain. What we do know from this experience is: aggression has additional causes besides capitalism; the masses can unite against invaders even without prior training or preparation; the methods of nonviolent struggle, although unable magically to overcome all odds, can mobilize considerable power.

In the French and Belgian invasion of the Ruhr, where the contending forces were more evenly matched, the outcome was considerably better for nonviolent resistance.

The invaders were forced by the German resistance to accept a rescheduling of reparations payments and to give up hopes of annexing the Ruhr. The Germans also paid a price for this in human and material terms, but nothing like the price of resistance on a similar scale with weapons. The workers of the Ruhr had more experience with striking than the workers of Czechoslovakia, but there was not the training and preparation for civilian defense which our revolutionary society would have.

In fact, the revolutionary process described in this book would give the best possible preparation for civilian defense. The people would gain the organizational and action experience which would make them invincible against a foreign invader. An alliance among the societies which have "trans-armed" to civilian defense would create an even match if a still-unchanged big power invaded a small nation. The small, regional states which will hopefully live in North America could aid each other in case of aggression.

To some readers this will not sound revolutionary enough. Preparing for civilian defense of small societies is suspiciously like the thinking of today's national military men. The military speak of defense and create hobgoblins. (In the United States, for example, there is a widespread superstition that the U.S. is preserved from invasion by its armed forces. No one who reflects for long on the cost of mounting such an invasion and occupying a country of this size and complexity will be fooled. The superstition masks the main function of the military. The U.S. occupies 275 major foreign bases and many more minor ones to be ready to suppress the movements for change, whether they be in the Philippines, Thailand, or the Dominican Republic.

While I admit that thinking in terms of defense only can be misleading and even negative, I think history gives ample illustration of the need for defense of societies against attack from outside. What could be clearer than Czechoslovakia in August 1968? What could be more painfully obvious than the inability of the Guatemalans in 1954 to defend themselves against CIA-sponsored attack?

A frequent objection to civilian defense is that it does not break sharply enough with nationalism. After all, nationalism has mobilized workers to fight workers and Christians to fight Christians. The obsession with national interest has slowed the growth of world community.

I agree that blind nationalism is often our enemy, especially when it is wrapped up in the trappings of the militarists. However, we should also see that people must live in community and one basis for community is in fact the nation. A common language and tradition inspire a natural affection among many. In this strategy for continuing the American Revolution, I argue for decentralization and even dismantling the nation-state as we now know it, but not for the eradication of the adjective "American," with its identification with Adams, Paine, Jefferson, Susan B. Anthony, Frederick Douglass, Lincoln, Debs, King, and the rest. To move forward we need not *deny* our history; black Americans are insisting that to move forward people need to accept their history because it tells them who they are.

Perhaps I will not be convincing on this score until I place these revolutionary societies in the context of transnational institutions.

COUNTER-INSTITUTIONS FOR WORLD COMMUNITY

Nearly everyone sees the need for world community, but there is frequent disagreement on what that phrase should mean. Many decentralists expect that world community means splitting the existing large nation-states into small ones and moving power back to local communities. They see the trend toward larger and larger political units over the past several centuries to be fundamentally anti-democratic and subversive of human values.

Advocates of world government, on the other hand, rejoice in the trend toward larger political units and find the problem in the stalling of the process at the point of today's national rivalries. They consider the arms races and hot wars inevitable without international organization and urge that a world government be created to end the violence.

I find that each side of the debate points to realities which the other ignores. The decentralists rightly complain that giant structures like the U.S. are incompetent to make many decisions they do make, because the decision should fit the community it affects and communities differ among themselves. But as the world government people correctly see, there is a *community* of humankind (community of interests, at any rate) which needs to have decisions which fit that community. What to do with the riches of the seabeds, how to relate to space, how to cope with pollution, how to redistribute wealth to the poor: these are humankind-sized problems which require humankind-sized solutions. We cannot always reduce the scale of decision-making to village level; some problems simply do not reduce.

The decentralists, however, are quite right to attack the tendency toward centralization and bigness which makes the individual a cog in a machine he cannot even comprehend. If an American finds little access to his federal government, what chance can he or she have to make him or herself heard in a world government? Or, to be more realistic (since the average citizen has never had much to say about the government): If large social movements have difficulty gaining change from the government of 200 million people, what chance will it have in getting a hearing in a government of 4 billion people?

An advocate of world government would want to put the question more precisely. What effect can a movement have now in preventing a nuclear war which might occur tomorrow or next week or next year? The lack of a world government means that the greatest decision of all—survival—is in the hands of no one, but will get made in the face-downs and struggles of a nuclear jungle. What could be more undemocratic than that? If the majority of the world's people decide they prefer survival and choose the instrumentality of world government to get it, it would be a step toward self-determination. And if a world parliament, democratically elected, made decisions about that which is now simply the result of cutthroat competition, the general public interest would gain.

The question of enforcement of decisions remains an awkward one, however. A government is, by definition, an agency which monopolizes the legitimate use of violence. Will a world government have more troops than anyone else? If it makes a decision contrary to the interests of a large number of people there may be civil war. Wars are not ended by setting up a world authority and calling the battles "civil conflict."

It seems to me that the strategy for revolution described in this book makes possible a program for world community which meets the most important points on both sides of the debate. By changing the context, the abilities of people, and the nature of the structures, movements might create transnational institutions that promote peace and human dignity. For decentralists who are not simply nostalgic for the good old earthy feudal face-to-face community, and world government people who are not simply projecting a bourgeois affection for order onto the world scene, the strategy may open a few new doors.

But now the working paper becomes still more tentative. This is not an apology, but simply a warning. The sketch of a world community which follows is not a blueprint, but a direction. The details are necessarily speculative, but may help to show new possibilities.

Transnational institutions are most likely in the context of revolutionary change. Today's large nation-states refuse to give up their sovereignty; they provide the major barrier to positive change. The large nations have occupied the space of world politics and must be dismantled even while transnational institutions are growing.

The Pentagon and its equivalents around the world will resist strongly the growth of a world institution which intends to monopolize the legitimate use of violence. Like the right-wingers whose instinct in times of change is to buy a gun, the nations' habitual recourse to military power is itself a hindrance to world community. Civilian defense, which provides a functional alternative for the legitimate defense needs of national communities, is therefore a necessary part of a realistic program for world community.

The massive injustice which exists in the world is another barrier to world institutions. A government cannot rest on the consent of the governed when it presides over such massive inequality as we now have. A world government must grow out of a greater degree of community than now exists, and that community can grow only from a greater degree of economic and social justice. Advocates of world government, whether they like it or not, must join the revolution against the imperialisms of the United States and the Soviet Union.

Programs for world government which propose the creation of a supreme layer of government in today's world are mechanical. Transnational institutions are realistic only in a world changing rapidly toward a condition where the hungry are fed, the empires dismantled, and the generals retired. On the other hand, a powerful movement opposing inequality and militarism will get farther if it has a program of counter-institutions which can supplant the old order. (On the transnational scene we should call it the "old disorder.")

The central concept for democratic world institutions is *people's enforcement*. In the revolutionary process outlined in this book, the people are learning how to struggle for change, and even to coerce the hardhearted, nonviolently. That kind of people's power might be harnessed to the growth of transnational institutions for use in enforcing decisions. Let us imagine that a World Seabed Commission, after months of study, finds that a certain miners' cooperative is extracting minerals in a way which runs against the best long-term interests of humankind. It directs the cooperative to stop the work, but the group, which has become corrupt and has underworld connections, refuses. The Commission then publicizes the issue and the voluntary associations around the world which have a special interest in conservation put pressure on the cooperative. The pressure might mount to a direct action campaign on behalf of the Commission's decision.

The Commission might itself have a weak case or be wrong; the test would be whether the voluntary associations would mobilize for a campaign, and whether, in the course of the struggle, new facts came to light which revealed that the miners were right after all. Compromises would be possible, as well as new solutions to the conflict that no one would have thought of in the beginning.

The Commission is the kind of structure which might meet the demands of both world government and decentralist camps. Commissions would be organized by function—for the seabeds, space, air pollution, world trade, currency, and so on. Each Commission would have a comprehensive view of our planet, would have a staff of experts, would be composed of respected and public-spirited men and women, and could make humankind-sized decisions for humankind-sized problems. Commissions would not lend themselves to tyranny because their major means of enforcement of decisions, where decisions were resisted, would be the people's willingness to struggle. Their composition would give them great legitimacy, however, and people struggling on behalf of their considered decisions would be quite different from the usual ad hoc campaigns.

The Commissions would deal only with world-sized problems; they would not try to solve problems that could be dealt with on a more local level. World and local perspectives would, on the other hand, occasionally clash. The Commissions' mandates would be supreme but could not be forced on a determined local opposition. Since the Commissions would have different functions, a locality at loggerheads with one Commission might be the most ardent supporter of another Commission; we would have what sociologists call "cross-cutting" conflicts, which help to stablilize the system and prevent civil war. War, in any case, would be very unlikely because the Commission would have no troops and many localities would have trans-armed to civilian defense.

A small force of world marshals would, I think, grow naturally out of a situation like the above. By marshals I mean "peace officers," men and women especially skilled in methods of conflict-containment. They would be needed for two reasons. First, a few of the Commission directives would likely be matters where time is of the essence; the world health authority might order a summer resort area quarantined if a new and dangerous virus epidemic broke out, yet the people on the scene might want to leave. Irrationality is not unknown in such circumstances, and persons might feel a sharp conflict between their own requirements and the needs of the larger community. Where speed of enforcement is critical the Commission cannot simply publicize, contact voluntary associations, and hope that in a few months its directive will be carried out! Prompt action might require world marshals to fly to the scene and protect the larger community.

Since this power is liable to abuse, a world's ombudsman might convene a panel of respected world citizens after each of these incidents, to investigate the whole case and decide whether the Commission was in fact justified in using police power. If the Commission were not justified, the published conclusion would be a deterrent against arbitrary action in the future.

The second reason for world marshals is to contain the social conflicts which spill over into violence. I have been arguing all along for a world order which is marked by a large amount of conflict, but conflict waged by nonviolent methods. Where the conflicts spill over into violence, the marshals can intervene to restore the conflict to its nonviolent, even though passionate, course.

Local police would continue to exist. In the places where revolution has already taken place, the police would be brought under community control. These local police will usually be on the job to enforce the urgent Commission directives and to contain the conflict spillovers. The number of marshals will be small, for only extraordinary circumstances require them.

But surely some conflicts will boil into large-scale battle, even if the participants have only clubs and knives to fight with? Rather than establish a large force of marshals for such a situation, I would rather depend on the people to act as peace-keepers, using tactics of intervention and noncooperation if need be. (When it seemed in newly independent Algeria that there would be civil war among elements of the liberation army, the people threatened a general strike and nonviolent intervention.)

Because the marshals will be used only under special circumstances, they will have a high degree of moral authority. When a team of world marshals is on the scene we will know there is a problem of world significance. The marshals would be linked to the world court, for putting the exercise of force under codified law is an important check to arbitrary police power. As with the world Commissions, the world marshals linked to the world court would be the supreme legal coercive institution, superior to local police and courts. When in conflict, the world court and marshals would take precedence over local courts and police. The check against centralized tyranny would remain in the people's ability to oppose it through nonviolent action.

Among the many problems in this proposal is that the checks and balances outweigh the coordination; the conflicts outweigh the integration. The Commissions are themselves coordinating agencies, deciding among alternative ways of harnessing resources to reduce pollution or provide inexpensive world transport. But the Commissions are not coordinated among themselves beyond the gross division of labor provided by function.

World referenda and a legislature are needed. They would come at a late stage of development because the revolutionary process is ragged and uneven, and a government of half the world becomes too easily a force against the other half. When the time is ripe, however, the imaginative use of television could make possible worldwide debates on pressing matters which could then be decided by electronic referendum. Since too-frequent referenda defeat their own purpose, a legislature could be elected by secret ballot to help give an integrating perspective to the segmented work of the Commissions and court. The Commissions, organized according to function, will have difficulty taking the systemic approach which some problems demand; the legislature can look at the specific problems more in terms of the whole.

This plan provides one picture of how community might be organized as the world revolution nears "completion." The three traditional branches of government are there—legislative, judicial, and executive—but the powers are circumscribed, the executive is broken up into Commissions, and the enforcement lies for the most part in the people. It is a central government in the sense that it has the authority to deal with humankind-sized problems, but it does not centralize the decision-making where this is best left in local hands. In fact, its very growth can help the process of centralization within the existing large nations. One of the arguments against breaking up large states has been security: in order to protect ourselves we have to band together in larger structures. With institutions of a world community aiding the security of all, that reason for mammoth states disappears, and many of the functions which Washington, London, Moscow, and Delhi have taken on can at last be returned to areas of a more modest scale. Further, the development of civilian defense provides a powerful barrier to tyranny on a world basis.

Clearly, the existing national governments will not build these transnational institutions. The people's transnational movement can grow them as the counter-institutions of its strategy for world revolution. An early task for the movement is already apparent— to enforce the rulings of the World Court. The Court is, in a sense, a counter-institution to the prevailing condition of every-nation-a-law-unto-itself.

Several proto-commissions already exist: the Universal Postal Union, the International Telecommunications Union, the Food and Agriculture Organization, the World Health Organization. The transnational movement could campaign in ways which would increase these agencies' ability to counter the pressure of the big powers and the corporations. Where the movement finds growing desire for a new Commission, it could help to set one up and enforce its demands even before the relevant centers of reaction have been fully undermined. When the transnational movement reaches the noncooperation stage on a large scale, the Commissions will grow to take more of the space left empty by the weakening big nations. Finally, in the stage of parallel institutions, the full flowering of Commissions will occur, to be followed by referenda and legislature.

In the last chapter I mentioned briefly that the national struggle would be integrated by coordinating councils on local, regional, national, and transnational levels. The transnational coordinating council will be useful in world boycotts of major corporations, world conscription refusal, and other forms of noncooperation. The council can help in the fifth stage of a national struggle (parallel institutions) by creating new Commissions to handle national functions which cannot be devolved to regional or local government.

DO THESE PROGRAMS ADD UP?

I have dealt with four programs which are often considered in contrast to one another: socialist revolution, nonviolent struggle, civilian defense, and world government. A newcomer to the movement may not see a basic incompatibility, but movement veterans are so used to the jarring overtones and undertones of the various programs that they may be puzzled by this chapter.

Our world is made miserable by many things, but surely four major culprits are militarism, monopoly capitalism, nationalism, and violence. These forces feed each other.

Capitalism stimulates militarism because it must, in the last resort, defend its exploitation by violence. Militarism stimulates nationalism because the god of wars is not very attractive and cannot admit his debt to mammon; super-heated patriotism obscures the guns in a steam of idealism. The habitual recourse to violence from schoolyard to television justifies militarism and forces the stereotyping of "goodies" and "baddies" on which nationalism thrives. Militarism stimulates capitalism by giving it enormous public subsidies; the United States pulled fully out of the 1930s depression only by preparing for war. Nationalism stimulates capitalism by providing the categories in which capitalism can justify its expansion; the "manifest destiny" of the United States was in reality the manifest will to profit-making of U.S. corporations. (The profit motive operates in non-capitalist economies as well, admittedly. At one point in the embargo of arms to South Africa, Czechoslovakia reportedly stepped in to fill the vacuum. The "people's state" needed some of that apartheid cash.)

Here is, then, a vicious circle of forces which push us down, which oppress us all whether we are living in an expensive suburb or in an urban slum. We need a beneficent circle which lifts us up, a series of programs which stimulate each other to the benefit of all.

Socialism of the participatory kind I have described substitutes people power for corporate power; it removes much of the basis for hunger, alienation, and inequality. Nonviolent struggle provides a means by which the people can find their power and retain it against threats from "socialist" managerial elites, party bosses, or military coups. Civilian defense undermines monopoly capitalism because, unlike the army, it cannot be used to defend exploitation. Civilian defense facilitates the growth of transnational institutions by undermining the generals who treasure national sovereignty.

World government of the kind I have described helps build socialism by allocating world resources fairly and eliminating irrational duplication of effort (e.g., space races). Nonviolent struggle helps world government by providing its chief means of enforcement. Liberation movements help build world government by undermining the Empires which stand in the way of its creation. Nonviolent struggle helps socialist revolution by making possible a populist transfer of power and mobilizing more disaffection within the oppressing states. World government in my conception aids decentralization because it undermines the large centralized state of today but does not substitute a vast centralized bureaucracy in their place. Civilian defense makes possible the decentralized societies' defense against any tyrannical trends in world government.

All these statements are brief, and therefore overly simple descriptions of tendencies made possible by the strategy for a living revolution. A cynic might say these programs add up to making the world safe for *conflict*. I readily admit that mine is not a vision of world order in the sense of tranquillity. But I note a good many people moving onto the land, climbing mountains, stealing cars, adventuring with drugs, acting very much as if they need challenge rather than a clockwork middle class life for all.

This vision of a world in process may seem to demand too much from "human nature," but that is hard to reckon without having a clear perception of the changes which people undergo as they develop their movements for life. Already the impatient ones are refusing to wait until "after the revolution" to change their life styles and unlearn their competitiveness, their sexism, and so on. The communes as crucibles for transformation in America show dramatically that personal change is being worked on even at this early point in the revolutionary struggle.

But is this struggle *ours*—yours as well as mine? Does this controversial strategy for continuing the American revolution make sense? In the final chapter are some arguments for and against.

IX
THE DIALOGUE BEGINS

The five stages of revolution that provide the framework for this book can be seen as tools not only for social but also for personal transformation. Empowering ourselves for peacemaking is not different from empowering ourselves for life—if we pursue a strategy for a living revolution. Our own cultural preparation involves respecting ourselves. We build strength for our lives by making friends. Propaganda of the deed means speaking truth. Noncooperation in the political and economic spheres is the logical extension of actively refusing to be a victim in all aspects of our lives. We create our own parallel institutions as we figure out new ways of doing our business and of living our lives based on the previous four stages.

When we build allies (a political way of talking about making friends) and involve them in dialogue with us about our plans, we give ourselves greater power to take action. The feedback I've received about this book suggests that the strategic framework has been most useful when the reader has discussed it with others. It's been easier to sort through what does and doesn't make sense to the reader when in conversation with allies.

For this edition I decided to invite four thoughtful allies—Richard Falk, David Albert, Jane Meyerding, and Bill Moyer—to start the process of dialogue even before the reader turns the last page.[1] The four were asked especially to consider what the last fifteen years suggest about the basic framework of this book.

Richard Falk describes a global perspective to reduce the confusion of our media-saturated world. When we can not see the forest for the trees, Falk's analysis of major trends gives us orientation. David Albert suggests that we nurture the seeds of creativity which, in social form, are called "alternative institutions" and enable us to get a taste right now of the vision of a new society.

Jane Meyerding offers a sense of unfolding from the richness of the feminist movement, where women heated the abstraction "nonviolence" in the fire of their own experience, melted it, and refashioned it into a more effective tool for liberation. Nonviolent action has historically been used mainly by the oppressed; Meyerding examines these dynamics and reports on an engagement between consciousness and a struggle technique which can move each of us another step toward liberation.

Bill Moyer empowers us by clarifying some of the ingredients for success in social change. In the process, he gives us back some of our recent heritage of peoples' movements and their concrete results.

RICHARD FALK

In the 1970s there was an important shift in the character of international relations and political life. From 1945 to 1970 or perhaps even to 1975— a period I refer to as the post-war world—the United States was dominant in the world. After the devastation of World War II, the United States was the only real center of economic strength. Other countries, such as Germany and Japan were greatly weakened by the war. Moreover, the United States had a monopoly on nuclear weapons, and even after losing that monopoly, it had a decided nuclear superiority and therefore military dominance. The U.S. also enjoyed political prestige as the country that "led the victory against fascism" and a reputation for promoting a more beneficial economic model. Our domestic economic success stood out in a world devastated by war. Moreover, the U.S. was not perceived as a colonial power. All this gave the U.S. the capacity to command the votes of the entire Western hemisphere in the United Nations.

At the end of the post-war world, in the 1970s, however, the military superiority of the United States eroded. The USSR achieved nuclear parity. And the Vietnam War showed how difficult it was to translate military superiority into political results in the Third World.

By the beginning of the 1970s, U.S. economic dominance had also been seriously threatened. Germany and Japan especially became major competitors and were increasingly able to challenge U.S. trading positions around the world. New industrial countries in the Pacific also became important economic rivals, and Japan took the place of the U.S. as the economic model for the rest of the capitalist world. The United States was not making the internal adjustments that were needed, resulting in lower productivity and level of quality. Japanese superiority in the auto and electronics industries was particularly striking. The Third World showed it could put pressure on the United States through the Organization of Petroleum Exporting Countries (OPEC). This shift in power also shifted the oil wealth from the U.S. to the Third World and especially to the oil producers.

The diplomatic influence of the United States was also declining considerably. One result of the defeat of the U.S. forces in Vietnam and the defeat of the U.S.'s long, unpopular effort to keep the People's Republic of China out of the United Nations was that the general image of the United States changed. The United States had taken the place of the colonial powers of Great Britain and France in resisting change and intervening throughout the Third World. Its lowered prestige and influence was especially evident in the United Nations where, instead of dominating, the United States was increasingly on the defensive, supporting isolated positions on issues such as South African and Israeli policies. The United States was also in a minority position resisting efforts represented by the "New International Economic Order" to reform the economy of the world.

This shift from undisputed world dominance to increasingly challenged leadership was reinforced by the continual ocurrence of national revolutions that seemed to be antagonistic to the United States: for example, Nicaragua, Angola, Mozambique, and Ethiopia.

In contrast to the situation during the post-war world when the major world conflict was seen as an East-West struggle between capitalism and communism, after 1970 the real conflict was emerging as one between the Northern and the Southern hemispheres. There were, in fact, two sets of antagonisms gaining prominence: one between the Third World and the industrialized nations and one within the capitalist world itself.

In response to this changing global situation, the two administrations of Richard Nixon and Gerald Ford, with the influence of Secretary of State Henry Kissinger, attempted to reorient U.S. foreign policy by seeking "detente," or limited accommodation with the USSR. We entered into an unclear bargain whereby we traded with the Soviet Union, in hopes that they would somehow not jeopardize our interests in the nonwestern world. We acted as if the USSR had the capacity and the will to turn off national revolutions in the Third World. When that did not happen and when national revolutions were actively supported by Cuba and other newly created socialist nations, detente was seen as having failed.

Under the Carter administration the effort to reorient ourselves to our changed position in the world shifted from security to economic issues through the Trilateral Commission. Consisting of North American, West European and Japanese elites, the Trilateral Commission's theme was that the future of international prosperity depended on the management of interdependence—a global bargain between the North and the South. It was an attempt, although unacknowledged to the public, to limit the influence of governments in economic policy in favor of the large banks and corporations.

This effort to regain a position of unchallenged dominance through the manipulation of economic power also failed. It did not adequately interpret the revolutions in the Third World (in which the embarrassing powerlessness of the United States was epitomized by the Iranian hostage crisis). In addition, it was attacked by the militarist argument that the USSR was moving to a position of superiority while the United States lacked the will and capacity to defend its interests.

Carter's policy was seen as a failure and a sign of weakness. Opposition to it culminated with the Soviet invasion of Afghanistan and Carter's over-reaction to that event. The invasion also confirmed the feelings of conservatives that the USSR was becoming bolder and that the future of the West depended on its willingness to show resolve, defend itself in more vigorous ways, and assert its power more unilaterally.

With the election of Ronald Reagan, this viewpoint became administration policy. The administration made no pretense of accepting the authority of international law or the United Nations. The United States determined policy solely by consideration of its own interests. Examples of this flouting of international authority included the rejection of the Law of the Sea Treaty, withdrawal from UNESCO, and repudiation of the legitimacy of the International Court of Justice to rule on a case brought against the U.S. by Nicaragua.

However, even this most recent effort to restore the sort of dominance reminiscent of the post-war period is likely to fail. It undermines the possibility for domestic economic reform by its emphasis on the military. It repeats the errors of Vietnam by trying to intervene against national revolutions in the Third World. It accentuates U.S. diplomatic isolation and repudiates cooperative approaches to problem solving. Such an attitude is inconsistent with the interdependence needed for international relations. Reagan's policy also tends to split the domestic society, favoring the winners and ignoring or punishing the losers. Finally, the Reagan administration pursues a foreign policy that is inconsistent with the values of a significant portion of the United States public.

I consider that there are four ways of bringing some stability and order back into international relations: renouncing nuclearism as an element of foreign policy; adopting a "live and let live" attitude toward the Third World by renouncing intervention; refraining from overt challenges to Soviet relations with Eastern Europe at a government-to-government level; and mobilizing the economic surplus for social reconstruction here at home, thus restoring vitality to the civilian sectors of economic life. These four developments, however, cannot occur within the present political party structure since neither the Democratic nor the Republican Party will make such changes, given their respective constituencies.

Therefore, there is a need for a nonviolent revolution. This, in my opinion, translates into popular politics—something like the Green movement of Germany, adapted to the realities of the United States.

We need a movement which provides security and promotes democracy by giving citizens more control over the policies of their government.

Our government at the moment is characterized by a strong central state which controls Congress, the media, the electoral process, and education to such an extent that the citizenry has no sense of what other alternatives there are. The entrenchment of militarism in government has also narrowed the scope of the public imagination. Public discussion, therefore, is so restricted in choice of options that the consideration of more appropriate responses is precluded.

There have been positive developments in the past fifteen years. One is the rise of the activist challenge to the state's dominance of society, in the anti-nuke movement, for example, or the activist religious communities in most major cities. Small groups of people are willing to devote their lives to stopping the arms race and are willing to accept imprisonment in order to dramatize their commitment. There is also a greater participation by the religious institutions in defining the limits of morally responsible actions by the government. The Catholic Bishops' pastoral letter on disarmament, for example, deepened public consciousness of the gap between the morality of society and the official policy of its leaders. The reality of this gap helps stimulate the impression that government is an illegitimate and even criminal enterprise because it violates fundamental precepts of morality.

There are many other examples: New Zealand's refusal to allow ships carrying nuclear materials to dock in its harbors; the publicity about the bombing of the *Rainbow Warrior*, the boat belonging to the activist environmental organization Greenpeace, which was preparing to sail into a nuclear test zone (Greenpeace subsequently sent other boats into the test zone, amid much international media coverage); the creation of nuclear free zones by eight governments in the Pacific; the Sanctuary movement; the various initiatives by the Pledge of Resistance in opposition to intervention in Central America; the case in Burlington, Vermont, in which citizens' rights to access to the state Senate in order to insist on lawful actions by their government were upheld; resistance to CIA activities; developments such as Solidarity, in Eastern Europe; continued efforts to achieve human rights and democracy; the European peace movement; the Green movement in West Germany; and the campaign of Jesse Jackson and the possibility that he could provide some continued leadership either within the Democratic Party or in providing an alternative. So there is some reason to hope.

Most important of all, we are coming to a new definition of peace. Peace depends on human rights and democracy even more than on decisions about which weapons to use. Because this book deepens our understanding of peace, George Lakey's discussion about what helps bring about a nonviolent revolution, a living revolution, continues to be a valuable contribution.

DAVID H. ALBERT

When *Strategy for a Living Revolution* was written, it attempted to stretch the limits of what we call revolution by showing that the overthrow of governments has not always required the use of violence. By reconstructing the ways in which people's struggles relate to governmental overthrow, George Lakey was looking for applicable models and explicit strategies for future nonviolent revolutions. This book was written during the height of the Vietnam War, by which time many people felt we had reached the limits of reform. While using examples from the Third World, it was written mainly for a Western audience and considered strategies and tactics in that context.

What has happened since has confirmed the optimism of Lakey's assumptions—and has made clear how important it is to understand the limitations on what we could expect from the overthrow of government alone. The idea of limits is nothing new to nonviolent action, the goal of which is to build the most just, humane and free society with the most minimal, elegant, and effective exercise of power. Yet in evaluating what a truly living revolution can achieve, we must include in our strategy new insights about limits.

In the past fifteen years, activists have deepened their understanding of the limits of the world's resource base and of the environment. Revolution, however, does not automatically bring more rational use of resources. In the African continent, for example, there are many so-called socialist and so-called capitalist governments, yet the resource depletion of that whole continent continues, irrespective of the economic system. Lakey is correct in focussing on the United States in this respect, because it is Western consumption patterns that cause this depletion of Third World resources. Revolutions in those countries cannot, in themselves, solve such a problem.

While Lakey's book devotes a chapter to the importance of cultural preparation, later thinkers have emphasized even more the importance of developing the radically new values which finite world resources and a fragile ecology demand. Rudolf Bahro, for example, argues that without a clear and early articulation of new social and ecological values, little will change. He sees organized labor as an appendage of post-industrial capitalism; major forces within it might indeed be alienated by such an articulation. Yet, to bring about the changes demanded by the limits to world resources, such emphasis on the need for lowered, not increased, production and consumption is essential.

In considering the revolutionary experiments of the Third World, we need to look for new models and methods of organizing which can be applied at home. One promising example is the development of Christian "base communities" in Latin America, which are unified around shared values rather than labor unions and modes of production. The example of these communities has helped shape the Sanctuary movement in the United States. It is also useful to note how cultural traditions can be used to create a context for rallying and building mass movements, as with the transformation of the mourning periods after funerals in Iran and South Africa from private religious events to public political mobilizations.

Values that come from an older time and could be considered reactionary have been useful, as many of Lakey's examples show. Yet they may have limitations. In the more recent Iranian revolution, the harkening back to traditional, broadly-held values did lead to a successful overthrow of a dictatorship, but it also led to the establishment of a reactionary traditional society. India is an exception where the nonviolent overthrow of a government did bring forth a whole series of new values, even though these have not been adopted by Indian society as a whole. One indication of Gandhi's success on this values front is the unbelievably small role the military has in Indian society. It has virtually no role in or influence over the government, and only a tiny percentage of India's GNP goes to arms spending, despite enemies on three sides.

Do new values come from working in coalitions or do they grow best in isolation? In both China and Nicaragua, revolutionary cadres initially spent much time off in the hills, all the while brewing new values, which they were able to put into practice once the revolutions succeeded. These examples would seem to argue for the hot-house-in-isolation theory. A focus on coalition-building , by implication, would encourage compromise rather than the formation of radically new values.

What social institutions in this country would foster the new values that are required to deal with newly-discovered global limits? The number of non–state-dominated cultural institutions in American society is rapidly diminishing; neither the universities nor the labor unions nor the churches have nearly as much power and influence over our society as they once did. The Moral Majority and the evangelical churches are currently doing the best job of putting out values that challenge those of the culture at large. Yet the lip service that these conservative institutions pay to the non-dominant values of family, simplicity and non-material ends falls far short of revolutionary consciousness. Alternative institutions on the left, while more likely to espouse revolutionary values, have yet to make a significant impact on the culture at large.

If you consider all the cases cited by Lakey for the nonviolent overthrow of governments or if you look at more modern cases (Bolivia, Poland, Iran, the Philippines), you find institutions of such strength, size, and moral force that they can actually challenge governments. In this country at present, however, the centralized state has extensive and powerful control over our lives and our minds. Activists who desire the spread of alternative values need to consider from where these values will emanate—and nurture the institutions that will bring them forth.

What about the power of the media to help overthrow governments? We are limited by our lack of control over the present mass media system and by our seeming inability to restrain ourselves and others to rely on other media sources. These sources are available; in Poland and in Iran, for example, people relied completely on tape cassettes for information and education. If, however, we are indeed going to change large numbers of people's hearts and minds, we must acknowledge the importance of access to the mass media.

None of these problems are insoluble, but the limits are difficult ones and ones we will have to confront. To give us hope, we can remember that, to the societies of the past which changed through the use of nonviolent action, the obstacles they faced must have seemed equally difficult.

The insights we have gained over the past fifteen years may cause us to rethink aspects of *Powerful Peacemaking: A Strategy for a Living Revolution*, yet Lakey's approach is more relevant today than ever. To even imagine the violent overthrow of Western governments, given the incredible destructiveness of current weapons technology, is pure fantasy. Moreover, the government's arsenal is growing to include not only weapons but new devices such as brain wave machines for crowd control.

The modern corporate system is built on and maintained through violence, and that violence becomes more naked to the eye as time goes on. The very philosophy of nonviolence, therefore, stands as the chief ideological value in opposition and can serve as a rallying point for a people's movement. In the case of the Iranian revolution, tapes made by Khomeini and distributed to his followers in Iran explicitly urged people not to pick up guns, but to use a tulip as a living symbol against the violence of the Shah. If nonviolence is a rallying point, as it was in the struggles for civil rights in the United States and for independence in India, then it must be promoted as a value, rather than just a tactic, and put forth strongly from the beginning.

In terms of values, Lakey's examples of Czechoslovakia, Hungary and France in 1968 show the centrality, not of economic issues, but of non-material values, such as democracy and free speech as opposed to dictatorships and censorship. Thus, rallying points for radical social change can indeed, and from my perspective must, be non-material and specifically related to value systems and how they are violated by the current state/corporate governments.

Lakey reminds us that the revolution is not the overthrow of the government alone, but what comes afterwards, and that what comes afterwards will most likely be a reflection of what we've done (or not done) before. In conclusion, this book remains a classic, and, seen within the context of the insights we have gained over the past fifteen years, it continues to be very useful to sincere students of the possibilities of nonviolence.

JANE MEYERDING

The publication in 1970 of Kate Millett's *Sexual Politics* was, for many U.S. activist women, the key that opened our minds to feminism. After a decade or more of involvement in male-dominated struggles for justice and peace, we suddenly discovered a perspective from which we could begin to acknowledge and examine our own experiences of injustice and victimization. Women who had remained unwaveringly nonviolent in the face of violence they and their male comrades recognized as political now began to doubt the value of nonviolence as a response to the privatized violence of sexism. Nonviolent action is most effective when it forces both the uninvolved and the actively unjust to recognize the violence and injustices of the oppressive status quo. In the early 1970s, however, there seemed to be no societal consensus on the true nature of sexism and therefore no shared assumptions to give the necessary weight to nonviolent acts of "political *jiu-jitsu*." Male violence against women was not even seen as violence for the most part; where the violence was recognized, it was considered an individual, private affair—and something for which the victim was largely to blame.

Andrea Dworkin's 1975 essay, "Redefining Nonviolence" (reprinted in *Our Blood*, Harper & Row, 1976) was tremendously liberating for those of us struggling to understand why our commitment to nonviolence seemed somehow to contradict our growing involvement in feminism. Surely it shouldn't be so, we complained to one another; surely nonviolent activists of both genders and all varieties should welcome feminism with open arms. After all, nonviolence and feminism were both about exposing and opposing the damage done to all people by violent social institutions such as racism, militarism, and sexism. So why did we nonviolent feminists feel so torn between our two "movements"? Why did we feel rejected sometimes by both our activist families?

Dworkin gave us the beginning of an answer to those questions by requiring us to see nonviolence in terms of our own oppression as women. We no longer felt at ease with—or accepted by—many of our former associates in nonviolence because we had begun to see that "any commitment to nonviolence which is real, which is authentic, must begin in the recognition of the forms and degrees of violence perpetrated against women by the gender class men." Without that basis, nonviolence is "a sham which will have, as its direct consequence, the perpetuation of your [i.e., women's] servitude." And for most of us the reality was that our male comrades in nonviolence had not even begun to think about sexism as an appropriate subject for serious political discussion, much less the basis for a nonviolent analysis or commitment.

Our other community, meanwhile, the growing community of activist feminists, was waiting for us nonviolent women to recognize that, as Dworkin put it, "As women, nonviolence must begin for us in the refusal to be violated, in the refusal to be victimized." We could not begin to build a bridge between our two worlds of nonviolence and feminism until we realized that, as women in a patriarchal society, "we must not accept, even for a moment, male notions of what nonviolence is."

In the five years following "Redefining Nonviolence," some women formerly committed to nonviolence rejected it altogether. Others, however, set out to redefine it, combining the best of the old analysis with the new insights of feminism. Many people have noted (some with pride, others with horror) that in virtually every facet of feminist activism, from publishing to direct action to shelters for battered women, lesbians have played a leading role, though our presence is not always openly acknowledged for one reason or another. Similarly, I suspect that women experienced in nonviolence have played a major role in almost every development of feminist political action, even though many of these women do not describe themselves as nonviolent for one reason or another.

The accessibility of nonviolence as well as its proven effectiveness are attractive to activists from every oppressed group. For many people, nonviolence also carries the appeal of being consistent with deeply held beliefs about how people should treat one another, whether those beliefs belong to an Indian Hindu, a U.S. Baptist, or a feminist atheist. The apparent consistency between nonviolent ethics and female sex-role stereotyping, however, has caused some major problems for U.S. feminists. Are women "naturally" nonviolent, or at least less violent than men? For a feminist, whether she looks back through history or around her at the state of the world today, it certainly is tempting to make that assumption. Men have always fought the wars, haven't they? And look, even the supposedly nonviolent men are sexist and therefore, by definition, violent. Not to mention the fact that everyone knows women are gentle, loving, nurturing, harmless creatures of nature.

Almost before anyone noticed what was happening, a significant number of feminists were well on their way down a flowery, apolitical path falsely labeled "nonviolence." The problem, this tempting path asked us to believe, is that men are violent and nasty. But women are nice. So the solution is that women can (and should) save the world. By being nice. And if this smacks of biological determinism, the old falsehood we thought we'd abandoned when we decided to put down racism, anti-Semitism, sexism, well, then, the problem is that society makes men violent.

Although it sounds ludicrous, there were times between 1975 and 1980 when feminist nonviolence really seemed to mean just this to many people. Not surprisingly, there were plenty of other feminists around who were more than ready to damn that "nice" lifeless version of nonviolence as unrealistic, apolitical, passive and a philosophical luxury item appropriate only for the privileged few. It was immensely frustrating for activist nonviolent feminists to see "real nonviolence," as we thought of it, thrown out by our feminist sisters along with the false nonviolence of nice-nice-nice.

Fortunately, that's not all that was going on. Women continued to work away, to weave, at the synthesis of feminism and nonviolence, many of us following in the footsteps of Barbara Deming as she moved deeper and deeper into an exploration of her own oppression—as a woman and a lesbian—and yet continued to remind us that "we are all part of one another." Nonviolence and feminism belong together not because men are nasty and women are nice, but because as feminists—and as lesbians, women of color, poor women, whoever we are in all our complexity—we need what nonviolence can be for us: a way to act strongly and effectively for change without violating (doing violence to) the complexity of a world in which each of us is both oppressed and oppressor, nasty and nice, a world in which, inevitably, "what goes around comes around."

Also during those years—and increasingly in the years between 1980 and now, feminism has developed a wider, more inclusive perspective. Those of us who are middle-class WASPs gradually—or suddenly—realized that the most powerful, most exciting feminism was coming from radical women of color and from white women committed to work against racism. More and more, the feminist chorus became a mixture of voices—women of color, Jewish women, disabled women, fat women, poor and working class women, victims of incest, survivors of addiction. And we began to look beyond national borders to women not only in Europe but in Central and South America, Africa, Asia.

My sense is that now, more than any time in the last twenty years, there are feminists ready to think seriously about radical social change. Because in our commitment as feminists we are poor as well as comfortable, colored as well as white, from Korea and Guatemala as well as the U.S., we can not settle for a program of surface reform. A major frustration facing us now is: How do we begin even to imagine a transformation as immense, as intense, as we want for our world? *Powerful Peacemaking: Strategy for a Living Revolution* is one good place to start.

BILL MOYER

The past twenty-five years have been a period of powerful peoples' social movements. Although these movements seemed suddenly to appear full-blown, they all occurred under certain social conditions and were preceded by a long period of unseen preliminary stages.

Looking at the development of these social movements, we can learn how, piece by piece, the conditions were built that enabled them to happen. We can see that, rather than emerging spontaneously and running a haphazard and uncontrollable course, successful social movements go through a series of stages, each with its own activities, goals, pitfalls, tactics, strategies, and other characteristics. Understanding these stages helps us launch and run new movements. Recognizing the success of many past social movements and the reasons for that success also helps people come to believe that they are powerful and able to create meaningful social change despite the formidable opposition of conservative centers of power.

A great success story is that of the anti-nuclear energy movement in the United States. The first time that nuclear power, and its opponents, became a major public issue was in 1977, when two thousand protestors occupied the construction site of the Seabrook, New Hampshire nuclear power plant. National and international news coverage put the public spotlight on this challenge to nuclear energy for two solid weeks, as fourteen hundred demonstrators were arrested and remained in armories that served as their jails.

Before the "take-off" of the anti-nuclear energy movement at Seabrook, however, there was a solid decade of ripening social conditions and quiet organizing. It is the care taken in these preliminary stages, invisible to major media coverage, that makes a social movement seem to appear from nowhere. Nuclear energy became a potentially "backyard" issue for almost everybody during that decade, as hundreds of nuclear power plant sites across the country were announced. Simultaneously, often unknown to each other, local citizens everywhere took the first steps: identifying nuclear energy as a problem; holding small demonstrations that went fairly unnoticed; and most importantly, showing that the normal channels of government were failing to protect the public interest. Citizens presented the opposition arguments at every hearing required for the state and federal licensing process for nuclear power plants. This process, which took years, helped citizens become their own energy experts, incensed local people enough that they were more ready to take action, and increasingly discredited the government in the eyes of the public, while enhancing the credibility of its opponents. The ending of the Vietnam War in 1975 helped fulfill another requisite for a social movement: it made available the energies of a network of people: those previously engaged in anti-war activities.

Finally, during all those years, there were people thinking about the movement as a whole, traveling around the country, encouraging people to get involved, and training them in nuclear site occupation and nonviolent action.

So when you have an action such as Seabrook, an action that puts the public spotlight on people in jail every day for two weeks, the issue becomes public. Through their actions, the Seabrook demonstrators spoke aloud the sentiments of millions of people across the United States who had begun to question the new nuclear power sites in their backyards but had felt powerless to challenge the big government and corporate forces behind this proliferation.

The Seabrook demonstrators provided not only inspiration but also a model for local action. Hundreds of new local anti-nuclear energy groups soon sprang into existence. Only months later came the occupation of the Diablo Canyon, California nuclear construction site. Within a few years, nonviolent blockades and occupations occurred at virtually every nuclear plant construction site in the country. This illustrates the process of creating social movements: after a period of largely invisible background work, a national event like Seabrook is launched, followed by similar actions such as Diablo at a regional level, and then local actions everywhere.

It is interesting to note the response to the 1979 accident at Three Mile Island. A TV interviewer called it a "lucky coincidence" for the movement and asked why we depended on such tragic events. I told him that, while we certainly wanted to alert the public to the danger of nuclear power, we depended on such accidents for building our movement less than the public depended on us for finding out about them. An equally serious meltdown occurred at the Enrico Fermi plant outside Detroit in 1969. Since there was no strong anti-nuclear power movement at that time, it went unreported for four years! (Read Fuller, *We Almost Lost Detroit.*)

It is important that activists and the general public know of the success of the anti-nuclear power movement and the reasons behind it, for the mass media is not about to tell us. We must recognize and take heart from our own victories.

There has been no new order for a nuclear power plant in the United States since 1978; every order made during the past eleven years has been cancelled. Moreover, there is no indication that there will be any new orders in the foreseeable future, despite the fact that the government and the electrical industry still want a nuclear America. If the trends of the past decade continue, there will be only about twenty-five operating plants in the year 2000 instead of the thousand projected by the government's "Operation Independence." Even those twenty-five operating plants will be closing down within the following decade.

The history of the anti-nuclear power movement exemplifies the prerequisites for establishing a large social movement: an issue that can be seen as a "backyard" or personal one for many people; a stage of going through normal channels to prove that they don't work; the creation of experts within the movement; a network of active people around the country; and adequate training for nonviolent action.

A second success story, the anti-nuclear weapons movement, demonstrates the interplay between U.S. and European initiatives and the way that different social movements build upon each other. In 1982 the social movements against nuclear weapons took off in the United States. Opposition to the arms race became a major public issue; it was in the newspapers, on the radio, and on TV. Citizens' groups sprang up all over the country opposing nuclear weapons. A demonstration in New York City in June of 1982 drew 750,000 people. How did all this suddenly happen?

The answer begins in Europe, where the anti-nuclear weapons movement took off in 1980 in response to the 1979 NATO decision to deploy U.S. cruise and Pershing-II missiles in England, Germany, Belgium, Holland, and Italy. All of a sudden, nuclear weapons became a "backyard" issue. The missiles were being placed on European soil, at European expense, with no democratic decision making, and worst of all, the United States had its finger on the button. The decision angered millions of European because it flew in the face of their sense of justice and democracy—and a full blown social movement emerged.

This European movement helped its U.S. counterpart to grow. The message that "the Europeans are ahead of us and we need to catch up" was a motivating force for that massive demonstration in New York. (European influence was also present in the anti-nuclear energy movement; the Seabrook action was inspired by the 1975 occupation of the Whyl nuclear power plant in West Germany.)

Different social movements also affect each other. When I started doing anti-nuclear power organizing in 1970, I was telling the peace leaders that we couldn't create a social movement on nuclear weapons in this country in that decade; the social conditions simply were not present. But we could challenge nuclear power—and later make the step to nuclear weapons. At all trainings and demonstrations in the anti-nuclear energy movement, we always had a speaker on nuclear weapons. Slowly people began to see the connection. The same process is now being repeated in connecting the anti-nuclear weapons movement to the anti-intervention movement.

Key to the new anti-nuclear weapons movement have been the women's peace camps, a historic coming together of the women's and the peace movements. The women's movement challenges patriarchy, domination by men, and destruction of lives; women in the peace movement saw the same forces at work in creating the nuclear arms race. The sense of power that happens for women in an all-women's space provided them with the strength to take a public stand on this social issue which they saw as being directly connected to the oppression of women and all of society by the patriarchal system.

The women's movement, in turn, grew out of other social movements, many of them inspired by the Gandhian movement in India. Martin Luther King, Jr. had studied Gandhi in seminary; James Lawson had gone to India and then held regular workshops back home with people who later became significant leaders of the civil rights movement. Quakers such as Glen Smiley and A.J. Muste did training based on their experience with Gandhi that influenced King and other future leaders of the Student Nonviolent Coordinating Committee (SNCC) and the Southern Christian Leadership Conference (SCLC).

With the 1964 Mississippi Summer Project, as many as one thousand whites went South to help out in black voter registration drives. They started with two weeks of training, and when they returned to their campuses, they took with them a model for nonviolence training and action, as well as the understanding of liberation from oppression that they had gained. The student movement was then launched by these participants in the civil rights struggle.

The groups most actively working for change in the 1960s—the New Left movement, represented by Students for a Democratic Society, SNCC, and SCLC—were still all steeped in patriarchy. They were attempting to empower and educate people to oppose the oppressive forces of the society, yet they reflected that society: men dominated leadership and decision-making while women did most of the work of implementation. Finally the women said, "Wait a minute! We're going to apply this to our own situation." Women in those groups, and in the anti-war movement that grew from them, started consciousness-raising sessions on the subject of their own oppression as women—a "backyard" issue for them all.

This history shows clearly how one movement for social change influences the beginning of another. The experience of these movements also shows that they depend not on the existence of one charismatic leader (a myth created mainly by the mass media which like to reduce complex issues to individual personalities), but on the influence of many dedicated individuals interacting with and supporting each other.

The end of the 1960s was a time of transition on many fronts. Some of us realized that we needed a way of training people to use the lessons we'd learned from the 50s and 60s to influence the new movements of the 1970s. The training center that we established in Movement for a New Society was, at that time, the only one in the country doing training in nonviolent action. This training expanded beyond training for actions into all sorts of other areas: group process; handling the "isms" (racism, sexism, classism, heterosexism, etc.) in ourselves and our groups; setting up alternatives to hierarchal organizations; and learning new, nurturing models of leadership, as opposed to dominant-doer, heavy-handed-individual models. Out of this training center came much of the leadership for the anti-nuclear power movement, both in the United States and abroad.

We also started to learn about the need for change from a larger perspective. By starting with this "macro" analysis—including international and Third World connections, environment and the limit to world resources, world-wide social and economic systems, and the needs of future generations—we would come to different conclusions than by looking at one social problem at a time.

Taking this larger perspective and trying to attack the roots was a significant change from the 1960s, when we just responded from the heart to what we saw. Rather than immediately giving food in response to hunger in the Third World, for example, we found that US food aid programs tended to flood the market in those countries and lower their domestic food prices—capturing a market for US farmers, but eroding Third World self-sufficiency. Education in this country and support of self-determination abroad would help more in the long run than just giving food.

In another example, a coalition of people from the anti-Vietnam War movement, the peace movement, and the welfare rights movement came together in the spring of 1971 to demand an end to the war and the arms race, a transfer from a military to a domestic budget (guns to butter), and a $6500 minimum income for everybody. I argued that, with a finite limit to the world's resources, we would have to switch from guns not to butter but to margarine. Cutting military spending would reduce our control over many Third World countries and limit our ability to exploit their resources. If we tried to raise everybody in the US to middle-class consumption levels, we would use up the world's resources in thirty years. Therefore, seen in terms of world justice, this demand for a minimum income posed a win/lose situation: if we got more, the Third World would get less, and the biggest losers would be the future generations. Rather than a $6500 minimum, a world-and-future-conscious goal would be a $6500 maximum income with a social welfare net under everyone to provide the basic necessities.

While new and different, such ideas need not be threatening if presented thoughtfully. For example, our standard of living would not really be reduced by protecting the environment and ending imperialism. Such changes would reduce our standard of consumption, waste, pollution and paternalism, but increase our well-being in the larger sense. Seeing change in these terms can present us with a big opportunity rather than a life-shattering problem and can lead to breakthroughs in our thinking.

The ecology movement is illustrative of many of these new developments and ways of thinking. Since World War II, we have lived with a societal assumption that technology will save us and that ever-increasing consumption is the way to happiness. A key role of the anti-nuclear power movement was to challenge one of the biggest symbols of that model: nuclear energy. The anti-nuke movement turned those assumptions upside down and posed an alternative way of living based on decentralized energy use and locally-controlled institutions. This new vision—of a system that can last for the long term and function on a democratic, human level—can serve as a model for all other areas of life.

A final development has been that of alternatives to the liberal/capitalist and marxist paradigms. In the 1950s and 1960s, a social reform model dominated. This model assumed that the United States was basically wonderful, but that there were a few problems to solve—i.e., race discrimination, poverty, the common cold. The goal was to bring the oppressed minorities into the mainstream of America, and similarly, the Third World into the mainstream of Western industrial democracies.

In the late 1960s, the achievability and even desirability of this goal were increasingly questioned. Many activists turned to another model—that provided by Marx. In this model, the masses of workers are organized to carry out an industrial revolution leading to a technological society with production controlled by the people instead of by the rich owners. Application of this model, however, has often included violence, centralization, a patriarchal society, and the same emphasis on growth and consumption.

The past fifteen years have provided a rich source for alternative visions and models of organizing for social change. The women's movement, MNS, and the struggles on the left all offer ideas of how to wage struggle in ways that are consistent with our vision of a new society.

George Lakey's book helps us by offering one model of how these changes might come about. Without such constructs, there is no basis to evaluate what we have done, whether we are moving in the right direction, and what we should do next. With no benchmarks of success along the road, it is easy to feel that we're making no progress or losing and then to burn out. By providing us with the model of five stages of a living revolution (cultural preparation, building organization strength, propaganda of the deed, political and economic noncooperation, intervention, and parallel institutions), Lakey can help us orient ourselves along the road toward a better society.

* * *

For me, these four commentators provide an excellent model of cooperative political dialogue. They take the argument further, refine it, and fill it out in light of their experience of this rapidly changing world. The reader may also have insights that further illuminate parts of the argument or experiences that would call some of it into question. I would love to hear from them, since each person's perception of reality must inevitably contribute to the clarity with which we see the whole. Dialogue cannot help but empower.

Yet, ultimately, the proof of the pudding for all these concepts lies in putting them into action. Academic discussion will never settle questions of strategy—as revolutionaries from Gandhi to Marx would agree. It's a big step out of theory and into practice—and it's very easy to feel discouraged when the tide seems to be turning toward conservatism, when so many people seem mired in victimization and apathy, when the problems appear so big and we so small. But to make the move, to start putting all our intelligence and theory to use, to begin building with our allies toward our visions, is a profoundly hopeful and life-giving process.

NOTES

INTRODUCTION

1. Robert Jay Lifton, *Death in Life: Survivors of Hiroshima* (New York: Random House, 1967).

2. Peter Seeger, "Rainbow Race," in *Survival Songbook* (Sanga Music, 1970).

3. The Nobel winners were from all branches of science and literature as well as six peace laureates. *Philadelphia Inquirer*, June 25, 1981.

4. *The Global 2000 Report to the President: Entering the Twenty-First Century* (Washington, D.C.: Government Printing Office, 1980).

5. *Washington Post*, November 4, 1979.

6. "I Don't Trust Any Economists Today," *Fortune*, September 11, 1978, p. 31.

7. *The Christian Science Monitor*, July 30, 1980.

8. In testimony to the Joint Economic Committee Hearing on Creating Jobs through Energy Policy, March 1978, cited by Hazel Henderson in *The Politics of the Solar Age: Alternatives to Economics* (Garden City, NY: Anchor Books, 1981), p. 44.

CHAPTER 1 — EMPOWERING OURSELVES FOR PEACE

1. Robert K. Merton, *Social Theory and Social Structure* (Glencoe, IL: The Free Press, 1949), especially p. 79.

2. Two recent publications of Sharp are: *National Security Through Civilian-Based Defense* (Omaha, NE: Association for Transarmament Studies, 1985) 96pp., and *Making Europe Unconquerable* (Cambridge, MA: Ballinger, 1985) 252pp. Both of these as well as other publications and a newsletter are available from Association for Transarmament Studies, 3636 Lafayette Ave., Omaha, NE 68131.

3. See Leghorn's essay in Pam McAllister, ed. *Reweaving the Web of Life: Feminism and Nonviolence* (Philadelphia: New Society Publishers, 1983).

4. From his article in Joseph Pleck and Jack Sawyer, eds. *Men and Masculinity* (Englewood Cliffs, NJ: Prentice-Hall, 1974) p. 136.

5. Reported by Dr. George Weinberg in his book, *Society and the Healthy Homosexual* (Garden City, NY: Doubleday Anchor, 1973) p. 131.

6. See the work of Marion Anderson of Economic Research Associates in East Lansing, Michigan.

7. See the Lucas report in Suzanne Gordon and Dave McFadden, eds. *Economic Conversion: Revitalizing America's Economy* (Cambridge, MA: Ballinger, 1984).

8. See, for example, Melman's book *The Permanent War Economy* (NY: Simon and Schuster, 1975).

9. "Defense Industry Profit Study, B-159896," U.S. Government Accounting Office Report to the Congress, March 3, 1971, p. 37.

10. See *The Global 2000 Report to the President: Entering the Twenty-First Century*, prepared by the Council on Environmental Quality and the Department of State. (Washington, DC: Government Printing Office, 1980).

CHAPTER 2 — POWER TO FORCE CHANGE

1. The material for this case was gathered from newspaper accounts and my own interviews in Paris in 1969. Candy Putter's 1969 Swarthmore College seminar paper, "The French Crisis of May-June 1968: A Case Study," helped me greatly. Patricia Parkman also helped me with this case. Newspapers included *Le Monde*, *The Times* of London, and the *New York Times*; periodicals included *Dissent*, *New Left Review*, and *Our Generation*.

2. The El Savador case study grows out of research by Patricia Parkman which has become her history Ph. D. dissertation "Insurrection Without Arms: the General Strike in El Salvador, 1944" (Temple University).

Some of the published sources are:

Charles Anderson, "El Salvador: The Army as Reformer," in *Political Systems of Latin America*, ed. Martin Needler (Princeton, N.J.: Van Nostrand, 1964), pp. 53–72.

Ben G. Burnett and Moisés Poblete Troncoso, *The Rise of the Latin American Labor Movement* (New York: Bookman Associates, 1960).

Miguel Thomas Molina, in Preface to Romeo Fortín Magana, *Democracia y socialismo, seguido de ostros breves estudios* (San Salvador, 1953).

Hubert Herring, *A History of Latin America from the Beginnings to the Present* (New York: Knopf, 1960).

William Krehm, *Democracia y Tiranías en el Caribe* (Mexico City, 1949).

Franklin D. Parker, *The Central American Republics* (London: Oxford University Press, 1964).

Mario Rodríguez, *Central America* (Englewood Cliffs, N.J.: Prentice-Hall, 1965).

Mario Rosenthal, *Guatemala: The Story of an Emergent Latin American Democracy* (New York: Twayne, 1962).

Mauricio de la Selva, "El Salvador: Tres Décadas de Lucha" *Cuadernos Americanos*, vol. 21, no. 1 (January-February 1962), pp. 196–220.

Thomas Lynn Smith, "Notes on Population and Rural Social Organization in El Salvador" *Rural Sociology*, vol. 10, no. 4 (December 1965), pp. 359–79.

Arthur P. Whitaker, "Pan America in Politics and Diplomacy," in *Inter-American Affairs*, ed. Arthur P. Whitaker (New York: Columbia University Press, 1945), pp. 4–7.

Also see the contemporary accounts in *The New York Times*, *Newsweek*, *Time*, *Inter-American*, and *Commonweal*.

3. *Newsweek*, May 22, 1944, "High School Revolution," p. 66.

4. In the Guatemalan case I also received the help of Patricia Parkman and Cynthia L. Adcock. The major sources were:

Richard N. Adams, "Social Change in Guatemala and U.S. Policy," in *Social Change in Latin America Today*, Richard N. Adams et al. (New York: Knopf, Vintage Books, 1960), pp. 231–84.

Victor Alba, *Politics and the Labor Movement in Latin America* (Stanford, Calif: Stanford University Press, 1968).

Carleton Beals, *Latin America: World in Revolution* (New York: Abelard-Schuman, 1963).

Ben G. Burnett and Moisés Poblete Troncoso, *op. cit.*

Archer C. Bush, "Organized Labor in Guatemala, 1944–49," mimeographed (Hamilton, N.Y.: Colgate University, 1950).

J. Halcro Ferguson, *The Revolutions of Latin America* (London: Thames and Hudson, 1963).

Amy Elizabeth Jensen, *Guatemala: A Historical Survey* (New York: Exposition Press, 1955).

William Krehm, *op. cit.*

John D. Martz, *Central America: The Crisis and the Challenge* (Chapel Hill, N.C.: University of North Carolina Press, 1959).

Franklin D. Parker, *op. cit.*

Mario Rodríguez, *op. cit.*

Mario Rosenthal, *op. cit.*

Ronald M. Schneider, *Communism in Guatemala, 1944–54* (New York: Praeger, 1958).

Kalman H. Silvert, *A Study in Government: Guatemala* (New Orleans, La.: Tulane University Press, 1954).

Arthur P. Whitaker, *op. cit.*

Also see contemporary accounts in *The New York Times, Newsweek,* and *Time.*

5. Richard N. Adams, *op. cit.,* p. 233.

6. *The Discourses of Niccolò Machiavelli* (New Haven, Conn.: Yale University Press, 1950), vol. 1, p. 254. For this and a number of other references, I am indebted to Dr. Gene Sharp.

CHAPTER III—CULTURAL PREPARATION

1. *Quotations from Chairman Mao Tse-tung* (New York: Bantam Books, 1967), p. 68.

2. *The Trumpet of Conscience* (London: Hodder and Staughton, 1968), p. 61. Also published by Harper and Row, New York, 1968, pp. 49–50.

3. Mohandas K. Gandhi, *Satyagraha in South Africa* (Ahmedabad, India: Navajivan, 1961), p. 78.

4. Quoted by Gene Sharp, "The Technique of Nonviolent Action," in *The Strategy of Civilian Defence,* ed. Adam Roberts (London: Faber and Faber, 1967), p. 97.

5. This generalization has been made by a number of students of the black church. See, for example, Benjamin E. Mays, *The Negro's God* (New York: Negro University Press, 1969), p. 245.

6. Adolf Hitler, *Mein Kampf* (New York: Reynal and Hitchcock, 1941), p. 388.

7. William P. Bundy, "The Missing Center," *Newsweek,* October 4, 1971, p. 46.

8. In the appendix Frantz Fanon gives a case history of a neurotic patient who was racked by guilt for having planted a bomb in an

Algerian café frequented by French people: *The Wretched of the Earth* (New York: Grove Press, 1966).

9. A useful analysis of the grape strike and boycott is by John Braxton, "The California Grape Strike," *Peace News* (Special Issue), January 16 and 23, 1970. The quote from Chavez is from a grape strike poster.

10. See Joan V. Bondurant, *Conquest of Violence* (Berkeley and Los Angeles, Calif: University of California Press, 1965), pp. 131–44. For more detail see the account by Pyarelal, *A Pilgrimage of Peace: Gandhi and the Frontier Gandhi Among N.W.F. Pathans* (Ahmedabad, India: Navajivan, 1950).

11. Jacob R. Fishman and Fredric Solomon, "Youth and Social Action: I. Perspectives on Student Sit-in Movement," in *Mental Health of the Poor*, eds. Frank Riessman et al. (New York: Free Press, 1964).

12. Dale Van Every, *Disinherited: The Lost Birthright of the American Indian* (New York: Morrow, 1966), p. 64. The Cherokee case and many other incidents of nonviolent struggle by Indians are described by Margaret DeMarco in "The Use of Nonviolent Direct Action Tactics and Strategy by American Indians," unpublished seminar paper (Chester, Pa., Martin Luther King School of Social Change, 1968).

13. For a handbook on how to conduct street meetings, see George Lakey and David Richards, "A Manual for Street Speakers," available from Friends Peace Committee, 1515 Cherry Street, Philadelphia, Pa. 19102.

CHAPTER IV—BUILDING ORGANIZATIONAL STRENGTH

1. In the distinction between classes and status groups I am following Max Weber. See Hans Gerth and C. Wright Mills, eds., *From Max Weber: Essays in Sociology* (New York: Oxford University Press, 1946), pp. 181–92.

2. Quoted in *The Monthly Review*, June 1961, p. 51.

3. *Newsweek*, January 14, 1972, p. 62.

4. Hannah Arendt, *On Revolution* (New York: Viking Press, 1966), pp. 252–53, 259–69. She notes that the revolutionary tradition has largely failed to link these spontaneous expressions of democracy to an organ-

izing strategy; because the councils arose outside the party they were
regarded as temporary phenomena rather than, in Arendt's words, "a
new public space for freedom."

5. A number of groups were formed under this name in the early 1970s
    within what became the Movement for a New Society (MNS) network.
    Later referred to simply as "collectives," they organized along the
    general lines suggested in this book. MNS can be contacted at PO Box
    1922, Cambridge, MA 02238.

6. Theodor Ebert, *Gewaltfreier Aufstand: Alternative zum Bürgerkrieg*
    (Freiburg: Verlag Rombach, 1968).

7. For a fuller description of the strategy game and other training meth-
    ods, see Theodore Olson and Lynne Shivers, *Training for Nonviolent
    Action* (London: War Resisters International and Friends Peace and
    International Relations Committee, 1970). It is available in the U.S.
    through Friends Peace Committee, 1515 Cherry Street, Philadelphia,
    Pa. 19102.

8. For a penetrating analysis of "the psychological man" as the character
    type of the emerging culture, see Philip Rieff, *The Triumph of the
    Therapeutic* (New York: Harper and Row, Torchbooks, 1968).

9. Such communities have existed within the MNS network (see 5 above).

10. "The California Grape Strike," *Peace News, loc. cit.*

11. Robert Michels, *Political Parties* (New York: Dover, 1959).

12. Eugene Nelson, *Huelga* (Delano, Calif.: Farm Workers Press, 1966),
    p. 26.

13. For this case I consulted the standard histories in English and the few
    books on the struggle and Ferencz Deák. The most useful single work
    is Arthur Griffiths, *The Resurrection of Hungary: A Parallel for Ire-
    land* (Dublin: Whelan and Son, 1918), most of which has been re-
    printed in Mulford Q. Sibley's collection of case studies, *The Quiet
    Battle* (Garden City, N.Y.: Doubleday, Anchor Books, 1963).

14. One factor, of course, was nationalism. In Hungary the people were
    gaining a new community of feeling and self-respect. In the early part
    of the century it had been considered in poor taste to speak Magyar,
    and sensible to look outside the country for anything good. A period

of cultural preparation came in Hungary before the political revolt began.

15. See Régis Debray, *Revolution in the Revolution?* (New York: Grove Press, 1967).

16. James McNeish describes the close call in his biography of Dolci, *Fire Under the Ashes* (London: Hodder and Staughton, 1965).

17. Ray Ginger, *Eugene V. Debs* (New York: Macmillan, Collier Books, 1962), p. 181; see also p. 159.

CHAPTER V—PROPAGANDA OF THE DEED

1. Eqbal Ahmad, "Revolutionary Warfare: How to Tell When the Rebels Have Won," *The Nation*, August 30, 1965, p. 96.

2. E. T. Hiller, *The Strike: A Study in Collective Action* (Chicago: University of Chicago Press, 1928), pp. 237–38.

3. Inez Haynes Irwin, *The Story of the Woman's Party* (New York: Harcourt, Brace, 1921), p. 196. In the course of researching this case I interviewed Alice Paul and consulted the publications of the Woman's Party. My analysis of the relation between the militant technique and their ethos was published in *Sociological Inquiry*, vol. 38, no. 1 (Winter 1968). For the militants' direct action in the context of the larger suffrage movement, see Eleanor Flexner, *Century of Struggle* (Cambridge, Mass.: Harvard University Press, 1959).

4. September 14, 1917, quoted in *The Suffragist*, vol. 8, no. 8 (September 1920), p. 222.

5. "Hayden Hails Chicago: The Elements of Victory," *The Movement*, October 1968, p. 4.

6. Eugene Nelson, *op. cit.*, pp. 36–37.

7. Krishnalal Shridharani, *War Without Violence* (London: Gollancz, 1939); a selection is included in Mulford Q. Sibley, *op. cit.*, where this quote can be found on pp. 234–44.

8. Leo Kuper, *Passive Resistance in South Africa* (New Haven, Conn.: Yale University Press, 1957), p. 126. The quotations are from *Flash*, a pro-campaign newspaper.

9. Here I am drawing on Gail Margaret Gillam's analysis in "A Choice of Weapons: Nonviolent Resistance in South Africa" (B.A. thesis Radcliffe College, 1966), especially p. 86.

10. *Ibid.*, pp. 63–64.

11. Gene Sharp, in a manuscript, "Politics of Nonviolent Action," p. 652.

12. "Communication Patterns as Bases of Systems of Authority and Power," in *Theoretical Studies in Social Organization of the Prison* (New York: Social Science Research Council), March 1960, p. 52.

13. *Current History*, September 31, 1931, p. 921. The student strike set off a civilian insurrection which led to the proclamation of a short-lived socialist republic. The case is described in the pamphlet by A Quaker Action Group, "Resistance in Latin America."

14. According to Glenn Smiley, executive secretary of the Coordinating Committee on Latin America, who learned of the incident while in Brazil.

15. Ernesto Che Guevara, *Guerrilla Warfare* (New York: Knopf, Vintage Books, 1968), pp. 6–8.

16. E. T. Hiller, *op. cit.*, p. 20. Hiller quotes Louis Levine, *The Women's Garment Workers* (New York: Huebsch, 1924), p. 288.

17. *Quotations from Chairman Mao Tse-tung, op. cit.*, p. 76.

18. George Katkov, *Russia 1917* (New York: Harper and Row, 1967), p. 273.

19. Theodor Ebert, "Resistance Against Communist Regimes?" in *The Strategy of Civilian Defence*, ed. Adam Roberts, p. 192.

20. For an account of these demonstrations see Michael Randle, April Carter, et al., *Support Czechoslovakia* (London: Housmans, 1968).

21. Milton Mayer, *They Thought They Were Free: The Germans, 1933–45* (Chicago: University of Chicago Press, 1955).

CHAPTER VI—POLITICAL AND ECONOMIC NONCOOPERATION

1. Letter from James E. Bristol from Lusaka, Zambia (dated October 8, 1966) to Stewart Meacham of the American Friends Service Committee.

2. Harrison Brown and James Real, *Community of Fear* (Santa Barbara, Calif.: Center for the Study of Democratic Institutions, 1960). In *The Pentagon Papers* (New York: Bantam Books, 1971), the sheer irrelevance of the Congress to top decision-makers is revealed. Genuine consultation with congressional leaders (including the Senate Foreign Relations Committee) is conspicuous by its absence.

3. For an account of this case with bibliography, see D. J. Goodspeed, *The Conspirators: A Study of the Coup d'État* (London: Macmillan, 1962).

4. Ernesto Che Guevara, *op. cit.*, p. 2.

5. *The Urban Guerrilla* (Chicago: Quadrangle Books, 1969), pp. 164–65.

6. *Strategy for Labor: A Radical Proposal* (Boston: Beacon Press, 1968), p. 73.

7. Lawrence Henry Gipson, *The Coming of the Revolution 1763–1775* (New York: Harper, 1954), pp. 210–12, 220.

8. William Z. Foster, *The Great Steel Strike and Its Lessons* (New York: Huebsch, 1920), p. 116, quoted by E. T. Hiller, *op. cit.*, pp. 145–46.

9. Patricia Parkman, "Violence and Nonviolence in the Belgian Struggle for Suffrage" (graduate history seminar paper, Temple University, 1968). A published account of the 1913 Belgian general strike is in Wilfrid Harris Crook, *Communism and the General Strike* (The Shoe String Press, 1960), reprinted in Mulford Q. Sibley, *op. cit.*

10. Jules Destrée and Émile Vandervelde, *Le Socialisme en Belgique*, 2nd ed. (Paris: V. Giard and E. Brière, Bibliothèque Socialiste Internationale, 1903), p. 259.

11. United Nations, *Report of the Special Committee on the Problem of Hungary*, supplement no. 18 to the Official Records of the Eleventh Session of the General Assembly (New York: United Nations, 1957).

12. "Lessons from Resistance Movements—Guerrilla and Nonviolent," in *The Strategy of Civilian Defence*, ed. Adam Roberts, p. 203.

13. Kalman H. Silvert, *The Conflict Society* (New York: American Universities Field Staff, 1966), p. 22. Silvert argues that "civilian opposition had previously so eroded the Batista Government's ability to impose itself as to leave the military with no choice."

14. From the memoirs of Heinz Ullstein, one of those arrested, quoted by Theodore Ebert, "Effects of Repression by the Invader," *Peace News*, March 19, 1965.

15. Victor Alba, *op. cit.*, pp. 221–22.

16. Adam Roberts, "Buddhism and Politics in South Vietnam," in *The World Today*, London, June 1964. Other useful material on the Buddhists in this period can be found in David Halberstam, *The Making of a Quagmire* (New York: Random House, 1965), and Jean Lacouture, *Vietnam: Between Two Truces* (New York: Random House, 1966).

17. Here I have followed Robert Levering's analysis in his seminar paper "The Buddhist Struggle Movement of 1966," (Chester, Pa., Martin Luther King School of Social Change, 1968).

18. Bart. de Ligt, *The Conquest of Violence: An Essay on War and Revolution* (London: Routledge, 1937), p. 239.

CHAPTER VII—INTERVENTION AND PARALLEL INSTITUTIONS

1. Candy Putter, "The French Crisis of May-June 1968: A Case Study," *loc. cit.*

2. Lawrence Henry Gipson, *The British Empire Before the American Revolution*, vol. 12, *The Triumphant Empire: Britain Sails into the Storm 1770–1776* (New York: Knopf, 1965), p. 313.

3. Arthur M. Schlesinger, *The Colonial Merchants and the American Revolution 1763–1776* (New York: Ungar, 1957), pp. 551–52.

4. Don Doane, Associated Press dispatch, datelined: Berlin, June 22, 1953, quoted by William Robert Miller, *Nonviolence: A Christian Interpretation* (New York: Schocken Books, 1966), p. 352.

5. Sidney Harcave, *First Blood: The Russian Revolution of 1905* (New York: Macmillan, 1964), especially p. 235; George Katkov, *op. cit.*, pp. 262ff.

6. David Dellinger, "The Future of Nonviolence," in *Nonviolence in America: A Documentary History,* Staughton Lynd (Indianapolis, Ind.: Bobbs-Merrill, 1966).

7. Gunnar Myrdal, "Gandhi as a Radical Liberal," in *Mahatma Gandhi: 100 Years,* ed. S. Radhakrishnan (New Delhi: Gandhi Peace Foundation, 1968), pp. 266–67.

8. *Quotations from Chairman Mao Tse-tung, op. cit.,* p. 26, Chap. 5, Note 17.

9. *Ibid.,* pp. 33, 34.

10. Quoted by Gunnar Myrdal, *op. cit.,* p. 263.

11. Gene Sharp, *Gandhi Wields the Weapon of Moral Power: Three Case Histories* (Ahmedabad, India: Navajivan, 1960), p. 167. See also p. 158 for a similar incident.

12. Arthur I. Waskow, *Keeping the World Disarmed* (Santa Barbara, Calif: Center for the Study of Democratic Institutions, 1965).

CHAPTER VIII—THE WORLD IN REVOLUTION

1. David M. Shoup, "The New American Militarism," *The Atlantic Monthly,* April 1969.

2. Harry Magdoff, *op. cit.,* pp. 45–54, 177–85.

3. In September 1970, Senator John Stennis successfully argued down a bid to ban the use of herbicides in South Vietnam: "The issue is very simple. Shall we take away one way of saving the lives of our men in Vietnam? There can be only one answer to this question—a categorical 'no!' "; reported in *Newsweek,* September 7, 1970, "Congress: The Odd Couple," p. 19.

4. Political scientist Nigel Young has argued for a careful analysis of the relation between military organizational requirements and politics in his article "On Wars of National Liberation," *Peace News,* November 21, 1969. This article, along with useful additional material, is available

in pamphlet form: "On War, National Liberation, and the State" from Christian Action Publications, London, 1972. It is also available from Housmans Bookshop, 5 Caledonian Road, London N1, UK or in photocopy from *Peace News*. Some of my argument here follows Nigel Young's important work.

5. Edward Goldsmith et al., *op. cit.*, p. 15.

6. See Frances Moore Lappe, *Diet for a Small Planet* (New York: Ballantine Books, 1971).

7. See Adam Roberts, "Resisting Military Coups," *New Society*, June 1, 1967.

8. *Quotations from Chairman Mao Tse-tung, op. cit.*, p. 20.

9. See the documented list in Gene Sharp, *The Politics of Nonviolent Action* (Boston: Porter Sargeant, 1973).

10. This brief account is taken largely from contemporary news reports in *The New York Times*, the London *Times*, the *Guardian*, the *Observer*, and the news magazines. A major book on the events is by Philip Windsor and Adam Roberts, *Czechoslovakia 1968: Reform, Repression, and Resistance* (New York: Columbia University Press, 1969).

11. For a study of the *Ruhrkampf*, see Wolfgang Sternstein's chapter in *The Stategy of Civilian Defence*, ed. Adam Roberts.

12. Heinz Schewe in the London *Observer*, August 25, 1968.

CHAPTER 9 — THE DIALOGUE BEGINS

1. Richard Falk teaches at the Center for International Affairs at Princeton University. David H. Albert is one of the founders of New Society Publishers. Jane Meyerding has been active in the feminist movement over the past fifteen years. Bill Moyer is a long-term anti-nuclear activist in both the United States and England.

Appendix:

QUESTIONS

For thinking through revolutionary strategy using the five-stage framework

What are your long-range goals? In other words, how do you want institutions to look in the new society (how work and trade will be organized, how decisions will be made, how the next generation will be nurtured, how play and culture will be communicated and supported, etc. etc.)?

STAGE I: CULTURAL PREPARATION

Who should you work with at first? In other words, where in the society will you find the initiative-takers (the "cadres") who will take responsibility, the people who can accept the job of moving things along in developing a revolutionary movement?

What are the changes these people need to go through in the way they look at *themselves*? What ideas about themselves do they need to change in order to be self-conscious revolutionists?

What are the changes they need to make in their view of the *world*? What kind of analysis needs to be developed? How can they get a clearer picture of what's going on without letting that picture freeze into dogma?

What kind of *vision* needs to be developed? How detailed does the vision of a new society need to be? How will people develop their vision—what methods will they use? What relation do you see at this point between short-term goals, medium-term goals, and the vision (long-range goals)?

What methods of consciousness-raising make sense for the kind of people you want to work with, for their cultural and economic background, etc.?

What kind of *strategy* approaches will be useful to the cadres? What new information will they need to understand how social change works with those strategy approaches? For example, if the debate is between electoral politics *versus* armed struggle *versus* nonviolent revolution, what do people need to know more about in order to make smart decisions?

STAGE II: ORGANIZATION-BUILDING

In your strategy, what forms of organization make sense? Remember to look back to where people are coming from (their historical experience with organizational structures), and also to look ahead to stage five and the need for strong organizations for the transfer of power. What experiments in forms of organization can be made now, in the light of feminist and other perspectives?

What is the role of alternative institutions in building the revolutionary movement? Of rank-and-file movements in labor? Of radical caucuses in the professions? Of action groups which develop campaigns? Of support groups?

How should the organizational units be linked? Informal networks? Formal networks? Hierarchical arrangements? Other?

Which allies need to be reached out to at this stage? How can honest and reliable relationships be built between revolutionists and non-revolutionary organizations and institutions, so each can help the other?

How can you build into organizations a learning process so they can learn from feedback and grow, and not become rigid or become dominated by elites?

STAGE III: PROPAGANDA OF THE DEED

Who is the "audience," the people who, when watching the drama of confrontation, can be won over to the side of revolution?

What are the central ideas you want the actions to communicate? (Remember, not everything can be said in a single action!)

What are the tactics, or methods, of confrontation which will communicate these central messages? (For example, a black sit-in showing discrimination.)

Who or what is the opponent in these confrontations?

What support do people need to get through this stage successfully, so they will not back down, become intimidated, or get isolated?

Conflict tends to split people and push them to take sides ("Which side are you on...?"). That process (polarization) also has some unfortunate side-effects (for example, some people get rigid). How can the side-effects be minimized?

STAGE IV: MASS NONCOOPERATION

In what ways is the system dependent upon the cooperation of the people to keep going? Whose cooperation is especially critical (for example, in Iran under the Shah, it was the oil workers')?

In addition to certain key areas of noncooperation, who can provide the mass base for noncooperation (if the masses are not in motion, it cannot be a true revolution)?

Which noncooperation tactics may be appropriate (strike, boycott, tax refusal, etc.)? (Gene Sharp lists dozens of tactics, with illustrations of each, in his book *The Politics of Nonviolent Action*. Excellent for extending our ideas of the possibilities.)

How will noncooperation be coordinated? How does the organizational work done in Stage II need to change in order to carry the scale and demands of Stage IV?

How will the movement's understanding of what is happening be gotten across to people in general, when the elite is trying to confuse the issue? (Remember, this is a stage of social upheaval, with a lot of confusion and fearful feelings.)

How can the movement reach out to opponents, and help individuals in the ruling class and the bureaucratic command posts come over to the revolution or at least be supportive in some ways?

What is the role of the movement (for example alternative economic institutions) in providing services in the middle of economic and social dislocation?

STAGE V: PARALLEL INSTITUTIONS

What are the legitimate functions of the old order, the things which have been done which actually need doing even though in different ways? (For example, growing food, providing transportation.)

How will the movement meet these legitimate functions? (This obviously connects with the vision process in Stage I, and also with the organization-building of Stage II.)

How can people show their acceptance of new institutions? (This grows organically out of Stage IV, which is a tussle between the old institutions and the people's determination to be free. The key is the fence-sitting part of the population, which did not actively participate in Stage IV but watched intently and now needs to decide whether to give the revolution the benefit of the doubt.)

What will happen to the old power-holders? What are the actual tactics of power-transfer? (For ideas, check Gene Sharp.)

What are the international connections in this process? (No revolution happens in a vacuum!)

How can we avoid the revolution freezing into new rigidities? How can we sow the seeds, even in this Stage V of power transfer, for continuing flexible growth of the new institutions? How can the empowerment of people continue to be deepened and strengthened after the excitement of getting rid of the old order wears off?

Bibliography

By George Lakey and Lynne Shivers

This bibliography offers references which readers may find interesting for additional study. These sources are all widely available, at least in libraries or from publishers.

Annotated sources are considered more important than the rest of the sources.

The bibliography is divided into four sections: analysis, vision, strategy, and next steps.

Analysis means the examination and interpretation of social, political, economic and cultural forces.

Vision means the presentation of desired alternative futures.

The *strategy* section explores the broad means to achieve those alternatives to present predicaments, and looks at how others have carried out strategies.

The *next steps* section offers sources which people can act on immediately. This contrasts with the earlier sections which offer sources suggesting programs which might take months or years to establish.

ANALYSIS

Arendt, Hannah. *On Revolution*. New York: Viking Press, 1966.

Barnet, Richard and Ronald Muller. *Global Reach: The Power of the Multinational Corporations*. New York: Simon & Schuster, 1974.

   See also Barnet's *The Lean Years: Politics in the Age of Scarcity*. New York: Simon & Schuster, 1980.

Barney, Gerald O., study director. *Global 2000, Report to the President*. New York: Viking/Penguin, 1979.

Bluestone, Barry and Bennet Harrison. *The Deindustrialization of America*. New York: Basic Books, 1982.

Bondurant, Joan. *Conquest of Violence*. rev. ed. Los Angeles: University of California Press, 1965.

This book provides a basic discussion of political theory of Gandhian nonviolent action with excellent case studies. This is one of the best sources on nonviolence.

Boulding, Elise. *The Underside of History: A View of Women Through Time*. Boulder, CO: Westview Press, 1976.

Carnoy, Martin, Derek Shearer and Russel Rumberger. *A New Social Contract*. New York: Harper & Row, 1983.

Carroll, Lakey, Moyer & Taylor. *Moving Towards a New Society*. Philadelphia: New Society Publishers, 1976.

Dellinger, Dave. *Revolutionary Nonviolence*. New York: Bobbs-Merrill Co., 1970.

Ehrlich, Sagan, Kennedy, Roberts. *The Cold and the Dark: The World After Nuclear War*. New York: Norton & Co., 1984.

Esquivel, Adolfo Pérez. *Christ in a Poncho*. Maryknoll, NY: Orbis Press, 1984.

Fuller, John G. *We Almost Lost Detroit*. New York: Reader's Digest Press, 1975.

Gandhi, M.K. *Nonviolent Resistance (Satyagraha)*. New York: Schocken Books, 1961.

Gutierrez, Gustavo. *A Theology of Liberation*. Maryknoll, NY: Orbis Books, 1973.

Harding, Vincent. *There Is a River: The Black Struggle for Freedom in America*. New York: Vintage, 1983.

Harrington, Michael. *Decade of Decision*. New York: Simon & Schuster, 1980.

King, Martin Luther, Jr. *The Trumpet of Conscience*. New York: Harper & Row, 1967.

Line, Les. ed., *What We Save Now: An Audubon Primer of Defense*. Boston: Houghton Mifflin, 1973.

McAllister, Pam. ed., *Reweaving the Web of Life: Feminism and Nonviolence*. Philadelphia: New Society Publishers, 1983.

This anthology of over fifty essays examines the relationship between feminism and nonviolence in theory and practice.

Meadows, Donella, et al. *The Limits to Growth*. 2nd ed. New York: Universe, 1974.

Melman, Seymour. *Profits Without Production*. New York: Alfred A. Knopf, 1983.

Melman might be called the father of the economic conversion movement in the U.S. His earlier books are valuable for vision as well as analysis.

Meyerding, Jane. ed., *We Are All Part of One Another: A Barbara Deming Reader*. Philadelphia: New Society Publishers, 1984.

Millet, Kate. *Sexual Politics*. New York: Doubleday, 1970.
>This influential book has provided initial inspiration and analysis for the modern women's movement.

Peace News. News and reflection on current nonviolent action and civil disobedience in Europe and worldwide: 25 issues annually. Peace News, 8 Elm Avenue, Nottingham NG3 4GF, U.K.

Schell, Jonathan. *The Fate of the Earth*. New York: Avon Books, 1982.
>This is a well-written description of the physical and human consequences of a nuclear war. See also Schell's article on Poland in the Feb. 3, 1986 issue of the *New Yorker*.

Schon, Donald. *Beyond the Stable State*. New York: W. W. Norton & Co., 1971.

Schumacher, Ernest F. *Small Is Beautiful: Economics As If People Mattered*. New York· Harper & Row, 1973.

VISION

Bahro, Rudolf. *Building the Green Movement*. Philadelphia: New Society Publishers, 1986.

Cheatham, Annie and Mary Clare Powell. *This Way Daybreak Comes: Women's Values and the Future*. Philadelphia: New Society Publishers, 1986.
>This source documents numerous projects carried out by hundreds of U.S. women today—experiments in communities, relationships, politics, art, networking technologies, international perspectives, and waging peace.

Civilian-Based Defense. Newsletter published by the Association for Transarmament Studies, 3636 Lafayette, Omaha, NE 68131.

Falk, Richard, Samuel S. Kim and Saul H. Mendlovitz. eds., *Towards a Just World Order*. Boulder, CO: Westview Press, 1982.

Ferguson, Marilyn. *The Aquarian Conspiracy: Personal and Social Transformation in the '80s*. Los Angeles: J.P. Tarcher, 1980.
>Ferguson reports on the most positive trends and experiments that embody a humanist vision.

Goble, Frank G. *The Third Force: The Psychology of Abraham Maslow*. New York: Washington Square Press/Pocket Books, 1970.

Goodman, Gerre, George Lakey, Judy Lashof and Erika Thorne. *No Turning Back: Lesbian and Gay Liberation for the '80s*. Philadelphia: New Society Publishers, 1983.

Gordon, Suzanne and Dave McFadden. eds., *Economic Conversion: Revitalizing America's Economy*. Cambridge, MA: Ballinger, 1984.
>The readings in this book are by many of the major experts and include case

studies and analysis as well as strategic reflections and a clear vision of what conversion makes possible.

Henderson, Hazel. *Creating Alternative Futures: The End of Economics*. New York: Berkeley Publishing Corp., 1978.

Lovins, Amory. *Soft Energy Paths: Towards a Durable Peace*. New York: Ballinger, 1977.

Piercy, Marge. *Woman on the Edge of Time*. New York: Fawcett, 1976, 1981.

Plowshare Press. Newsletter published by the Center for Economic Conversion, 222C View Street, Mountain View, CA 94041.

Rowbotham, Sheila and Jeffrey Weeks. *Socialism and the New Life: The Personal and Sexual Politics of Edward Carpenter and Havelock Ellis*. London: Pluto Press, 1977.

STRATEGY

Ansbro, John J. *Martin Luther King, Jr., The Making of a Mind*. Maryknoll, NY: Orbis Books, 1984.

Bacon, Margaret. *The Quiet Rebels: The Story of the Quakers in America*. Philadelphia: New Society Publishers, 1985.

Bosrup, Anders and Andrew Mack. *War Without Weapons: Non-violence in National Defense*. New York: Schocken Books, 1975.
This is the most sophisticated book on the strategy of nonviolent action yet produced—a theory of strategic analysis, borrowing from the classic work of Clausewitz.

Boyte, Harry. *Community is Possible: Repairing America's Roots*. New York: Harper & Row, 1984.

Brinton, Crane. *Anatomy of a Revolution*. rev. ed. New York: Vintage Press, 1965.
This is one of the few widely available books that deals with stages of revolutions. Its frame of reference is a common one used by others in the field. Compare with Skocpol's newer treatment of stages (see later in this bibliography).

Cooney, Robert and Helen Michalowski. eds., *The Power of the People: Active Nonviolence in the United States*. rev. ed. Philadelphia: New Society Publishers, 1987.

Easwaran, Eknath. *A Man to Match His Mountains: Badshah Khan, Nonviolent Soldier of Islam*. Petaluma, CA: Nilgiri Press, 1984.

Gandhi, M.K. *Satyagraha in South Africa*. rev. ed. Ahmedabad, India: Navajivan Press, 1961. Dist. in U.S. by Arthur Harvey, Greenleaf Books, Weare, NH 03281, USA.

Hooks, Bell. *Feminist Theory: From Margin to Center*. Boston: South End Press, 1984.

King, Martin Luther, Jr. *Why We Can't Wait*. New York: Signet Books, 1963.
This in-depth case study details the 1963 desegregation campaign in Birmingham, Alabama.

Lynd, Staughton. ed., *Nonviolence in America: A Documentary History*. New York: Bobbs-Merrill Co., 1966.

Mabee, Carlton. *Black Freedom: The Nonviolent Abolitionists from 1830 through the Civil War*. London: Collier-Macmillan Ltd., 1970.

Macy, Joanna Rogers. *Despair and Personal Power in the Nuclear Age*. Philadelphia: New Society Publishers, 1983.

This is a primary work for overcoming "psychic numbing." It includes sections on awakening in the nuclear age, relating to children, guided meditations, affirmations and other group exercises. See also *Death in Life*, an account of "psychic numbing" in Nagasaki/Hiroshima survivors: Robert Jay Lifton, New York: Basic Books (Harper & Row), orig. ed. New York: Random House, 1968.

Narayan, Jayaprakash. *Prison Diary*. Edited by A.B. Shah. Bombay: Popular Prakashan, 1977.

Oppenheimer, Marty. *The Urban Guerrilla*. Chicago: Quadrangle Books, 1969.

Peavey, Fran with Myra Levy and Charles Varon. *Heart Politics*. Philadelphia: New Society Publishers, 1986.

Piven, Frances Fox and Richard A. Cloward. *Poor People's Movements: Why They Succeed, How They Fail*. New York: Vintage, 1979.

Randall, Margaret. *Sandino's Daughters: Testimonies of Nicaraguan Women in Struggle*. Edited by Lynda Yanz. Toronto: New Star Books, 1981.

Roberts, Adam. ed., *Civilian Resistance as a National Defense*. Harrisburg, PA: Stackpole Books, 1968.

This is one of the most important sources about Civilian-Based Defense, as the concept has come to be known.

Sharp, Gene. *Making Europe Unconquerable*. Cambridge, MA: Ballinger, 1985.

_____. *National Security through Civilian-Based Defense*. Omaha, NE: Association for Transarmament Studies, 1985.

_____. *The Politics of Nonviolent Action*. 3 vols. Boston: Porter Sargent, 1973.

This monumental work provides a nonviolent perspective on the process and analysis of social change as well as an examination of almost 200 tactics of nonviolent action with case studies.

Sibley, Mulford. ed., *The Quiet Battle*. Garden City, NJ: Doubleday/Anchor, 1963.

Skocpol, Theda. *States and Social Revolutions: A Comparative Analysis of France, Russia, and China*. New York: Cambridge University Press, 1979.

Weschler, Lawrence. *The Passion of Poland*. New York: Pantheon Books, 1984.

This case study of the Polish Solidarity movement, covering 1980 to September 1983, first appeared in the *New Yorker* magazine. Includes a chronology.

Woodrow, Peter. *Clearness: Processes for Supporting Individuals and Groups in Decision-Making.* Philadelphia: New Society Publishers, 1976.
The clearness process is a special kind of group meeting enabling a person to get support from friends when the person faces a difficult decision or a personal crisis.

NEXT STEPS

Blood, Peter & Annie Patterson. eds., *Rise Up Singing.* Easton, PA: Sing Out Corporation, 1988.

Bodner, Joan., ed., *Taking Charge of Our Lives: Living Responsibly in the World.* American Friends Service Committee, San Francisco. San Francisco: Harper & Row, 1984.

Coover, Deacon, Esser, Moore. *Resource Manual for a Living Revolution.* rev. ed. Philadelphia: New Society Publishers, 1985.
The primary source of training tools that Movement for a New Society members have used since 1971.

Jackins, Harvey. *The Human Side of Human Beings: The Theory of Re-evaluation Counselling.* rev. ed. Seattle, WA: Rational Island Press, 1978.

Kahn, Si. *Organizing: A Guide for Grassroots Leaders.* New York: McGraw-Hill, 1982.

Lappé, Frances Moore. *Diet for a Small Planet.* Tenth Anniversary Edition. New York: Ballantine, 1982.
Lappé's book analyzes why people of developed countries consume at a higher level through eating off the top of the food chain. She goes on to explain how complementary vegetable protein is ample nutrition. Numerous recipes as well. A revolutionary book in its implications.

Taylor, Richard. *Blockade: A Guide to Nonviolent Intervention.* Maryknoll, NY: Orbis Books, 1977.
This case-study of a campaign carried out in 1971 (a blockade of ships sending arms to Pakistan during the Pakistan/Bangladesh war) gives information and perspective to this book's "Stage Three," as carried out by a small group. The "manual" section outlines how to organize a nonviolent action campaign.

Wollman, Neil. ed., *Working for Peace: A Handbook of Practical Psychology and Other Tools.* San Luis Obispo, CA: Impact Publishers, 1986.

INDEX